PSYCHIC ST

Essays, lectures and sermons on the implications of psychic experience for Christian thinking.

PSYCHIC STUDIES
A Christian's View

by

MICHAEL PERRY

Archdeacon of Durham

THE AQUARIAN PRESS
Wellingborough, Northamptonshire

First published 1984

British Library Cataloguing in Publication Data

Perry, Michael
    Psychic studies.
    1. Christianity and psychical research
    I. Title
    133.8   BR115.P85
    ISBN 0 85030 345 1

*The Aquarian Press is part of
the Thorsons Publishing Group*

Printed and bound in Great Britain

Contents

		Page
Introduction: Building bridges		7
PART 1: SIGHTING SHOTS		19

Chapter

1. A psychic word for the Church		21
2. The psychic and the spiritual		26
3. Psychical research and religion		29
PART 2: LIVING		37
4. The quest for the transcendent	—	41
5. Faith, reason and evidence		52
6. May a Christian investigate the paranormal?		66
PART 3: DEATH AND DYING		85
7. Death		87
8. What is dying like?		96
PART 4: SURVIVAL		111
9. The theological approach to survival		113
10. Life after death – what will it be like?		121
11. The spiritual implications of survival		133
PART 5: RESURRECTION AND		
REINCARNATION		149
12. Resurrection		151

13. Reincarnation – three reviews   167
14. Reincarnation – a Christian option?   175
    PART 6: PREACHING   191
15. A centenary sermon   193
16. Fascination with the occult   197
17. Angels   202
18. The mystery of incarnation   206
19. Hell harrowed   210
20. All souls   214
    Periodicals   217
    Index   221

Introduction
Building bridges

Records of allegedly psychic happenings go back to the very dawn of civilization, and those who read their Bibles are well aware that the religious literature of Judaism and early Christianity is shot through and through with accounts of the paranormal. The established Churches, however, have been very loath to have much to do with the practitioners of the psychic. In some other cultures people who claimed to have some sort of psychic awareness, who were able to read minds, to tell the future, or to be in touch with entities from a world beyond the visible one, were part of the religious set-up of the culture concerned. Not so in Western Europe. In the age of Christendom, such people were part of the religious underground. The medievals had their cunning people, wise women and folk healers; but they worked apart from the Church and knew that repressive measures might be taken against them at any time.

As a result, there is a deal of confusion in the records and much ignorance generally – in particular, the confusing of mediumship with witchcraft, which was something of quite a different order. Since all were thought to be supping with the devil, whom you kept at arm's length, you were not choosy about analysing precisely what he was up to. Much of this is fascinatingly told by Keith Thomas in his *Religion and the Decline of Magic*[1] – an enormous, erudite, and magnificently entertaining volume of over eight hundred pages, which chronicles the magic and astrological practices of the late medieval world (with compelling detail from contemporary records) and the reaction against them of the reformers of the sixteenth and seventeenth centuries. Parapsychologists might complain that some of Thomas' conclusions are somewhat reductionist, but they cannot complain that the evidence has not been fairly set out and the case competently argued. It is clear that those who had the reputation of possessing paranormal gifts – whether they were wise women, astrologers, or healers – were regularly consulted by serious enquirers at all levels of society, from the peasantry to Royalty. But the Church (at official level, whatever the practices of individual members) regarded it coolly at best, and normally with disfavour.

By the nineteenth century, when the gulf between science and religion was arguably at its widest, one might have expected there to have been a study of paranormal phenomena as a part of the scientific endeavour of understanding the world and the way it worked. There was; but not before religion had beaten science to it, by about a generation. The phenomena beginning in 1848 and centring round the Fox sisters at Hydesville in New York State were interpreted as evidence that discarnate spirits existed and that they could communicate with this earth. A new religion, Spiritualism, was founded, and spread like wildfire.

The new religion was no more unified than Christianity. Some Spiritualists had time for God and some had not. Some regarded the new teachings as a substitute for Christianity, some as a supplement to it; some thought it dealt with a set of brute facts that taught us something about the nature of man but had nothing to say about his relation to God either one way or the other. As far as the vast majority of Churchmen were concerned, the fact that anything parapsychological was grist to the Spiritualists' mill was enough to turn them even further from the possibility of giving the psychic a sympathetic and critical theological evaluation. A few brave clerics studied the data with care and discrimination, but the more usual Christian reaction was either to scoff or to issue penny tracts warning the faithful off the forbidden territory.

The religious aspect of the paranormal was not the only way in which the nineteenth century reacted to the subject. The century was also the great age of Science (the capital S was frequent), when the mysteries of the Universe were to be unlocked by all who could examine them with patient care through the scientific method. So it was that a group of friends, mainly Cambridge philosophers and scientists, formed the Society for Psychical Research in 1882. The scientific optimism of late Victorianism was in full flood, and psychical research was part of the attempt to apply rigid scientific criteria to human experience.

The Church was happier with psychical research than with Spiritualism, and there has been a smattering of Christians active in the field ever since. The first part of the SPR *Proceedings* carried an article on some experiments in 'thought-transference' done by a Derbyshire clergyman (A.M. Creery) in the true spirit of the country parson of literary, historical, or scientific pursuits. By the time the second list of supporters was published in 1883, the wife of the then Archbishop of Canterbury, Mrs E.W. Benson, appeared on the list of 'Associates, Honorary and Corresponding Members' of the Society.

Interest in the paranormal as a scientific pursuit has, however, always been a minority concern amongst Christians. The suspicion has been that those who 'dabbled' in such matters were well on the way to slipping down the primrose path to perdition to join the heretics and schismatics for whom no fate was bad enough. (Incidentally, I would love to know who first applied the verb 'to dabble' to those with an amateur interest in the psychic. He has a lot to answer for; the term has been pitifully overused for a very long time, and deserves to be given a rest.) The number of Christians who have attempted to engage in this field in a theologically literate way has been small indeed. And yet it is very close to Christian concerns. To quote Morton Kelsey, an American Episcopal (i.e. Anglican) priest and psychotherapist with a considerable knowledge of parapsychology:

If the Church does not take ESP data seriously and integrate these experiences into its thought and practice, people will deal with them *without* the wisdom and understanding that the Church can provide ... Clairvoyance, telepathy, precognition, psychokinesis and healing have been observed in and around the lives of many religious leaders and nearly all Christian saints. If these phenomena are not accepted and given a legitimate place in religious life, they will be sought outside of the Church and for other than religious reasons ... ESP is a natural phenomenon of the human psyche. It can be used for the glory of God and the enrichment of human life when it is understood and placed in the service of divine love, the love expressed in and through Jesus Christ.[2]

Fortunately, bridges are being built between the Churches and this whole area of knowledge. As long ago as 1920, the Lambeth

Conference of the bishops of the Anglican Communion received a report on Spiritualism that recognized that this religion was a protest against materialism and a materialistic way of life, but that criticized it (very properly) for not having at its heart what the Christian faith regarded as central – the revelation of the incarnation of God in Jesus Christ. Spiritualism, it said, was more concerned with survival than with God, and its teachings advocated no moral struggle for purity to help the soul to grow. But the report realized that some people do have psychic gifts, and it was legitimate for them to use them – though with caution and restraint.[3]

The General Assembly of the (Presbyterian) Church of Scotland appointed a Committee as long ago as 1922 to explore this area. It expressed the hope that those Christians who had been vouchsafed special psychic manifestations 'should be encouraged to share in the life of the Church rather than to withdraw themselves from its communion'.[4]

A second Anglican document was written in 1939 but was not published in full till forty years later.[5] This was the report of a committee appointed by Archbishop Lang of Canterbury 'to investigate the subject of communications with discarnate spirits and the claims of Spiritualism in relation to the Christian faith'. A minority report of three members urged the Church to have nothing to do with any of this, but the other seven saw some good in Spiritualism, though they were critical of much within the movement. They urged that representatives of the Church should keep in touch with intelligent Spiritualists (presumably they thought they should let the unintelligent fend for themselves?).

Churchmen did not do so, except as individuals rather than representatives, and after 1939 it was many years before any official Christian body re-opened the subject on a wider front and in the light of more modern studies. In 1971, the Archbishops' Commission on Christian Doctrine (Church of England) produced a report entitled *Prayer and the Departed* which contained an Appendix on 'The Evidence of Psychical Research'.[6] Its conclusions were remarkably cautious: 'The whole subject is full of uncertainties and alternative explanations and we have no criteria for distinguishing true information from false.'

Across the Atlantic, the United Presbyterian Church of the USA received a report (in 1976) from a Task Force on Occult and Psychic Activities.[7] This presented guidelines for pastors and Sessions, to help discriminate between such practices as honoured

God and witnessed to him, and such practices as did not. They are eminently well worth reproducing here as an example of the questions Christians need to ask about psychic manifestations.

1. Does the psychic event or phenomenon lead us as total persons – heart, soul, and mind – to love the Lord our God, putting no other gods before him, and to love our neighbours as ourselves?

2. Does it witness to the sovereignty of God as the ultimate source of possibility, power, and resources; or is it ego-centric and manipulative, concerned primarily with private power?

3. Does it honor God's chosen means of self-revelation: his Son, his Word, and his Spirit?

4. Does it honor God's creation, both nature and humanity, in terms of fostering wholeness, reconciliation, and a posture of self-sacrificial servanthood rather than exploitation in both personal and societal terms? Is the 'unloveable' and the enemy given at least equal status within this redemptive framework? Is human need, bodily as well as spiritual, an item of concern and action?

5. Is it open to the infinite variety of God's work in the world, with humble recognition that 'His ways are not our ways', leaving room for unknowns, for natural and general revelation, for fellowship with any and all human beings, whatever their faith, ethnicity or theology, providing they do not despoil the human or seek to subvert love and community?

6. Does it produce in the long run, the 'fruits of the Spirit': Love, joy, peace, patience, kindness, goodness, faithfulness, gentleness, and self-control?

7. Does it promote humility, a recognition that we do not yet see God 'face to face' but only 'through a glass darkly', that much is yet incomprehensible or unknown, that we yet have much to learn and perhaps to relearn about his ways?

These are searching questions, and much that is vaunted as being of importance in the psychic world would not survive examination in the light of them. But they need to be asked. The fact that a Christian church has produced them as criteria for the assessment of this body of evidence shows that the task of Christian discrimination is getting well forward.

In many respects it is still an uphill task to get the 'official' Church to recognize the importance of this field. On 29 October 1981 the House of Bishops of the General Synod of the Church of England considered a paper in which they were asked to set up a group to examine the subject and report on it, particularly because such an initiative might well have profound results on relationships with Spiritualists and also on that larger body of people who are at a loss to know what to make of their psychic sensitivity and who would like to hear the Church saying something to show it has some understanding of their condition. Sadly, their minutes record that they doubted whether the time was yet ripe for a fresh investigation.[8] Some workers in the field believe that the time is so over-ripe that things will go rotten if the synodical Church does not wake up to the fact that psychic sensitivity is a fact of life for many people, and that they are longing for some word of encouragement and understanding from their Fathers in God.

Although the English bishops would not commission a further study, they did at least officially acknowledge the work done by the Presbyterians north of the border. The General Assembly of the Church of Scotland in 1976 had received and published[9] the report of a working party on parapsychology which took a puzzled look at many of the alleged phenomena, wondered what on earth to make of them, and concluded that the matter ought to be kept under review by a special sub-committee. By 1982, after seven years, it had not yet met.

The Scottish report was clearer about the status of exorcism. The Church of Scotland, it recommended, should have nothing to do with any such ceremony, which can only do more harm than good, and appears to give a kind of quasi-magical power to the minister (the Scots have always been mistrustful of anything smacking of priestcraft). The year before, Archbishop Coggan, speaking on behalf of the bishops in General Synod, had laid down pastoral guidelines for the exercise of 'the ministry of deliverance' in the Church of England.[10]

So, on the level of its official bodies, the Church has occasionally looked at the psychic dimension, but seems remarkably disinclined to take it really seriously and to give it prolonged theological consideration. But, as ever, the running is made by individuals and groups who believe that private enterprise is a good way to keep a subject in the churches' consciousness. Two such organizations are, in England, the Churches' Fellowship for Psychical and Spiritual Studies, and, in the USA, the Spiritual Frontiers Fellowship.

CFPSS was founded in 1953. The Fellowship believes that many people who have become estranged from the Church have found their way back again because a psychic experience has brought alive for them the Communion of Saints. Yet there are dangers in the psychical if it is sought for its own sake and not approached through the spiritual. Problems arise when individuals with no desire to use their psychic gifts to the glory of God become involved in practices which can destroy the personality and bring intense suffering to themselves and others. The leadership of the Fellowship believes that it is very important that it remain a *Churches'* Fellowship, ecumenical but firmly anchored within the mainstream of the life of the Christian community. Only so can it act as a bridge and an interpreter between orthodox Christianity and the psychically gifted, whilst at the same time fostering a truly critical theological discrimination of all the many claims and counter-claims that abound in the psychic fraternity. CFPSS publishes two periodicals. Its *Quarterly Review* is the members' forum for notices, correspondence and shorter articles of a more 'popular' character. *The Christian Parapsychologist* is its theological quarterly, carrying articles, reviews, correspondence and abstracts of relevant material from a wide range of other periodicals. The Fellowship has honoured the present writer with the task of editing *The Christian Parapsychologist* since 1978, and he finds it a stimulating and worth-while enterprise.

Spiritual Frontiers Fellowship is three years younger than CFPSS (1956) and is an organization less firmly rooted in the life of the Christian churches,[11] so that it feels freer than CFPSS to venture into less orthodox realms and ideas. Its 'academic affiliate' is the Academy of Religion and Psychical Research, whose quarterly *Journal* carries articles of interest to those concerned with a wide spectrum of religious studies, not only the specifically Christian.

These two organizations hope to build up in the Churches an informed body of responsible opinion which is aware of the importance of the psychic within Christianity, but on the other hand does not fall into the trap of letting that interest degenerate into one-track-mindedness. It is all too easy for enthusiasts to inflate their favourite subject well beyond its true importance. In this instance, they could do the Christian Church a grave disservice by their lack of balance and discrimination. The psychic is not the spiritual, and it is easy for it to assume a very much more important place than it deserves. But equally, it exists, and – especially for those people who are psychically sensitive – it must be understood and come to terms with, within a Christian understanding of the whole of life – not as determinative of that understanding, but contributing to it. Like any human gift, psychism has its spiritual opportunities and its spiritual dangers. If it goes sour, or gets out of hand, it can lead to overbalance, mania, idolatry, devil worship, psychic and spiritual disease. But so can – for example – money, which is just as much a spiritual power which can be used for good or misused for evil and overbalance its devotees! We need to put Jesus at the centre of our spiritual life and see how he relates to all our human potentialities, our human abilities, and our human destiny.

The psychic dimension will reveal to us some things about human abilities which may be rather unusual and may exert a kind of fascination over those who do not know much about them. Psychic gifts have to be exercised only to the glory of God and the honouring of Jesus, or they are not being Christianly used. The person with psychic ability may be able to lift some part of the veil that lies between us and the truth about human destiny. He may be able to reveal things that would otherwise be unknown to us about survival of death and about what we might expect to happen to us after this life is over; but the Christian believes that this veil is only truly transparent to the person who puts his trust in Jesus, the conquerer of death, the resurrection and the life. All we learn from parapsychology about what lies beyond the barrier of death has to be set within a faith in which Jesus is central and in which God matters a great deal more than man.

Our belief and trust has to be belief in God, and belief in survival only through him. Otherwise it degenerates into a selfish and self-centred search for personal certainty, personal assurances, and personal existence, in which God only comes as a necessary and perhaps rather tiresome condition, and in which the really determinative factor is the human individual rather than the Divine Reality. The theologian will find such an attitude redolent of the archetypical and original sin. Human beings in their fallen state are eccentric. They tend to look for their centres in themselves, when the true centre should be God, his purpose and his will. Only a radical reversal of this tendency – only a conversion bringing about a complete right-about-face – will cure this fatal condition. Such a conversion can only come about when the individual finds his meaning, not in his own self and its possible survival, but in Christ.

That is true of the whole of life as well as of the psychic dimension within it. I believe paranormal phenomena to be no less part of God's creation than other natural phenomena, and research into them to be no less legitimate for Christians. Yet it is possible to fix on psychic phenomena in such a way that they feed our sinful self-centredness, instead of opening us to the glories of God through contemplation of the wonders of his creation.

If that happens, psychism is preventing spiritual growth, and there is need for drastic action. Christian parapsychologists need to work responsibly. If sensitives begin to lose their spiritual balance, the experimenter will realize that some work with some sensitives is too dangerous to proceed with. The ethical committees which are such a prominent feature of medical research should become a standard part of parapsychology also, for the good of all who engage in it. But the only true and safe way, in any course of action, is to be rooted and grounded in the knowledge and love of Jesus. The 1976 report of the American Presbyterians, to which we have already alluded, had these wise words to say:

Our Lord has warned us that when one devil is driven out, seven more will take his place unless the vacuum is filled with the good. It is clear that many cults and novel psychic enthusiasms are pursued because of a religious vacuum in people's lives. This is a judgement on the Church, and it behoves us to ask in what ways we have failed to fulfill our whole task in the world. It is also a signal call to the Church to proclaim in more timely and effective ways the Lordship of Christ and to witness to his living power.[12]

Amen to that! There are many cults around these days, and many of them make overblown claims. Some of them touch on the world of parapsychology. The more we know about the subject, the less we are likely to be blown off course by incredible claims based on flimsy evidence. Certainly the more we know about Jesus and the fulness of the Christian religion, the more we can get the psychic into perspective. If this happens, then perhaps the bridges that are being built between the Christian and the parapsychological communities may become strong enough to bear the weight of traffic they need to sustain for the good of both. Perhaps this book may be a part of the process. That is certainly why it has been compiled.

Over the last few years, in particular, I have attempted to be a bridge-builder, and have had the stimulation and privilege of being asked to address a number of groups on subjects in the field of overlap between Christianity and parapsychology. I remember in particular the week of 13-17 July 1981 when I lectured and taught a group at one of the Summer Schools organized in Richmond, Virginia, by the Presbyterian School of Christian Education. This introductory chapter and a great deal of material to be found in the subsequent pages of this book were delivered there, and I am grateful to Dr Charles Melchert for his invitation and to Dean Geri Jones and others who looked after me so marvellously on that occasion.

Most of what follows in this volume has appeared in print before, but it has been scattered in a large number of periodicals both in the UK and in America. Some of them are specialist-interest publications with a very small circulation. It seemed good to put them together to see whether they would 'jell' as the expression of a way of looking at reality from a position on a bridge between two communities that have for too long been too ignorant of one another and too distrustful of one another.

I am grateful to the various editors and proprietors who have been unfailingly generous over copyright and reprinting arrangements, and have allowed me freely to modify and adapt what I had originally written for them so that it could exhibit a greater consistency of approach and less repetitious overlap. There still remain places where it has not been possible to avoid saying the same thing twice in different contexts, and I hope my readers will forgive me. Perhaps it will show that there are certain things about which I feel strongly enough to say them more than once.

There is only one thing to add, and that is that the more I learn of the world of the psychic, the more I realize that the depths of my ignorance are truly inexhaustible. The same is true of whatever exploration I have been able to do into the mysteries of understanding the love of God shown forth in Jesus Christ his Son, our Lord. In religion and spirituality, in every human science, and in psychical research, we stand on the shoulders of others in order to try to see further than they have been able to do. If that is what I have done, I shall be satisfied, and if others can use what I have written in such a way as sets their own thoughts into motion, I shall be even more gratified. The word for 'bridge-builder' in Latin is *pontifex*; but the last thing I want to do is to pontificate.

Michael Perry
The College, Durham
24 December 1982

References

1. Keith Thomas, *Religion and the Decline of Magic* (Weidenfeld and Nicolson, 1971; Penguin Books, 1973).
2. Morton Kelsey, *The Christian and the Supernatural* (Augsburg, 1976), p. 143.
3. 'Report of the Committee appointed to consider and report upon the Christian Faith in relation to (a) Spiritualism; (b) Christian Science; and (c) Theosophy' (Committee of the 1920 Lambeth Conference under the chairmanship of Bishop Burge of Oxford). In *The Lambeth Conferences (1867-1930)* (SPCK, 1948), pp. 106-117. This and the following reports are discussed by Angus H. Haddow in 'The Churches and Psychical Research: A review of some twentieth-century official documents', *The Christian Parapsychologist*, Vol. 3, No. 9 (December 1980), pp. 291-303.
4. *Report on Supernormal Psychic Phenomena.* A paper of the General Assembly of the Church of Scotland, 1922 (see Haddow, *art. cit.*, n. 3 *supra*, pp. 299-300).
5. *The Christian Parapsychologist* Vol. 3, No. 2 (March 1979), pp. 40-73.
6. Appendix 1 (pp. 61-66) of *Prayer and the Departed: A Report of the Archbishops' Commission on Christian Doctrine* (SPCK, 1971).
7. *Report on Occult and Psychic Activities* adopted by the 188th (1976) General Assembly of the United Presbyterian Church (USA). Reprinted (minus appendices) in *The Christian Parapsychologist* Vol. 1, No. 6 (December 1976), pp. 77-81.
8. See *The Christian Parapsychologist* Vol. 4, No. 5 (March 1982), p. 138.
9. *Report of the Working Party on Parapsychology.* A paper of the General Assembly of the Church of Scotland, 21 May 1976. Obtainable via 121 George Street Edinburgh EH2 4YN.
10. *General Synod: July Group of Sessions 1975: Report of Proceedings* (Vol. 6, No. 2), p. 361 (Church Information Office, 1975).
11. For a useful recent critique, see Leslie Price, 'American Perspectives on Christian Parapsychology', *The Christian Parapsychologist*, Vol. 4, No. 8 (December 1982), pp. 252-5.
12. *Op. cit. supra*, n. 7.

Part 1
Sighting shots

There is so much suspicion between the Church and psychical research, and so much of it is simply the result of one party knowing woefully little about the interests and method of approach of the other, that I find it difficult to refuse occasions for explaining each to the other. Sometimes the opportunity arises of producing a brief article in which only the broadest of introductions can be given, and it seemed a good idea to begin this present volume with three examples which could then preface the closer studies of particular aspects of the field which follow.

John Bluck heard me lecture in New Zealand in 1976, and when he became editor of *One World*, the monthly magazine of the World Council of Churches, published from Geneva, he asked me if I would do a brief and popular article showing why Christians ought to be interested and knowledgeable about the psychic scene. I originally called it 'Chi-Rho and Psi', but John very properly re-titled it 'A Psychic Word for the Church'. My title referred to the closing words of the article, in which I wrote of the Christian symbol of the Chi-Rho, the first two letters of the word 'Christ' in Greek, and the Greek letter Psi, which indicates the subject-matter of parapsychology. (They are combined in the symbol used for the cover of this present volume.) This article first appeared in *One World* for October 1977 (No. 30, pp.19–20) and was reprinted in the June 1978 issue of *The Christian Parapsychologist* (Volume 2, No. 2, pp. 30–33).

The second of these 'sighting shots' was published as the 'Saturday religious article' on the Court Page of *The Times* for 20 February 1982, one hundred years to the day from the occasion on which the Society for Psychical Research was formally constituted.

As part of the centenary observances of the SPR, Ivor Grattan-Guinness assembled a team of twenty-nine contributors to produce a book introducing psychical research to those outside its discipline. It was published by the Aquarian Press on 16 September 1982 as *Psychical Research: A Guide to its History, Principles and Practices, in Celebration of 100 Years of the Society for Psychical Research*. Part Four of this collective venture, on 'Psychical Research and Other Subjects', contained a chapter on 'Psychical Research and Religion', which forms the third section of what follows. A very similar article had appeared in *The Christian Parapsychologist* for March 1982 (Volume 4, No. 5, pp. 139–145).

1
A psychic word for the Church

The year was 1950. I was in my final year at school before going on to National Service and University. Chemistry and physics were the subjects I found completely absorbing. The sciences had probed to the very building-blocks of the material universe, and had taken the atom apart and put it together again with a blast so powerful that, five years previously, it had within days ended the greatest war known to man. Every day something new was being discovered, and now I was on the verge of joining the fellowship of the discoverers.

My other interest was the local church, where I said my prayers, read my Bible, taught in Sunday School, sang in the choir, and organized the youth fellowship.

Every now and again I was told that I was living a schizophrenic existence, and that I would some day have to choose between being a scientist and being a Christian. But, at seventeen, the world is too full of things to discover. There isn't time to ask whether one is being entirely self-consistent. (That is just as well – otherwise one would miss such a lot.)

One of our duties as members of the Upper Sixth was that each of us in turn had to deliver a paper to the Scientific Society. I used to read every paperback I could find on scientific subjects, and I had just come across a Penguin book by G.N.M. Tyrrell entitled *The*

Personality of Man. It was so different from anything I had read before that I determined to base my paper on it.

It talked of some of the capabilities of man which neither my religious home nor my scientific school had even mentioned. It explored a world of apparitions and intuitions, of knowledge passed from mind to mind without physical link, of occasions when the causality of time seemed to have gone backwards, of trances in which people wrote or spoke things of which their conscious minds were entirely unaware, yet which tapped either the minds of others here on earth, or of those who had died. It showed me that the human mind was a thing of even greater complexity and mystery than those mysteries of the atom which were fascinating me. I had discovered psychical research, and the beginning of a lifelong interest. The paper was delivered a week or two later, but a whole generation afterwards I know I am still only on the outskirts of an understanding of this field.

Since then, I have learnt that it is not necessary to make a choice between being a scientist and being a Christian. One can be both – and ought to be. Linking the two communities is the bridge of psychical research – parapsychology, or the study of psi phenomena.

Parapsychology, like science, deals with observed facts, and tries to fit them into a framework of understanding so that they can be seen in the context of a total world-picture. Science, for me up to that moment, had dealt only with mechanical or material or electromagnetic facts. The observer was left with a feeling of being not only unrelated to these facts, but irrelevant to them. It seemed also that the observer as a person needed to be explained (if at all) in terms of the same kinds of material or mechanical or electromagnetic forces.

But psi phenomena opened up, for scientific examination, aspects of man which had previously been the preserve of the poet, the mystic, the religious. Perhaps here was a way in which, with scientific rigour and impartiality, the religious nature of man could be examined and the claims of religion be validated.

The phrase used by the founding fathers of psychical research, those worthy Victorians who set up the Society for Psychical Research in 1882, was 'to examine without prejudice or prepossession and in a scientific spirit those faculties of man, real or supposed, which appear to be inexplicable on any generally recognized hypothesis'. Was this to be a bridge between the world of scientific explanation and the world of religious claim?

Unfortunately, bridges (unless they are like the medieval London

Bridge) are not built to be lived on, and most people seem to be happier on one side or the other of the water. Or, to change the metaphor, a border-post manned by UN peace-keeping patrols is not a comfortable place to be. You tend to be misunderstood by both sides, and sniped at by everybody.

That is certainly the case with psi. By and large, the scientific establishment is not disposed to take it seriously. The climate *is* changing, but very slowly. Courses on the subject are now offered at undergraduate level in a number of British, Continental, and American universities, and it is possible to do postgraduate research in it, leading to doctorate status. But it is still a minority interest, at which the greater number of scientists look askance. The repeatable experiment is elusive, there is no standard theory within which to place its findings, the boundaries of the subject are ill-defined, and such results as there are challenge too many scientific orthodoxies about space, time, and causality.

The religious establishment is just as cool. For centuries the tradition has been to distrust psychically sensitive people as representing the pagan religion from which the Christian faith has liberated the countries into which it has percolated. This is as true of the First World as it is of the Third, though Christianity took such a hold in Europe that the indigenous religions are now no more than vestigial, and apathy or irreligion are greater threats by far than paganism.

But in Europe, the Church had driven the psychic into the underworld. It never disappeared; but it was always threatened, so that it allied itself with pagan rather than with Christian ideas, and it never had the advantage of a probing and critical theological understanding. The Church was too busy persecuting the witches to ask what their psychic sensitivity was saying about the nature of man and his relation to spiritual reality. (In fact, witchcraft and the psychic were largely unconnected, as modern scholarship has demonstrated; but those who were antagonistic to both were not all that careful how accurately they described those people whom they believed to be tarred with the same Satanic brush.) So psi was left to proliferate amongst 'Jews, Turks, Infidels, and Hereticks' and to be the preserve of spiritualists, occultists, magicians (black, white, and any shade in between), theosophists, Swedenborgians, or simply those who were regarded as too feeble-minded to have a proper grasp of theological orthodoxy. This then reinforced the establishment Church's prejudice that the psychic was the realm of Satan. And when supping with him, even the longest spoon was too short.

Here again, though, the tide is turning. There are signs that

Christians are treating psychic sensitivity seriously, understanding rather than condemning, and sifting critically rather than exorcizing wholesale. As with the scientific establishment, the signs of a deluge are at present no more than a cloud the size of a man's hand.

Two such signs are, in England, the Churches' Fellowship for Psychical and Spiritual Studies (CFPSS), and, in America, the Spiritual Frontiers Fellowship (SFF).

CFPSS was founded in 1953 'for the study of the wide reaches of the paranormal and extra-sensory perception in their relation to the Christian faith. The field of study includes psychical phenomena, mysticism, creative meditation and spiritual healing. The psychical includes such phenomena as telepathy, clairvoyance, clairaudience, precognition and psychokinesis'.

SFF dates from 1956 and exists 'to sponsor, explore and interpret the growing interest in psychic phenomena and mystical experience within the Church, wherever these experiences relate to effective prayer, spiritual healing and personal survival. The Fellowship has as its goal the development of spiritual growth in the individual and the encouragement of new dimensions of spiritual experience within the Church.' Both bodies are ecumenical. CFPSS invites membership from all who belong to Churches which acknowledge Jesus Christ as Lord and Saviour of the world. SFF tends to membership which is less tightly theologically defined. The difference shows in the titles of their respective theological or academic publications – CFPSS issues *The Christian Parapsychologist*, whilst SFF's academic affiliate is the Academy of Religion and Psychical Research.

In addition, there are individual theologians who include the psychic as part of their remit – recently and notably John Hick, whose book *Death and Eternal Life* takes the evidence for survival provided by parapsychology very seriously indeed. Hick's treatment is significant in that it is in an inter-faith as well as in an international context. He is well aware of cross-cultural currents which necessitate a new way of doing theology for a new age.

In this kind of setting, psi can be seen as something which needs to be taken more seriously in ecumenical circles than it appears to have been so far. We need theologians from all traditions and cultures trying to relate the truth of Christ to human experience. A *World* Council of Churches could do this more effectively than any purely Western-based organization. If so, the pages of the Bible could be illuminated, the pastoral problems of many people better handled, and the faith itself better related to the men and women for whom the Gospel is intended.

Is it time for the Chi-Rho of Christianity to take more seriously the Psi of parapsychology? Can the World Council of Churches help this to happen?

2
The psychic and the spiritual

On 20 February 1882, the Society for Psychical Research (SPR) was formally constituted. One of the things its founders looked for was an end to the sterile old debates between religion and science. Thirty or so years previously, the table rappings at the home of the Fox sisters in up-state New York had set off a world-wide movement which soon claimed followers at all levels of intellectual and social life. It was even rumoured that Queen Victoria was in contact with the spirit of Prince Albert through the mediumship of her 'fey' Scots retainer, John Brown.

But Spiritualism was a religion, and accepted the purported data with an attitude more of faith than of critical inquiry. The founding fathers of the SPR were pledged to approach the subject 'without prejudice or prepossession of any kind, and in the same spirit of exact and unimpassioned inquiry which has enabled Science to solve so many problems, once not less obscure nor less hotly debated'.

They approached their tasks with optimistic enthusiasm. It was an enthusiasm I remember sharing when, as a schoolboy more than thirty years ago, I picked up a copy of G.N.M. Tyrrell's *The Personality of Man*, in Penguin, and thought I had found a subject that could form a bridge between my scientific studies and my religious aspirations.

Alas, things were not as easy as that, and both the scientific and

the religious establishments have been markedly cool towards psychical research (or parapsychology). Scientists look for repeatable
experiments without multiple interpretations, and parapsychologists
seem to be as far away from that state of affairs as ever. Nevertheless, scientific scepticism on, for example, the existence of
telepathy seems to be on the wane and it is the 'hard' scientists, such
as physicists, who are the more open-minded. Psychologists, as a
group, remain notably sceptical.

Mainstream religion has been as chary as mainstream science,
though with honourable exceptions, such as Bishop Boyd Carpenter, who served a presidential term at the SPR in 1912 and
Dean W.R. Matthews of St Paul's, who delivered its Myers
Memorial Lecture in 1940. The Lambeth Conference in 1920
recognized that some people had psychic gifts, but advised caution
and restraint in their use; the Archbishop of Canterbury received a
report on the subject in 1939 but it was consigned to the Lambeth
archives for forty years before publication was allowed. A
sympathetic and balanced report on parapsychology was received
by the Church of Scotland in 1976.

Religion dismisses the psychic aspect of life at its peril. It poses
special pastoral and theological questions to the churches that have
wide ramifications. For example, several of the bishops now have
their advisers to whom they refer correspondents troubled by
poltergeist outbreaks or by their own psychic sensitivity and the
results of its exercise. What counsel should they give? If there is
such a thing as psychic sensitivity, is it essentially a gift from God
(like other gifts such as musical or artistic sensitivity) and therefore
to be exercised, albeit with fear and trembling and in prayerful
discretion, to God's glory? Or is it a Satanic ruse, to be eschewed
by all faithful Christians?

If Christians find themselves to be psychically sensitive, is this a
faculty which they should develop with the help of a sound spiritual
director, or should they exclaim at the discovery, 'Get thee behind
me, Satan'? What is the theological and pastoral propriety of taking
note of psychic communications, especially when they appear to
straddle the gulf of death? Do they provide a corroboration of some
Christian doctrines about the life beyond death? Or do they
faithlessly seek proof where trust in God is the more appropriate
attitude?

As usual, private enterprise runs ahead of official cognisance. The
Churches' Fellowship for Psychical and Spiritual Studies was
founded in 1953. Its meetings try to help those who wish to

integrate their psychic sensitivity with their spiritual life, and its quarterly, *The Christian Parapsychologist*, aims to promote awareness of the psychic dimension within Christian thinking and tries to offer a discriminating discussion of the whole subject and its implications within theology.

There are two opposite dangers in all this. One is to make the psychic into the centre and mainstay of a person's religion. The other is to ignore it altogether. The first is the temptation of Spiritualism. The second has been the temptation of the religious establishment. After one hundred years of the SPR and nearly thirty of the CFPSS, there is still much work to be done.

3
Psychical research and religion

A religion is a system of belief in which man seeks self-understanding and an understanding of the world about him. It makes unprovable assertions about the nature and destiny of man, and of humanity's relations with an unseen world and its human and non-human denizens. Those beliefs are expected to have certain implications in terms of conduct and behaviour. The term 'religion' is generally applied to the behaviour-system (including – if applicable – worship), while the underlying beliefs and their intellectual ramifications are spoken of as 'theology'.

Like all definitions of 'religion', this one can be criticized. Is scientific materialism a religion? Its unprovable assertions about man are that he is ultimately explicable in physico-chemical and electro-physiological terms, that he ceases to exist on the death of the body, and that there is no unseen world to have denizens, let alone to be interconnected with our visible universe. Is Communism a religion? Its unprovable axioms of belief cover such matters as the relation of the individual to the collective, and the ultimate end to which history tends. Certainly religion does not need to be theistic to qualify under any comprehensive definition, or the purer forms of Buddhism would not qualify. Perhaps one should not try to define too comprehensively, but simply accept 'religion' as a recognizable phenomenon, and to enquire about areas of overlap with psychical research.

Psychical research and Christianity

Psychical research arose within a society familiar with the Christian world-view. In its classical form, Christianity holds (among other doctrines) that the world was created by, and is sustained by, God. He designed men and women for eternal fellowship with himself and with other beings (sub-human, human, and super-human) in a world unseen from, but interpenetrating, this present and visible one. Because of man's inability to achieve this calling, God became incarnate in Jesus of Nazareth who, though killed by his contemporaries, rose from death and still enables those with faith in him to share his life in heaven. This belief system is not empirically provable; indeed, within it, 'faith' is reckoned as a virtue and is contrasted with 'sight' or 'proof'.

Psychical phenomena loom large within the foundation documents of Christianity (which shares a common origin with both Judaism and Islam). They are also well attested in Christian history. Basic to a Christian conception of prayer, for instance, is the belief that man can converse with God (a two-way traffic) without the use of sensory channels. In the Catholic devotional tradition our intercession with God also involves the saints — those humans who departed this life in a condition of exceptional holiness. Sometimes it seems that our sensory channels can be extra-sensorially activated so that the devotee can see or hear the entity with whom or through whom this converse takes place — visions of the saints or angels, or even of God himself. But prayer and visions are not the only ostensibly paranormal phenomena with which the student of religions is familiar. Within the Christian tradition, for example, it is obvious that 'when we begin to examine the Bible in terms of the categories of the paranormal, we are confronted with an almost embarrassing abundance of parapsychological riches. Examples of telepathy, clairvoyance, precognition, mediumship, psychokinesis, and out-of-body experiences abound.'[1]

Divination and oracles played an important part within Biblical religion, as did such practices in the religions of many nations, not only in the ancient world.[2] Mediumistic practice was far from unknown in ancient Israel, but there are various estimates as to the attitude of the Biblical writers to it.[3] Paranormal healings — often at a distance from the sufferer — are alleged as a commonplace within the ministry of Jesus of Nazareth, and accounts of such go back at least as far as the time of Elijah in the ninth century BC. The resurrection appearances of Jesus[4] are *prima facie* an example of paranormal phenomena, and have been interpreted as collectively perceived veridical apparitions of the recently departed. The paranormal and the miraculous are not identical phenomena, though they overlap; to remove either from the pages of the Bible would be to emasculate it intolerably.

Christian history continues the story, and its writings, particularly the lives of the saints, are full of wonder stories.[5] A psychical researcher needs, of course, to separate mis-observation or exaggeration and pure fantasy from fact; but it is clear that their contemporaries believed that odd phenomena could accompany those who were notably close to God. Indeed, if a person was to be enrolled in the Kalendar of Saints, miracles both during and after the candidate's lifetime had to be proved to the reasonable satisfaction of the Church authorities, who employed a *promotor fidei* (or, as he was popularly called, a 'devil's advocate') to do all he could to discredit the stories.

One such 'advocate' was Prospero Lambertini (1675-1758), whose treatise *De Servorum Dei Beatificatione et Beatorum Canonizatione* has earned him the title of 'the father of Christian psychical research' for his careful attention to methods of enquiry into allegedly paranormal occurrences. He ended his life as Pope Benedict XIV, and Renée Haynes has written his biography under the title *Philosopher King* (Weidenfeld and Nicolson, 1970). Within the Christian tradition, reported miracles have included

levitation, telekinesis, . . . 'seeing without eyes' and multiplication of food. The majority fall within the more ambiguous domain of extreme physiological manifestations . . . These include stigmata (appearance of the wounds of Christ), tokens of espousal (physiological deformation to produce structures with the appearance of wedding rings or other symbols of the mystical marriage with Christ), generation of light by the body, inedia (not eating for weeks, months, or years), production of intense heat ('incendium amoris'), capacity to sustain prolonged contact with fire, boiling water, etc., without pain or injury, and several peculiarities manifested by saintly corpses (incorruption, absence of rigidity, continued ability to bleed after weeks, months, or years).[6]

Such phenomena are by no means confined to Christian holy men, but are known in a variety of religious traditions. The issue of *The Christian Parapsychologist* for December 1979 contained a number of articles examining the claims made on behalf of Sri Sathya Sai Baba, a contemporary Indian holy man (Volume 3, No. 5, pp. 156-171). Most such saints and gurus insist that the unusual phenomena are unimportant, and secondary to their main purpose and personal sanctification. Indeed, they often regard them as an embarrassment and try to hide them.

Partly as a result of the Reformation, but mainly through the influence of the scientific revolution, there began to be a more careful distinction drawn between faith and what was known as 'superstition'. Amongst 'superstitions' which fared ill in the centuries of the Enlightenment were beliefs in astrology, divination, claims to prophecy and second sight, magic, witchcraft, and the miracles associated with canonizations. For an excellent account of the early stages of this development, it would be hard to better Keith Thomas' *Religion and the Decline of Magic* (Weidenfeld and Nicolson 1971, subsequently issued by Penguin Books). As the centuries drew on, religion and theology in the Christian West were becoming emancipated from superstitions which had earlier been associated with them, whilst scientific orthodoxy – which generally meant a materialistic view of man and a debunking one of paranormal data – made enormous inroads, not only on religious belief, but also on any view of man as other than materially explicable. By the mid-nineteenth century, both were in full flood.

Fortunately, paranormal phenomena refused to go away. As a result, there was a reaction in the name of the empirical data. It had two aspects to it, the one religious and the other scientific.

Reactions to psychical claims

The scientific reaction was, of course, what led to the founding of the Society for Psychical Research, which attempted to examine those faculties (or alleged faculties) of man 'without prejudice or prepossession and in a scientific spirit'. But it is doubtful if the scientific reaction would have come had it not been preceded, a generation or so beforehand, by the religious one, in the shape of Spiritualism. The paranormal rappings experienced by the Fox sisters at Hydesville, USA, in 1848, which they interpreted as communications from the departed, set off a movement which has claimed followers at all levels of intellectual and social life from the Universities and the Court to the populace. It was even rumoured that Queen Victoria was in contact with the spirit of Prince Albert through the mediumship, first of Robert Lees and then of her Scots retainer, John Brown. However unfounded (and see Elizabeth Longford's *Victoria RI* for its detailed refutation), it is a rumour that even today is not without its protagonists.

The Church, however, had little to do either with Spiritualism or psychical research. There were honourable exceptions – the wife of the Archbishop of Canterbury was on the list of Associates of the Society for Psychical Research by 1883, Bishop Boyd Carpenter was its President for 1912, and the Dean of St Paul's, Dr W.R. Matthews, delivered the Myers Memorial Lecture in 1940 – but the more common view was that the whole enterprise was a seeking after evidence where faith would have been more appropriate, or that Spiritualism was a wicked and pernicious heresy and psychical research was too close to Spiritualism to be safe. To quote Dean Matthews' Myers lecture on *Psychical Research and Theology* (SPR, 1940, p. 1):

The attitude of the Christian Church to psychical research in the past has been, on the whole, one of antagonism, or at least of suspicion. This has not been, in the main, due to scepticism concerning the phenomena which are the subject-matter of the enquiry, but rather to a conviction that they were real and that they came from a source only too well known . . . The general opinion has been that abnormal and supernatural phenomena could be produced by evil spirits.

In more recent times, several branches of the Christian Church have appointed official commissions or committees to enquire into the relation between psychical research and Christian theology or religion. A useful list of these reports, together with a discussion of their contents, can be found in Angus Haddow's article entitled 'The Churches and Psychical Research: A Review of some Twentieth-Century Official Documents' in *The Christian Parapsychologist* for December 1980 (Volume 3, No. 4, pp. 291-303). This covers Churches on both sides of the Atlantic.

In 1953 there was founded in England a body subsequently to be known as the Churches' Fellowship for Psychical and Spiritual Studies, and the Spiritual Frontiers Fellowship followed in the USA in 1956. There is in addition a large penumbra of belief systems arising from psychical data, some of them coming under the definition of 'religion'. The Inner-Space Interpreters' Service of Burbank, California, produces a useful annual guide to the multitudinous and ever-changing number of publications that such groups sponsor.

Implications for religion of psychical phenomena

Psychical research touches religious concerns at a number of points. What is the relation between psychical ability and spiritual stature? Does man survive death and if so, is there any spiritual content to his survival? Is reincarnation a rational option? (This is a question which has greatly concerned many of the Eastern religions but about which Christianity has, until recently, appeared to have very little to say, though Western interest in it is increasing.) Is mankind alone in the Universe? This question involves angels, demons, the existence of God, even unidentified flying objects – Barry Downing, in his book *The Bible and Flying Saucers* (Lippincott, New York, 1968) reckons that they have considerable religious significance. What about prayer, spirituality, and mysticism? Can we learn anything about them from a study of altered states of consciousness? Is there anything objective here, or are we simply dealing with self-induced psychological states?

Whether psychical research can bring knowledge and certainty in place of opinion and faith is another matter. Spiritualism as a religion invests almost the whole of its spiritual capital in the answer to the question, and avers that we can *know* what otherwise would be within the sphere of faith. Psychical researchers are more aware of the ambiguity of so much of the evidence, and sometimes despair of ever reaching a clear-cut solution to any question.

Mainstream Christians prefer to hedge their bets. They believe that the dead survive; but a belief in the possibility of communication with the dead is not a part of their creed. It is, for them, a matter for empirical investigation. For the Spiritualist, a belief in communication is almost the totality of his creed, and critical investigation is therefore felt by him to be highly threatening. The Christian believes that psychic phenomena have a place in his beliefs, but only a place, and they must be kept in proportion. To quote Laurence Tunstall Heron,

Enthusiasm for psychic insight and communication must not overbalance and override other equally essential facets and strands of faith, tradition, and action. Specifically, psychical lore and practice ought not to become the center and mainstay of religious observance ... In the web of the Judaeo-Christian tradition ... a score of crafts and disciplines contribute their important strengths. Through this web the psychic element weaves just one luminous filament.[7]

A knowledge of psychical research will not replace faith; the relation between faith, reason, and evidence is a subtle and complex one, whether in orthodox science, psychical research, or religion.[8] But men of religion who are ignorant of the findings of psychical research are missing a dimension of great value to them in their thinking. Let me end by quoting from Richard Neff's book *Psychic Phenomena and Religion*:

The Church particularly should pay close attention to what is happening in parapsychology. Religious experience, I am convinced, has a psychic dimension, and if we are to handle this area of life, we must keep current on the advances made in understanding it. Psychic phenomena and religious experience are not synonymous terms ... but the facts and theories related to parapsychology aid in our understanding of religious phenomena, and they help some people to see that their leap of faith is credible.[9]

References

1. Boyce M. Bennett Jr., 'Vision and Audition in Biblical Prophecy as Illuminated by Recent Research in Human Consciousness', in *Psi and States of Consciousness* (edited by Betty Shapin and Lisette Coly, the Parapsychology Foundation, New York, 1978), p. 112.

2. See L. Loewe and C. Blacker (eds.), *Divination and Oracles* (Allen and Unwin, 1981).

3. For different assessments, see G. Maurice Elliott, *The Bible as Psychic History* (Rider 1959), and the present author's paper reprinted as Chapter 6 on pp. 66-83 below.

4. See Michael C. Perry, *The Easter Enigma* (Faber and Faber, 1959).

5. See *The Physical Phenomena of Mysticism* by H. Thurston SJ (Burns Oates 1952) and many later articles, particularly two by Rhea White: 'An analysis of ESP Phenomena in the Saints' in *Parapsychology Review* for January – February 1982 (Vol. 13, No. 1, pp. 15-18), and 'Saintly Psi' in the *Journal of Religion and Psychical Research* for July and October 1981 (Vol. 4, Nos. 3 and 4, pp. 157-167). There is also a useful cross-cultural article on 'Saints, Shamans, and the Paranormal' by D. Scott Rogo in *Theta* for Autumn 1981 (Vol. 9, No. 4, pp. 2-6). See also the articles on St Joseph of Copertino and Padre Pio by Jule Eisenbud and Michael Grosso respectively in *The Christian Parapsychologist* for September 1982 (Vol. 4, No. 7, pp. 211-226).

6. E.F. Kelly and R.G. Locke, *Altered States of Consciousness* (Parapsychology Foundation, 1981), pp. 18ff.

7. L.T. Heron, *ESP in the Bible* (Doubleday, New York 1974), p. 50.

8. See the article on 'Faith, Reason, and Evidence' reprinted on pp. 52-65 below as Chapter 5.

9. R. Neff, *Psychic Phenomena and Religion* (Westminster Press, Philadelphia Pennsylvania 1971), p. 170.

Part 2
Living

Parapsychology investigates the powers and capabilities of the human mind, and is as concerned with the potentialities of men in this world as with their survival into another. Although the majority of the essays in this collection are concerned with death and its sequel, it is important that we should begin with a consideration of what is (or may be) possible to us in the here and now. Two of the pieces in this section are particularly concerned with the status and interpretation of evidence, and the third is an attempt at seeing how far the Biblical narratives are permeated with parapsychological data, and at what that says for our interpretation of them.

In 1972, I was invited to be one of the lecturers at the fifty-fifth Annual Conference of the Modern Churchmens' Union, held at Balls Park College, Hertford from 24-28 July. Its general theme was 'The Search for Meaning', and two speakers were asked to lecture on 'The Quest for the Transcendent through the Paranormal'. My paper was followed by a similar one by the Revd G.S. Whitby, a founder of the Unitarian Society for Psychical Studies. It was printed in *The Modern Churchman*, Vol. 16 (n.s.), No. 1 (October 1972), pp. 70-77, and reprinted in *Spiritual Frontiers*, the quarterly journal of the Spiritual Frontiers

Fellowship (then of Evanston, Illinois, now of Independence, Missouri), Vol. 5, No. 3 (Summer 1973), pp. 131-9. Its opening pages were reworked and expanded as the fifth of my Selwyn Lectures given at St John's College, Auckland, New Zealand, in 1976, on 'Worship and Mystery' and printed as *The Paradox of Worship* (SPCK, 1977); but there it was developed without reference to parapsychology at all. It will be obvious how much the paper owes to Bishop Ian Ramsey's concept of the 'disclosure situation'. I was much looking forward to sending a copy of the printed form of the lecture to him and to asking him what he made of it. His comments were always illuminating and often astringent, and would have helped me to see whether I was thinking along the right lines. Alas, on 6 October 1972 he suffered his second and fatal heart attack, and the Church on earth is permanently the poorer without his physical presence.

That paper on 'The Quest for the Transcendent through the Paranormal' began to explore the bearing of two relationships on each other – the relationship, on the one hand, between evidence and interpretation, and – on the other – between parapsychology and Christian faith. But it needed to be taken to a deeper level and teased through more adequately. When, therefore, I was asked if I would present a paper at the Annual Conference of the Unitarian Society for Psychical Studies which was meeting that year in Newcastle upon Tyne, I took the opportunity to return to that topic by lecturing on 'Faith, Reason, and Evidence in Religion, Science and Psychical Research'. By that time, George Whitby had died – another great loss to the earthly Church – and the session was ably chaired by his widow Florence ('Tim'). That was on 14 April 1981. The lecture was published in No. 29 of *Psychical Studies* (the journal of the Unitarian Society for Psychical Studies) for Autumn 1981, pp. 1-16. It also appeared in *Theta* (published by the Psychical Research Foundation of Chapel Hill, North Carolina), Vol. 9, No. 3 (Summer 1981), pp. 2-7, and was translated into Dutch for *Bres* No. 91 (November/December 1981) pp. 19-29 as 'Kan een gelovig mens parapsycholoog zijn?'.

'Psi in the Bible' was originally a lecture delivered before the Society for Psychical Research in London on 7 November 1978. It appeared under that title in *Parapsychology Review* (published by the Parapsychology Foundation Inc., New York), Vol. 10, No. 3 (May/June 1979), pp. 9-14, and in Dutch in *Bres* No. 77 (July/August 1979), pp. 24-37, as 'Parapsychologie en de Bijbel'. For this collection, I have re-titled it 'May a Christian Investigate the Paranormal?' The original title promised more goods than the paper even attempted to deliver, and the main thrust of this piece is to use Biblical evidence to examine the propriety of Christian involvement in psychical studies rather than to make an exhaustive study of Biblical accounts of paranormal occurrences.

4
The quest for the transcendent through the paranormal

How does a man become aware of the transcendent? For some people, there is a moment of numinous consciousness within the setting of natural or man-made beauty. Beauty of form or sound – flowers or trees, a windswept crag, sunset and seaside, a haunting melody – can take a man outside himself and flood his soul with the realization that there are things beyond our seeing or touching or handling; can give him what T.S. Eliot has described[1] as 'a tremour of bliss, a wink of heaven'. Others go in search of their experience of the transcendent through prayer, through the techniques of meditation, through the dangerous avenue of a drug-induced psychedelic state. But whatever apprehension comes to them, they find it has its own sovereign freedom. It cannot be commanded or manipulated; it comes unbidden and cannot be forced. A man is surprised by joy.

There are, of course, other avenues. For some people, the transcendent is found through moments of failure when they come to the end of their tether. As they face a situation of basic need, be it bankruptcy, or divorce, or alcoholism, or bereavement, or illness, or redundancy, or the knowledge that their own life has not got much further to run – or as they find themselves let down by people they thought they could trust – they reflect on the ephemera of love or the unreliability of human nature. Then, *de profundis*, there wells up within them the feeling that if there is the impermanent, the imperfect, then somewhere, somehow, there must be the permanent, the perfect. There comes to them what Bishop Ian Ramsey has spoken of as a 'disclosure situation', an apprehension of the transcendent which hides behind the shifting veils of sensory awareness. This is the raw material of religious experience. It is not specifically Christian, but basically and elementally human. If it comes to religiously-minded men, or in a religious setting, then it may be overlaid with symbols from religious ideology, as it was for Isaiah when he described what he experienced in terms of the Lord high and lifted up, surrounded by winged seraphs and a ceaseless sound of 'Holy, Holy, Holy'; or as it was for an exile in a strange land on the Lord's day, who wrote down what he saw as the Book of the Revelation to John. If it comes to secularized men, or in a secular setting, of course, it can easily be brushed off as emotion, or a quirk of physiochemistry, and laughed off into the harsh lethal light of common day.

Which all goes to show that no experience comes to us without its interpretation. But experience may be followed by reflection, and it is at that stage that the question is asked, 'Was this a valid experience of an objective transcendent, or, if we are honest, ought we to rationalize it away?' Reflection is an attempt to disentangle experience and interpretation, and one must stand at some distance from the experience itself in order to do it. Often, and for many people, reflection enables them to explain their feelings, and the explanation takes all the numinous magic out of it.

> There was an awful rainbow once in heaven:
> We know her woof, her texture; she is given
> In the dull catalogue of common things.
> Philosophy will clip an Angel's wings.[2]

But there are also many cases where the transcendent reference, once recognized, stays with a man all his life, and shapes the whole of the rest of his days. One thinks of the revelation to Brother Lawrence in the winter tree, or to Francesco Bernadone in the face of a leper.[3]

The fact is, that everybody recognizes how subjective is the type of numinous experience about which I have so far been talking. A tree in winter, a leper by the roadside, a golden sunset, a haunting melody, do not *have* to trigger off an apprehension of the transcendent. And when they *do*, they are seen to be no more than triggers. That which is apprehended is seen to be a reality which is greater and more significant than the avenue by which it was apprehended. The winter tree enabled Brother Lawrence to see inside another world, and throughout the rest of his pilgrimage he was validating within his own experience the realization that had come to him in that moment that there *was* another world, and that the transcendent *was* real and objective. But there are many people about who will claim that the poor man was deluded and that there was *no* objective referent either to his initial experience or to his subsequent Practice of the Presence of God.

This is where the paranormal comes in. Ordinary numinous experience is so subjective. Its interpretation depends on faith and not on sight. Is it possible to be in touch with the transcendent in a way which brooks no denial, and where the empirical evidence is *there* objectively, so that the sceptic (even the sceptic who has not himself had the experience) can be forever silenced? At first sight, paranormal phenomena provide the answer.

Experience of the paranormal may come completely unsought, or it may be part of a quest deliberately entered upon. In the former category, perhaps the most unnerving thing to happen to a person is to see an apparition. It can be something as vague as the grey hooded monk seen by moonlight in the ruins of the priory, or as specific as the figure of C.S. Lewis which was seen shortly after his death by J.B. Phillips and which spoke a few words of encouragement to him before dissolving into the thin air from which it came.[4] Or it can be as apparently ordinary as the figure of Fr. Burrows seen reading his breviary as he walked on the terrace in front of Heythrop College. It was only later that Fr. Crehan, who saw the figure, discovered that Fr. Burrows had had a motor accident earlier that afternoon and that what he had seen was an apparition, observed within an hour or two of the death of Fr. Burrows in the Radcliffe Infirmary at Oxford.[5]

Another type of paranormal experience is that of the poltergeist. Something strange and inexplicable happens in a house. There may be noises, creaks, footsteps, there may be movements of objects, crashings and breakings; there may be apports. The person concerned feels – sometimes with curiosity, more often with apprehension, occasionally with sheer terror – in contact with the transcendent.

All these are examples, not so much of man's quest for the transcendent, but of the transcendent popping up and taking a man by surprise. It is possible, however, for the initiative to come from our side – by experimenting with table-turning, or planchette, or the ouija board, or by discovering that one can produce automatic writing, or by consulting a medium, or even by the more exotic method of joining a group practising white or black magic.

Sometimes nothing happens. The table won't turn, or planchette spells out nonsense, or automatic writing produces nothing but a mass of unintelligible squiggle; or the medium 'fishes' for information and patently produces nothing which is specifically relevant to the sitter or to the departed spirits with whom she claims to be in contact. Sometimes – particularly with planchette and occasionally with automatic writing – there are messages which show that here we have a method whereby the censorship which the conscious mind exerts upon the unconscious can be relaxed, and repressed material be brought out into the open. This, I am sure, is why so many people who play around with planchette 'for kicks' become frightened and drop it. Very often, not long after planchette begins to produce intelligible messages, it starts to spell out threats to the life of one of the circle, or prophecies of his forthcoming death. I believe that the sitters in such a case are not in touch with malevolent spirits so much as with the malevolent contents of their own repressed subconscious, and especially with the violence which lurks not far below the surface of urbane and civilized humanity.[6] But at other times it really does look as if this is a method by which we can be in touch with discarnate entities. To the person concerned, this *may* be felt to be completely matter-of-fact. This is the way the world is made, and why get excited about it? It no more calls for a transcendent explanation if a man survives death than if he survives sleep every night and wakes up again in the morning. But this is an unusual attitude. Generally, the person who has seen an apparition or been involved with a poltergeist or become mixed up in the occult, takes the matter far from unemotionally. For him, here is an indication that materialism is just not on as an explanation of the world, that there is a spiritual world beyond this present one but in some mysterious way interlocking with it, and that man must – if he wants a complete explanation of the world – come to terms with the transcendent.

I want now to ask what we are to think about the paranormal, and what we ought to say to people who come to us because they believe they have found, by such means, an avenue into awareness of the transcendent.

In the past, the Church has been noticeably hostile towards the paranormal and its practitioners. It has assumed that such phenomena are the work of the devil and that we should have short shrift with the black gentleman, whose specialities are the deceits of magic and sorcery. Society ought to be cauterized by the removal from its midst of the defiling wizards who chirp and mutter.[7] If they appear to have no baleful effect, even if they seem to have a therapeutic role to play, even if they speak of God and of Jesus, this is all the more reason to be ruthless, for it is one of the devil's more mischievous wickednesses to disguise himself as an angel of light in order to lure the unwary into his clutches.[8] Faced with that sort of a reception, small wonder that psychic sensitives steered well clear of the Church and were thereby denied the theological guidance of which they were so much in need. If the Church had been friendly – or even neutral – we should never have had some of the more amazing superstructures of heretical metaphysics which adorn the pages of some theosophical or spiritualist publications. As so often happens, the sects are an indictment of a Church which has refused to engage intellectually and pastorally in an area where competent scientific, philosophical and theological investigation is desperately needed.

There are signs that the climate is changing, but the damage of centuries will not be put right in decades. It is still not easy to get responsible Church bodies to look at the data, still less to think about the subject in an open-minded way. In 1937, Archbishop Lang appointed a committee under the chairmanship of Bishop Underhill of Bath and Wells and containing such distinguished members as Dean Matthews of St Paul's, Professor L.W. Grensted, and Professor William Brown. Its terms of reference were 'to investigate the subject of communications with discarnate spirits and the claims of Spiritualism in relation to the Christian Faith'. Eleven members were appointed; Evelyn Underhill resigned after the first meeting. Of the ten who remained, seven viewed psychic phenomena with such lack of condemnation that the Archbishops took fright and the Bishops' Meeting never allowed the publication either of the majority or the minority reports. Had it remained even semi-private, this piece of archiepiscopal timidity would have reflected them little credit; as it was, a copy leaked to a Spiritualist newspaper, which printed the conclusions of the majority in full.[9] In today's climate of opinion there is less of that kind of censorship in Anglican circles; but it still seems to be easier to publish a report than to have it debated. The report of the Archbishops' Commission on Christian Doctrine entitled *Prayer and the Departed*, with its appendix on the evidence of psychical research, was published on 14 January 1971 but not debated by the General Synod until 8

November 1972, by which time its Chairman, Ian Ramsey, had tragically died.[10]

Not that the auguries are favourable for the reception of that Appendix to the Doctrine Commission report by the majority within the Church of England. As the report on *Exorcism*[11] by the then Bishop of Exeter's group admirably indicates, the Church seems more interested in banishing the spirits than in testing them to see if they be of God; more concerned with exorcism than with understanding. Too many Christians, when confronted with the paranormal, simply want a spiritual DDT-spray to rid them of unwanted pests, and are insensitive to warnings that they may not always be dealing with basically malevolent spirits but with disturbed human beings (in this world or another one) who need skilled pastoral care. The signatories to the Exorcism Report knew this, but little of it comes through from a reading of their document, and with Christian prejudices running the way they are, it needs to be spelt out in foot-high letters if it is to sink in. As a result of the prevalence of this kind of attitude, precious few people with an experience of the paranormal, or of seeking the transcendent through the paranormal, will come within miles of a Churchman to ask for advice or for help towards understanding.

But if (almost *per impossibile*) someone *does* come to you with an experience of the paranormal, and asks you for help in fitting it into his understanding of the world and of God, what then?

There are two aspects to the problem, and though they will be closely intertwined in practice, they need to be thought about separately. The first is whether the ostensible explanation of what has happened is the true one, and the second is whether the experience can be a valid way in to an apprehension of a genuine transcendent.

We must discuss with the enquirer the worth of his experience in terms of the disciplines of psychical research. Here there are two basic approaches. One is that of the scientist, and the second is that of the believer.

The scientist knows that all possible normal explanations of an event have to be exhausted before a paranormal explanation can be admitted. For some people, normal explanations take an awful lot of exhausting – so much so that the normal explanation can seem to the objective outsider as even more far-fetched than the paranormal one. Poltergeists are linked with underground water,[12] telepathy is explained away by hyperaesthesia, mediums have subconsciously stored away the details of obituary notices published decades ago in the provincial press at the other end of the country which they could conceivably have glanced at during their summer holidays, and so on. As a result, the paranormal is whittled away to almost nothing, and what is left has no mystery in it, no wonder, no doorway into the transcendent. Philosophy has clipped the Angel's wings.

The believer is at the other end of the spectrum. For him, the benefit of every doubt has to be given in such a way that there is no question as to the paranormal nature of the event concerned. He believes that the Church is missing out on half its heritage if it does not accept *at face value* the accounts of even the most bizarre of paranormal experiences. There is little attempt to seek for non-paranormal explanations of the accounts, no attempt at cross-checking or independent verification of the anecdotal material, or at taking seriously the possibilities of misremembering, exaggeration, or misinterpretation of the evidence. And interpretation is as freely accepted as experience. As a result, the person who takes his story to this sort of a listener gets far more sympathetic treatment. He is likely to be helped in his search for a transcendental understanding, and to be given a framework in which he can progress spiritually. The only question is, is it a true one? Many people find it impossible to take seriously the accounts put out by this end of the spectrum, because they believe that the stories they read are retold by folk who have not so much as heard that Occam ever had a razor. It is perilously easy to put an interpetation on one's experience which is by no means necessarily entailed by the empirical facts, and to forget that one man's experiences cannot be determinative for theology in the way that the reflection of centuries may be.

My own approach is, I suppose, somewhere between the extremes which the two previous paragraphs have caricatured.[13] If anybody came to me with an experience of the paranormal which had for him evoked a sense of the transcendent, I would try to begin as a good scientist. I should have to examine the experience itself and insist that it does not necessarily entail the transcendent deductions that have been made from it, and that even the deductions about the paranormal which can be drawn may be mistaken or over-simplistic. The outsider can see flaws in the evidence far more easily than the experient can. To the outsider, it may be patently obvious that here is a chance-coincidence, or a puzzling event with a perfectly normal explanation, or a feeling with no objective counterpart, or an hallucination brought about by psychological means, or a dream with no external significance. He must measure the account against the criteria he uses when he is assessing parapsychological data, and if he is a good psychical researcher, these will be stiff criteria. So the first move with an enquirer is to point out that the parapsychological or transcendent interpretation is only one possible explanation amongst many, and that it might not be logically entailed by the data.

But to end there would be disastrous. Whether or not the man's experience had any objective paranormal content, it has pointed him in the direction of the transcendent, and it is our Christian duty to explore in that direction with him. The exploration will involve pastoral care and spiritual direction.[14] Particularly if our enquirer has been experimenting with the occult, we may find that he has been going about his quest for the transcendent in quite the wrong way and may need drastic reorientation. For many people, dabbling in the occult feeds their neurotic tendencies. They may approach the subject in the frame of mind of the magician – a basically selfish frame of mind which tries to manipulate the unseen powers for egotistic ends. Or there may be in a man something of the gnostic who wants to feed his sense of self-importance by pretending to arcane knowledge for which the common herd is unfit. It is no good going about the quest for the transcendent with motives like those. Only the pure in heart will see God; the rest will find their quest leading them only to a deep well in which they dimly descry a distorted image of their own unrecognized countenance. But if one can be purified of such base motivations, if one is genuinely seeking a faith in something greater than one's self, a benevolent power which has to be acknowledged as sovereign over one's self, then the paranormal experience can be a significant starting-point for a spiritual quest. And our exploration of the transcendent aspects of the experience will be largely independent of the judgement to which we have come about its worth as evidence for the paranormal.

At the beginning of this paper I spent some time in discussing the avenues by which the numinous – however evoked – can be a 'disclosure situation' which unlocks the door to more than is logically or empirically demanded by the bare facts of the situation. I believe that a paranormal experience, or reflection on the paranormal experiences of others, can similarly be an avenue to a transcendent realization which can point us towards belief in God. The disclosure *may* never come. We may for ever be locked within a naturalistic understanding in which the paranormal is simply a set of facts to be put alongside the normal in the dull catalogue of common things, and in which the transcendent penny never drops. Or there *may* be a disclosure which opens for us a world beyond our understanding, the world of the transcendent, a spiritual world, a world in which the word 'God' has got a meaning. Neither *need* happen, but either *might*.

Paranormal experiences can be variously interpreted; in natural or supernatural ways, along theistic or atheistic lines, in an orthodox or heretical manner. But then so can aesthetic or numinous experiences. A melody can be analysed into sound-waves or seen as an open door into heaven, and similar things can be said of a painting, or a tree in winter, or the sight of a leper. The paranormal by itself is no more necessarily transcendent than a tree in winter; but for a soul which is set on a quest, both can be pointers. We need to let our enquirer know that his experience has alternative explanations, and that any transcendental explanation is always and necessarily a disclosure beyond the empirically verifiable. Not even when we look at the paranormal will we find a scientific, logically irrefragable, knock-down justification for our talk of the transcendent, let alone for talking about the transcendent in Christian – or even in theistic – terms. The man who has felt it can only point to what has been a disclosure for him, and hope that it may evoke a similar disclosure in others. He may hope it, but he cannot demand it; for the transcendent, like the numinous, cannot be commanded or manipulated, and one cannot force Christian orthodoxy out of a mystical or numinous or transcendental experience. We must not take Peter on the mount of the transfiguration as our exemplar.[15] We cannot build three tabernacles and cage the transcendent within them, like a scientific specimen always available for cold objective study.

It all boils down to the simple fact that whenever we talk of 'the transcendent' or of 'God', this world is a world of faith and not of proof. There is a quest for the transcendent, and some people will find pointers within the paranormal which will help them in their quest. The danger of a purely logic-centred or objective scientific approach is that it vetoes the quest before it has begun. The danger of the approach of the committed believer in a particular interpretation of the data is that it misunderstands the difference between a pointer and a proof. Christianity, on the other hand, insists that in this life we walk by faith and not by sight, and the Christian who comes across the paranormal can help people see where knowledge ends and faith takes over.

References

1. T.S. Eliot, *Murder in the Cathedral* (Faber, 1935), Part II.

2. John Keats (1795-1821), *Lamia*, Part 2, lines 231-4.

3. Nicolas Herman of Lorraine (1610-91), 'Brother Lawrence', told Monsieur Beaufort on 3 August 1666 that 'God had done him a singular favour in his conversion at the age of eighteen. That in the winter, seeing a tree stripped of its leaves, and considering that within a little time the leaves would be renewed, and after that the flowers and fruit appear, he received a high view of the providence and power of God, which has never since been effaced from his soul. That this view had perfectly set him loose from the world, and kindled in him such a love for God that he could not tell whether it had increased during the more than forty years he had lived since.' (Page 9 of the edition of Brother Lawrence's *Practice of the Presence of God* made by Hugh Martin, SCM Press 1956.) Francesco Bernadone was St Francis of Assisi whose conversion included an encounter with a leper in Rome.

4. J.B. Phillips, *Ring of Truth* (Hodder and Stoughton, 1967), pp. 88-90; discussion by Andrew MacKenzie and K.M. Goldney in the *Journal* of the Society for Psychical Research, Vol. 45 (December 1970), pp. 382-91 and by M.C. Perry *ibid.*, Vol. 46 (September 1971), pp. 203-5, where the chronology of the occurrence is corrected.

5. Andrew MacKenzie, *Apparitions and Ghosts* (Arthur Barker, 1971), pp. 90-93.

6. In another (but perhaps related) connection, it has been suggested that the glossolalia of the Pentecostal revival may be a means whereby conscious censorship may be by-passed, and psychological release at a deep level achieved. In this case, it is spiritual blockages which are done away with and there is a therapeutic result. See Simon Tugwell, OP, *Did You Receive the Spirit?* (Darton, Longman and Todd, 1972), p. 68.

7. Isaiah 8:19 (RV translation).

8. 2 Corinthians 11:14.

9. The forty-year embargo on the publication of the Report expired in 1979, whereupon *The Christian Parapsychologist* published it in its entirety (Vol. 3, No. 2 (March 1979) pp. 40-73; see also 'Lang, Underhill and the 1939 Report' by Michael Perry in *The Christian Parapsychologist* Vol. 3, No. 3 (June 1979), pp. 83-6).

10. The paper on which this section is based was delivered on 27 July 1972. Ian Ramsey had suffered his first heart attack on 1 April 1972; at more than one session of the General Synod he came

prepared to lead the consideration of this Report, but it was deferred because of pressure of business. He died on 6 October 1972 and the Report was presented by Professor Nineham in the following month.

11. *Exorcism*, edited by Dom Robert Petitpierre, OSB (SPCK, 1972). There was an admirably balanced article about this report in *View Review*, Vol. 23, No. 2 (July 1972), pp. 36-8, by Rosalind Heywood, a respected psychical researcher who was neither a Christian nor a Spiritualist. It came to my notice after the original form of this paper went for setting. Mrs Heywood made a number of the same points as I did (and made them better than I do!).

12. See 'Poltergeists: A Physical Theory' by G.W. Lambert in the *Journal* of the Society for Psychical Research, Vol. 38, No. 684 (June 1955), pp. 49-71.

13. See 'How Long a Spoon?' by M.C. Perry in *The Modern Churchman* Vol. 12 (n.s.), April 1969, pp. 201-210.

14. The careful reader of *The Mystery and Magic of the Occult* by John Stevens Kerr (SCM Press, 1971) will pick up a good many hints to help him understand the need for this.

15. Mark 9:5.

5
Faith, reason and evidence in religion, science and psychical research

Two great planks in the Unitarian platform are Reason and Conscience. Anglicans add others, and insist on the threefold foundation of Scripture, Tradition, and Reason. Whatever our differences (and they are, of course, substantial), we agree on the importance of reason. We could not happily become *sannyasin* of the Bhagwan Shree Rajneesh. Devotees who come to him to don the orange robe and to find the truth about themselves and the universe are told that shoes and minds are to be left outside, at the gate of the *ashram*. That would not suit us.

Yet, however great an importance we give to reason, we are also men and women of faith. Many people nowadays misconstrue the nature of faith. Like the Red Queen in *Alice Through the Looking-Glass*, they think it means believing as many as six impossible things before breakfast. Christians, they think, have a great list of impossible things to believe in. Three of them are

1. that within man there is something – call it mind, call it soul, call it spirit – which makes him akin to divinity;
2. that this cannot be destroyed by physical death; and
3. that the departed and ourselves are not in incommunicable isolation from one another.

If we are men and women of reason as well as men and women of faith, then these beliefs are not simply three random early morning impossibilities. There must be some evidence for them. It was, I suspect, the hope of finding evidence for what had formerly been purely a matter for faith that motivated the founding of the Society for Psychical Research. It was certainly what impelled Reginald Lester to start what is now known as the Churches' Fellowship for Psychical and Spiritual Studies, and to take as its motto those words from 2 Peter 1:5 – 'to faith add knowledge'. And it was the same question about evidence behind belief which led George Whitby – that able philosopher whose loss we so much mourn – to belong both to the SPR and to the CFPSS and to found the Unitarian Society for Psychical Studies. Though he is no longer with us in the flesh, we salute his memory and rejoice to have Tim so graciously in the chair for us this afternoon.

The men who founded the SPR were beginning to get tired of the old sterile debates between faith and unbelief. They thought they might be able to resolve them by using a new tool which had in their century been used in other areas of thought and had led to quite staggering gains in knowledge and understanding. That tool was not simply evidence. Evidence had multiplied over the previous thirty or forty years with the advent of Spiritualism, which was still in its early flush and arousing intense interest. What distinguished the psychical researchers from the Spiritualists was that Spiritualism was a religion and treated the evidence in a way characteristic of, and appropriate to, a religion. The founding fathers of the SPR believed that they could better solve the enigmas of human potentialities, human powers, and human survival with the tool of scientific method. Their first manifesto set out their aim, which was to approach the subject 'in the same spirit of exact and unimpassioned inquiry which has enabled Science to solve so many problems, once not less obscure nor less hotly debated'.

The scientific optimism of late Victorianism was in full flood (notice the telling capital S for Science in that quotation). Provided inquiry was exact and unimpassioned, progress would be assured. Physics had just about completed its electro-magnetic explanation of the nature of reality, and there were going to be no surprises round the corner as the proud nineteenth century sailed majestically on towards its conclusion.

How wrong can you be? We all know what happened to science as the Victorian certainties gave way to that whole new and entirely unanticipated world of relativity, of quantum mechanics, of the

Uncertainty Principle, of the statistics of probability, and of the still unfulfilled search for a unified Field Theory. Science has never been the same since the secure base of nineteenth-century thinking was shattered into as many pieces as the indivisible atom. And the attitude which characterized these great discoveries was far indeed from unimpassioned. Let me quote some sentences from *Physics and Beyond* by Werner Heisenberg, whose Uncertainty Principle did so much to revolutionize the scientific thinking of this century. He had reached a crucial point in his calculations:

When the first terms seemed to accord with the energy principle, I became rather excited, and I began to make countless arithmetical errors. As a result, it was almost three o'clock in the morning before the final result of my computation lay before me. The energy principle had held for all the terms, and I could no longer doubt the mathematical consistency and coherence of the kind of quantum mechanics to which my calculations pointed. At first, I was deeply alarmed. I had the feeling that, through the surface of atomic phenomena, I was looking at a strangely beautiful interior, and felt almost giddy at the thought that I now had to probe this wealth of mathematical structures nature had so generously spread out before me. I was far too excited to sleep.[1]

That catches, I think, the sheer numinous awe that came upon those men whose discoveries changed the very structure of scientific thought. Science is not a matter of sitting down before the facts as a little child, without prejudice or prepossession. It is making bold (and sometimes mind-bending) adventures of the imagination, and seeing where another and different set of prepossessions to the currently acceptable ones can get you. But prepossessions there must be. When the possibility of a new set of them comes upon that man of genius who is able to conceive of them, then comes the painstaking work of seeing whether his hunch will lead to a model of the universe which hangs together in a logically satisfying way – and there, too, in the concept of precisely what is meant by 'logically satisfying', there are bound to be prepossessions. Within scientific discovery there is a subtle blend of faith, reason, and evidence. The imagination, the heart, and the mind are all involved.

What is more, a new scientific theory does not take over from an old one simply because some new evidence has turned up which makes the old one untenable. It is nothing like as simple as that. What generally happens is that we begin with a situation in which the old, accepted, view of things is satisfying to everyone. But then, at odd spots or on odd occasions, there crop up new and troublesome data which don't fit. They do not, however, overthrow the established theory. What happens first is that they are simply ignored. Perhaps they are artefacts of a badly-designed experimental set-up. Perhaps they are just errors in measurement. Perhaps they will not crop up again when a different set of experimenters, in a different laboratory, tries to replicate the data. Perhaps they are the results of unknown or uncontrolled independent variables. Perhaps they will just go away if we don't worry them.

And, often enough, they *do* go away. If they were accepted, they would call into question the rationality of the whole of the rest of the scientific structure. Never mind that a belief in the rationality of the structure of scientific thought is an article of faith. It is an article of faith without which the whole of the scientific enterprise would founder. So, rather than call into question the 99.9 per cent of human experience which is given understandability and rationality by scientific explanation, we ignore what will not fit in.

This is not at all unusual. The history of science is littered with the debris of unexplained facts which have found no logical resting place within any overall view of the universe. It is simply impossible to recast the whole of science to fit one or two knobbly observations. If we try to do so, if we bend the structure at that place, then it warps out of true so much in another place that we simply have to let it straighten itself out again. The attempt has created more anomalies than it solves. That is why we have to live with a residue of the unexplained. We can find page after page of unexplained facts (for example) in the *Fortean Times*[2] or the many journals which chronicle and investigate unidentified flying objects. And, whatever our niggling sense of unease, most of us do not recast our philosophy to allow ourselves to believe in the spontaneous combustion of human beings, or in the surveillance of our planet by intelligent creatures from outer space. We just shrug our shoulders and get on with the job of interpreting the 99.9 per cent of our experience which is interpretable within existing scientific paradigms.

But then the awkward phenomena multiply, and it becomes necessary to fit them in, because the success rate of the existing theory is falling too far below the acceptable 99.9 per cent. At first, this means adjusting the old theory to fit them in. This is what happened to the geocentric view of the universe. Those who believed, with Ptolemy, that the earth was the centre of the universe and that the sun and stars moved round it in circular orbits, found that the more accurate their observations, the less satisfactory their theory. So they saved the appearances by saying that there must be little orbits superimposed on the main ones. When even this did not do, and the little orbits had to have pimply excrescences of sub-orbits, it became like that verse that pointed out that:

> Great fleas have little fleas
> Upon their backs to bite 'em,
> And little fleas have lesser fleas
> And so *ad infinitum*.[3]

The appearances were saved, but only at the cost of a theory which was beginning to be more complicated than the data it sought to set in order.

At that stage, when the old theory can be tinkered with no longer, there is need of a quantum leap forward. A bold and imaginative thinker throws aside the presuppositions which once seemed so self-evident and yet had led us into so many difficulties, and starts from a fresh perspective – not without prepossessions, but with a new set of starting-points. There is a Copernican revolution.

And it works! There is a period of intense confusion, when the old and the new co-exist. There are innumerable rearguard actions by those who cannot see why the old ways cannot be adapted a bit more and a bit longer, and who cannot see reality from the new standpoint. But in the end, the new theory wins. Partly it wins because its explanation covers a wider field than the old theory did. Partly it wins because it leads to predicted results which are confirmed by experiment, but partly it wins because it seems a more elegant and satisfying theory than the old one. And elegance belongs more to the realm of faith than to that of evidence.

Mind you, it never lasts for ever. For all we feel that the new for-mulation is perfect and that it affords us insights into the structure of reality that our forefathers had been denied, the inevitable happens. No scientific theory seems to be endowed with immortality. For all that Alexander Pope was able to say that

> Nature and Nature's laws lay hid in night:
> God said, *Let Newton be!* and all was light,[4]

within a couple of centuries, Hilaire Belloc could make his riposte:

> It did not last: the Devil howling 'Ho!
> Let Einstein be!' restored the status quo.[5]

The relation between faith, reason, and evidence in the history of science is a subtle and changing one. Evidence needs interpretation, and interpretation involves faith. Sometimes (as in the epicycles which temporarily shored up the Ptolemaic theory of an earth-centred universe) the faith which is exercised is faith in a bad theory which has really had its day. Often, faith is faith in a brilliant and elegant new idea which strikes its discoverer with the force of a great revelation. And, often, that brilliant new idea has not got the experimental verification it needs, and yet it seems so *right* that its discoverer cannot doubt that when the experiment is done, the result will bear him or her out.

We are on dangerous ground here. A scientist's faith in the validity of his or new idea may be so overwhelming that it seems quite legitimate to cut a few corners here or there. That is what happened in Mendel's pioneering experiments in genetics. The theory was so elegant, yet the results did not exactly accord with it. They were almost right, but not quite. Mendel did not know enough about statistics (nobody did at the time) to realize that results on biological material had a wide spread of deviation from the norm and that his figures were well within what would have been expected. So they were ever so slightly doctored to make them absolutely irresistible. It was only a generation or more afterwards that statisticians showed that the published results of Mendel's experiments on his pea seedlings were just too good to be true.

By then, genetics was an established science, and the fudging had done no harm. But if the hunch is not a correct one, what damage can be done by giving way to temptation! Is this what happened in the case of Dawson and the Piltdown Man? Is this what happened in the case of S.G. Soal? When he carried out his experiments in the 1940s on Basil Shackleton and claimed that they proved the reality of precognitive telepathy, people were so amazed at his change of view from sceptic to believer that they exclaimed 'Is Soal also among the prophets?' But Betty Markwick has now shown[6] that he had doctored his data-sheets and that the scores he claimed were spurious.

Soal did incalculable harm to the still-fledgling science of parapsychology, because there is as yet no generally-accepted world-view within which our kind of data might fit. His action means that for many years to come, genuine data will be as suspect as doctored ones.

Why did he do it? In a fascinating article Anita Gregory tells us that

A pioneer engaged in truly novel investigation, then, may be far more likely to be tempted to stray from the rigorous path of literal truth for quite a variety of complex reasons ... Since he may become persuaded rightly or wrongly that he knows the truth which others are too stupid, ignorant or ill-meaning to recognize, he may succumb to the temptation of building spurious foundations to support what is deeply felt to be a certainty. He may consider that truer and firmer foundations are sure to be devised later, once the new vision is accepted.[7]

Anita Gregory illustrates her thesis with examples from the work of Sir Cyril Burt, 'a great man in his day, a man of prodigious intellect ... as learned and widely read as anyone is ever likely to be'. Yet, she reminds us, 'it seems that the evidence forces us to accept that he cheated and lied'.

It is clear that there are times in science when faith, reason, and evidence jostle each other very uncomfortably. What, then, are we to do about it? Outlaw faith entirely from scientific thinking? Work towards the elimination of the personal equation?

No. That would prevent all scientific advance. We need to recognize that faith has its place in all aspects of life and that science is no exception. What we must do is to observe at what point it enters the argument — not so that we can blackball speculations or explanations from then on, but so that we can say, 'At this stage, we begin to deal with an hypothesis held on faith. It may turn out to be a useful working hypothesis, but if our faith proves to be misplaced, it is open to us to find a better one — if we can.'

After that long excursus, let us get back to the bearing of parapsychology on questions of religion. Can we hope, by bringing parapsychological data to bear on questions of religious belief, to add knowledge to faith, and to be possessed of certainty where before we could only offer opinion?

If we are to pursue this question, we need first to look at the data, and then at their interpretation.

It is difficult enough to be sure of the data. In the whole of science, you will find no more sophisticated set-ups than you get in experiments to test psi capacities. That is because experimenters have three things to guard against. The first are sensory cues. That does not mean *normal* sensory cues. They do not know the limits of hyperaesthesia and so they have to take abnormal precautions to exclude it. Sam Weller, you will remember, said that his vision was limited because he only had a pair of eyes, not 'a pair o' patent double million magnifyin' gas miscroscopes of hextra power'.[8] His sarcasm would be lost on parapsychologists. Secondly, experimenters have to exclude all extrasensory cues except the ones for which they are testing. Since psychical researchers know next to nothing about the powers and limits of extrasensory perception, their task in this regard is about as near a definition of impossibility as we are likely to get. And thirdly, they have to guard against conscious or even unconscious fraud on the part either of the agent, or the experimenter, or of both in collusion.

The wonder is that there are any experimental data at all. But there are; because we know that nothing less than consistent data, honestly obtained, will do as a foundation. This is hard, because it seems as if the repeatable experiment does not exist. We do not yet know the full range of independent variables, each of which could completely scupper the repeatability of an experiment. So, suggestive results are obtained, and, since they are not repeated by the next experimenter, they remain to tease us, but not to enlighten us or to help us formulate a new and fuller vision of reality which takes account of them.

To those of us who are convinced that parapsychology is on to something and who wish desperately to get orthodox science to take notice of psychical studies, this is hard to take. But we have got to take it and we cannot risk those tempting short corners. One short corner which I have already mentioned is the short corner of outright fraud. An even more tempting one is that of claiming more for the data then they will bear. Let me give you one warning example.

A little while ago, a friend wrote to me to tell me about an amazing experiment conducted by Dr Karlis Osis in America. Alex Tanous is a sensitive who claims to be able to indulge in out-of-body travel, and Dr Osis asked him to travel in this way into a sealed room in which a picture was exhibited. Not only was he asked to describe this unseen picture, but there were strain gauges in the room which would be activated if anyone was physically present to look at it. My friend told me not only that Tanous had been 'able to perceive precise details of 114 pictures concealed' in the room, but that 'each time' he did so, the strain gauge showed that something was present in the room. Was this not proof positive that Tanous was able to project something out of his body which was able to look at pictures in a sealed room and affect a physical instrument there whilst he was doing so?

It sounded too good to be true, but I knew that Dr Osis was a careful and a scientific investigator, so I looked up his paper.[9] In it,

Karlis Osis and Donna McCormick describe how Tanous was asked to project himself into a shielded chamber in which an optical image device displayed at random a series of stimulus pictures. He was then asked to guess the colour (one of four), the quadrant in which the picture appeared (one of four), and which of five possible drawings was exhibited. A 'hit' was counted if *any one* of these three aspects was guessed correctly. That meant that the probability of a hit was 55 per cent. Out of 197 guesses, Tanous scored 114 hits, or 56.3 per cent. The scoring rate was absolutely at chance level. Nobody expected it otherwise. The experiment was so arranged that hits should be about as frequent as misses. The whole point was not to see whether an unduly large number of hits was scored, but to compare the strain gauge readings on hits with those on misses. My friend who had told me that Tanous had been able, while 'astral travelling', to guess the nature of 114 pictures 'in precise detail' was about as far up the pole as he could get.

Nor was he much better on the significance of the strain gauge results. He claimed that 'each time Tanous made a hit the concealed strain-gauges recorded an increase'. What Osis and McCormick actually found was that the predicted effect (i.e. that the gauge should be activated more when hits were scored than when Tanous got the target completely wrong) did occur, but by no means each time. The score was only slightly above chance expectation, at no more than a five per cent level of probability. Other, non-predicted, effects were observed at a greater degree of statistical significance. The whole experiment was suggestive rather than compelling, and Dr Osis ended by reporting that 'our interpretation must be very tentative'.

The tentative nature of the interpretation had been completely lost on my friend. When I pointed this out to him, he told me that he had not seen the article in question but had relied on an account of it in a letter from an American friend of his.

I tell this cautionary tale to show how dangerously easy it is to claim more than the data warrant. Gossip is as fecund in this field as it is in other walks of life. Never accept a statement in para-psychology until you have checked it for yourself. You are quite likely to find that the will to believe has led your informant to exaggerate. We want evidence, not hearsay.

But even when we are sure of our data, we are far from out of the wood. When we come to interpret data and to relate them to theory, we find that the path is even more bestrewn with difficulties. It seems as if no two people can agree as to what the observed data *mean*. The cynic says that parapsychology is unique among the sciences in that it is the only field of scientific endeavour in which there has been no progress whatever in the last hundred years. We are still as unsure of the interpretation of the phenomena as our great-grandfathers were. That is untrue. Admittedly, their optimism about progress was over-facile. Admittedly, the great questions about human destiny remain as controverted as ever. One reason why this is so is that the lesser questions are getting well on their way to having acceptable answers. Extra-sensory perception, for example, is far more generally believed in nowadays than it was a hundred years ago. On 20 December 1980, *The Times* published the results of its questionnaire on the paranormal. Out of 1314 respondents, 83 per cent believed in ESP; 51 per cent thought it was an established fact and another 33 per cent thought it a likely possibility. On the other hand, when it came to contact with the dead, the percentage of believers dropped to 38 per cent.[10]

This may be because, once we allow ESP, we can explain almost all the data concerned with contact with the departed in terms of ESP in this present world. Notice, however, that we can only do so if we put practically no limit on the powers of ESP between living agents (and, in ESP, we have to include not only telepathy and clairvoyance, but precognition and the picking up of latent material by paranormal means even though it has lain dormant for decades or even centuries). The 'super-ESP' theory accounts for all the data without having to have recourse to the hypothesis that the human self survives physical death and can on occasion communicate from beyond that barrier. The only trouble with the super-ESP theory is that it has to assume paranormal powers so wide-ranging as to be staggering – more powerful by an astronomical factor than anything that has been experimentally demonstrated. That is why Dr Osis has described the super-ESP hypothesis as 'that strange invention which shies like a mouse from being tested in the laboratory but, in rampant speculations, acts like a ferocious lion devouring the survival evidence'.[11]

Why do people feel a need to bring in the super-ESP hypothesis rather than accept survival evidence at face value? Clearly, it is not a matter of evidence but of its interpretation – in other words, of belief. It is much easier for many people to believe in ESP between the living – even in ESP of a strength and range for which there is not a shred of independent evidence – than it is to believe in survival of death and communication thereafter.

Renée Haynes, a Roman Catholic lay person who has written a

good deal about psychical research, has produced a new and engaging term for use in this context. It is the 'boggle threshold'.[12] The person who approaches the data has ready-made assumptions as to what he or she can or cannot believe. Up to a certain stage, a person can accept the evidence of his or her eyes. But then, the mind begins to boggle, and thereafter the kind of defensive theory of which super-ESP is an example, takes over. Before you reach your boggle threshold, the *prima facie* explanation of the data satisfies you. Thereafter, you are allowed to be as devious as you like in finding reasons which seem good to you for insisting that things are not what they seem to be.

Where does your boggle threshold lie? Can you accept telepathy? Apparitions which are private to the observer? Apparitions which are shared by the bystanders? Precognition? Psychokinesis? Poltergeists? Mental mediumship? Physical mediumship? Floating trumpets? Materializations? Unidentified flying objects? Little green men getting out of their space-craft and taking you to their leader? 'Orrible 'airy spiders as big as Alsatian dogs running up and down the walls of the ward? All right, you have got to stop somewhere. But where, and on what criteria? And do the criteria bear any relation to the cogency of the data or the strength of the argument? The boggle threshold seems to be an entirely subjective matter. The average reader of *Psychic News* seems never to reach his threshold, whatever he is told, and earth is crammed with so many wonders that he stops marvelling at them. If you are a follower of CSICOP (The Committee for the Scientific Investigation of Claims of the Paranormal) you boggle before you begin, lest you be led astray by the apparent reasonableness of what you are being asked to investigate. Many people will accept any mental phenomena, but boggle as soon as the physical world is involved. Others will accept anything referring to this world, but as soon as survival is mooted, wriggle like a worm on the hook.

There is no end to the possibilities of speculation in seeking a theoretical construct to bring sense to the many disparate types of paranormal data. Only those who refuse to boggle will be able to appreciate them all. Those who do appreciate them will have the far greater task of trying to make a rational choice between them. The scientist's job is not over when he has made his theoretical construct, any more than Archimedes had nothing more to do after he had shouted 'Eureka!' than to retrieve his bath towel. The next job is to devise tests to choose between alternative scenarios – preferably tests based on predictions which will be different on different hypotheses. We do not seem to have got as far as that in para-psychology, because the repeatable experiment still eludes us, and without repeatable experiments we cannot make rational choices between hypotheses. All we can do is amass data and try and find a way of looking at them which makes tolerable sense.

Does this mean, then, that the Churches' Fellowship for Psychical and Spiritual Studies is naïvely mistaken in taking as its motto the phrase 'to faith add knowledge'? Or, on the other hand, does it mean that the parapsychologist who tries to understand his data rather than simply to amass them, ends up in a morass of subjective judgement, with faith counting for more than reason or evidence? I hope that neither of these accusations describes the true situation. I hope that all who study the paranormal (with whatever set of motives or interests) will be open to the evidence – critically open, testing all things, never satisfied with any standard of evidence lower than the best, always ready to question – but, in the end, always open to look at the shape of the evidence as it piles up before them.

Often, that evidence will take us beyond our boggle threshold. If we are honest, we will then have to say that we suspend our judgement. We have an overall world-view which it has taken us all our lifetime so far to build up and to test against the available evidence, and it holds together for us in a way which we find convincing. We are simply not prepared to abandon it on the basis of a few maverick observations which don't fit in. If we were to accept them at face value, it might relieve the pressure at that point, but only at the cost of creating bigger and more intolerable pressures elsewhere. So the odd and knobbly bits of evidence are filed, as it were, in the 'pending' tray. We cannot see where they go. We cannot say that they do not exist, but we cannot say that they are so crucially important that because of them we have to abandon all the sense we have so far made of the universe.

That is an uncomfortable predicament to be in, but anyone except the most obtusely self-satisfied person has been in it at some point or other. There is not one of us who has a philosophy of life, or a viewpoint on the world of phenomena, which adequately explains every facet of the observed universe. All of us see through a glass, darkly, and it is disingenuous to deny it.

If, however, the pressure mounts, and the evidence grows, we may find we have to do something about it. There are many people about today for whom the evidence for telepathy has grown so big and so pressing that they can simply no longer file 'telepathy' in their pending tray. There are many for whom the evidence for survival has come into that category. There are many for whom the evidence for God is like that. Some of them have come to a conviction of the nature of man, his destiny, and his purpose in the mind of almighty God through the convergent pressure of many lines of evidence – human, scientific, mystical, yes, even parapsychological. Psychical studies may not add knowledge to faith in a simplistic way, but they can point in the same direction as faith points, and they can help to make the leap of faith a great deal more credible. Many of us started from a world of pure materialism, but were troubled by things which would not fit into that kind of world-picture. Eventually, the attempt to ignore the oddball facts became too much. The attempt to fit them in to the old picture became less and less convincing, the epicycles became more and more complicated and incredible, and, in the end, we had to come to our Copernican revolution. It had become intolerable for us to do anything otherwise. That is the way it happens in science, when a new idea takes over. That is the way it happens in parapsychology, when a sceptic is finally convinced. That is what happens in religion, where the phenomenon is known as 'conversion' and the St Pauls of this world let a new apprehension of reality wash over them and engulf them, and they find release from the intolerable tensions of maintaining a discredited world-picture.

The new viewpoint will not be perfect. There are still difficulties in a parapsychological view, or a theistic view, or a Christian view. For example, I still bow before the mystery of reconciling my view of an omnipotent God of love with the fact of animal suffering, or undeserved and unredemptive human suffering, particularly the suffering of little children. But the difficulties are less than the difficulty of ditching the whole scheme, because no other scheme will cover half the ground half as well.

So that is why I am a Christian parapsychologist. My overall world-view is one in which my Christian faith and the discoveries of psychic studies come together in a convergent way. Faith, reason, and evidence have produced their subtle amalgam. That does not mean that I have no more discoveries to make, and no more adjustments to look forward to. If I thought there were no points at which the mounting evidence might ever lead me to reconsider my present views, I would be highly alarmed. I have no wish to become intellectually ossified into a position from which there is no chance of movement and none of growth. I am a man of faith, and I hope that my faith is a reasonable faith which has considered the evidence and has matured in the process; but I take great comfort in some words St Paul once wrote to his friends in Philippi. It was not, he said, as if he had already attained or were already perfect. 'This one thing I do', he wrote; 'forgetting those things that are behind, and reaching forth unto those things that are before, I press toward the mark for the prize of the high calling of God in Christ Jesus' (Phil. 3: 12ff.). Hold to Christ; but always be on the move!

References

1. Werner Heisenberg, *Physics and Beyond* (Allen and Unwin, 1971), p. 61.
2. The *Fortean Times* is 'the journal of strange phenomena', which chronicles anomalies and occurrences which, by all the laws of expectation, ought not to have happened.
3. Augustus de Morgan, *A Budget of Paradoxes* (1872), p. 377.
4. Alexander Pope, *An Epitaph Intended for Sir Isaac Newton.*
5. Hilaire Belloc, *Epigrams*, 'Answer to Pope's Epitaph for Sir Isaac Newton'.
6. Betty Markwick, 'The Soal-Goldney Experiments with Basil Shackleton; New Evidence of Data Manipulation', in the *Proceedings* of the Society for Psychical Research Vol. 56 (1978), pp. 250-277.
7. Anita Gregory, 'Why do Scientists Engage in Fraud?'; *Parapsychology Review*, Vol. 11, No. 6 (1980), pp. 1-6.
8. Charles Dickens, *The Pickwick Papers*, Chapter 34.
9. Karlis Osis and Donna McCormick, 'Kinetic Effects at the Ostensible Location of an Out-of-body Projection During Perceptual Testing', in the *Journal* of the American Society for Psychical Research, Vol. 74 (1980), pp. 319-329.
10. A more recent survey of leaders in the scientific 'Establishment' gives less encouraging figures. Only 29 per cent of respondents thought ESP was an established fact or a likely probability. See 'A Survey of Elite Scientists' by James McClenon, *Journal of Parapsychology* Vol. 46, No. 2 (June 1982), pp. 127-152.
11. *Research in Parapsychology 1978*, ed. W.G. Roll (Metuchen NJ, Scarecrow Press, 1979), pp. 30-31.
12. Renée Haynes, 'The Boggle Threshold', *Encounter,* Vol. 55 Nos. 2-3 (1980), pp. 92-97.

6
May a Christian investigate the paranormal?

The Bible is a bewilderingly rich collection of books, covering many centuries, and chronicling many diverse forms of ostensibly paranormal phenomena. Is it possible to find within its pages a coherent position for the Bible student to adopt towards the study of parapsychology? And, if so, where can we begin?

I suggest that as useful a place as any is the twenty-eighth chapter of the first book of Samuel. This is part of the narrative of the life and times of King Saul, and deals with the period at the beginning of the Israelite monarchy, round about 1000 BC. We pick up the story as the Israelite army was encamped at Gilboa and their Philistine enemies at Shunem. Saul wanted to know how to conduct the campaign, and was sorely missing the advice he might have got from the prophet Samuel, who had died some time before. Like a good Israelite, he enquired of his God, but none of the normal and acceptable forms of extrasensory guidance were successful – no dream, no divination by the sacred Urim, no prophecy. The Lord was silent. Now Saul, we are told, 'had put away from the land those that had '*oboth*, and the *yidde'onim*'. But in view of the urgency of the occasion, Saul asks his servants to seek one out for him. As usual, official clamping-down had been neither complete nor totally efficient, and his men were able to tell him that there was a woman who had an *'ob* at En-dor. So Saul, like a modern-day sitter who does not want to give unnecessary clues,[1] goes to the woman at dead of night and in disguise, and asks her, 'Divine unto me, I pray thee, by the *'ob*, and bring me up whomsoever I shall name unto thee'.

The first thing we want to ask is, 'What on earth was an *'ob*, and what kind of person was a *yidde'oni?*' Nobody seems to know exactly what an *'ob* was. When we consult Hertzberg's standard commentary on 1 and 2 Samuel,[2] we read that the word is usually translated 'ghost', but that that will not do here, because the apparition which the woman calls up is called, not an *'ob*, but *'elohim*, and is brought up 'with the help of *'ob*'. So, says Hertzberg, *'ob* 'describes not the ghost itself but the mechanism or means whereby the conjuring of the ghost is brought about' – and off we go along the anthropological parallels and the Australian aboriginals with their bull-roarers, which the shaman uses to bring himself to the required pitch of frenzy for his professional activity. The *'ob* must be some item from the paraphernalia of the *yidde'oni* that she uses to bring about her conjuration.

And the woman herself, the *yidde'oni?* King James' men in most places translated that by 'wizard', which is etymologically reasonable, since the English 'wizard' and the Hebrew *'yidde' oni'* both mean 'one who is wise'. She has been traditionally called the 'Witch of En-dor', after the chapter heading (but not the text) of the King James Bible.

The parapsychologist has probably been reading with mounting exasperation for the last couple of paragraphs. If Saul goes to a woman with an *'ob* (and we have seen that *'ob* is usually translated 'ghost'), and asks her to use her *'ob* to call up from the dead whomever he names, what more likely that she is a medium, that King Saul is her sitter, that the *'ob* is her spirit control, and that she claims to be in contact via her control with the departed souls with whom her sitters wish to communicate?

The King James Version translated *yidde'oni* as 'woman with a familiar spirit' or as 'wizard'. To call the woman 'the Witch of En-dor' confuses mediumship with witchcraft; but witches are not mediums, and do not necessarily have psychic sensitivity. Margaret Murray a generation or more ago tried to revive the idea that the witches of the European Middle Ages were hereditary mediums and practitioners of an ancient folk-religion of a Spiritualistic kind, but that theory has not stood the test of scholarly examination. Any confusion between witches and mediums is partly caused by the fact that the word 'medium' as used in parapsychology did not come into the English language until 1853, so that there was no precise word by which a psychic sensitive could be called when she was engaged in commerce with the spirits of the departed. But part of the trouble arose because the earlier Bible translators did not know enough about either witches or sensitives to make a clear distinction between them. In the words of Keith Thomas, whose *Religion and the Decline of Magic* carefully documents the beliefs and attitudes of the late medievals of England, 'at a popular level every kind of magical activity, including any unacceptable brand of religion, might be lumped together under the blanket title of "witchcraft".'[3] When you are supping with Satan, they believed, you use a long spoon and keep your eyes on your own plate.

The American Revised Standard Version, correcting King James, calls the woman a 'medium'. So long as we do not import too much of our modern knowledge of mediumship into our use of this word, it will serve to describe her accurately enough. We will examine the account, and see if it makes sense as the story of a consultation with a psychic sensitive who claims to contact departed spirits through her control. There are differences between ancient and modern practice. The woman at En-dor seems to have been ready to contact whomever her sitter wanted her to, whereas most modern sensitives profess to be more passive in this regard and simply to pass on whatever messages come to them without guaranteeing beforehand that any particular departed person is going to come to them. They would certainly not claim to command any spirit to come at their bidding, though they frequently do have a knack of finding a spirit (often *the* particular spirit) whom the sitter is anxious to contact. This difference between the woman of En-dor and a modern trance medium has led Manfred Cassirer[4] to suggest that the Biblical figure was, 'as distinct from a medium . . . one who calls up the dead by an act of conjuration in an altered state of consciousness at the request of a client'. That is a clumsy way of referring to her, though it is certainly exact. The fact is that we know too little either about trans-cultural variations of the phenomenon of mediumship, or how far back in history the characteristic activities of mediums of the last century or so go. True, nowadays most mediums are lightly entranced if at all, and most claim no control over their communicators, but it has not always been so. Heavily tranced mediums were far more common a couple of generations ago, and it is anybody's guess how a medium would behave in Israelite culture of the eleventh century BC. It looks, therefore, as if the woman of En-dor was not exactly the same as a modern medium. Nevertheless, she was probably close enough to enable us to use the word 'medium' of her without gross anachronism. She may well have been a member of a class of people from whom the modern medium has evolved. Mediumship, like prophecy, was probably differently exercised in different eras.

That having been said, let us go on, using the term 'medium'; but realizing that there is some residual danger of anachronism by doing so.

The king asks the woman to call up whom he shall name. She demurs. Surely the man knows how King Saul has put away the mediums and their controls? Her life is in danger if she agrees to give a sitting. Saul swears she shall come to no harm, so the woman ask whom to call up. He answers 'Samuel' – the prophet who anointed Saul at the beginning of his reign, and whose advice he so much misses.

Now what happens? The text immediately continues, 'When the woman saw Samuel appear . . .' Presumably, she does the usual. But what is 'the usual'? We guess – but it is no more than a guess – that she goes into a trance and establishes contact either with her control or with the spirit whom the sitter has asked her to call up. The text nowhere says that King Saul saw Samuel, so it may be that the woman was telling what she saw in her mind's eye rather than with her physical sight; or there may have been a hallucination which she did not share with her sitter.

What kind of altered state of consciousness did the woman enter? There are several different kinds of such states described in the Old Testament, but biblical scholars seem to concern themselves far more with the experiences of the prophets than of the *yidde'onim*. There is an instructive recent article by Simon B. Parker of Boston, Massachusetts, entitled 'Possession Trance and Prophecy in Pre-Exilic Israel'[5], in which he discusses the phenomenon in the light of cross-cultural studies of trance states. First he distinguishes between two kinds of altered state of consciousness: 'visionary trance' and 'possession trance'. In visionary trance, which is characteristic of many of the later, 'writing', prophets of Israel, the prophet sees a vision whilst he is in his altered state of consciousness. There is no claim to be possessed by god or spirit, and on regaining the normal state of consciousness, the prophet remembers his vision and can interpret its meaning. In 'possession trance', on the other hand, the person entering it is believed to be inhabited by the spirit of another person or supernatural being. When he returns to normal, he retains no conscious memory of what he said and did whilst in the altered state of consciousness. His words, therefore, are regarded as words of the possessing entity, and he is not responsible for them. This seems close to the deep trance of some present-day sensitives.

Possession trance may be further divided into two types, 'mediumistic' and 'personal and compensatory'. The latter is a matter of observed behaviour, without alleging any communication from a god or spirit. It is characterized by wild behaviour such as Saul encountered when he met a band of ecstatics on their way down from the High Place, led by lute and drum and pipe and harp, when a spirit from the Lord overwhelmed him, so that he joined in their wild practices (see 1 Samuel 10: 5-7; also the similar incident in 1 Samuel 19:20ff.). This kind of behaviour was either compensatory — i.e. its purpose was to 'provide subjective, expressive compensation for personal or social stresses through the emotional satisfactions provided by the possession trance experience itself' (Parker, p. 275); or it was used to legitimate the status of being the divine nominee — as it did for Saul in the example we have just quoted, where he was recognized as being the Lord's chosen one because he had been overwhelmed in trance by the Lord's spirit.

Mediumistic possession trance, on the other hand, is trance which claims to mediate a message from the spirit world, whether that message purports to be from a deceased human being or from a god. The practice of this kind of trance came to Israel from Phoenicia, but its earliest known example is Egyptian. The *Report of Wen-Amun* (eleventh century BC, almost contemporary with the En-dor incident) contains the remark that 'while he was making offering to his gods, the god seized one of his youths and made him possessed'.[6] The word for 'possessed', as indicated by the form of hieroglyph, denotes some form of quasi-epileptic frenzy.

There is a wide cross-cultural study of trance states in J. Lindblom's book *Prophecy in Ancient Israel*. He draws attention to the similarities between the prophet of the Old Testament and the Arctic shaman, the Arab *kahin*, and the dervish. All laid claim to parapsychological gifts. For example, the *kahins* were 'expected to interpret dreams, reveal thefts, discover lost objects, know where strayed camels were to be found, etc. Usually they were rewarded for their services according to the circumstances of the applicant'.[7] This sounds very like 1 Samuel 9, where young Saul goes off to find some strayed asses of his father's. The search is unsuccessful, and when they have got a good way from home, Saul's servant says to him, 'There is a man of God in the city here who has a great reputation, because everything he says comes true'. Saul wonders what to offer him and the servant turns out his pockets and finds a quarter-shekel. The seer turns out to be Samuel, who is able to tell Saul not to worry about the asses because he knows (paranormally?) that they have been found.

Simon Parker believes that prophecy in Israel did not involve the claim to possession at all. The Hebrew word for 'prophet' is *nabi'*, and this is certainly used in the account of the incident when Saul met the band of *nebi'im* and was himself infected by their frenzy. Parker would have us believe that there are two quite distinct meanings of the word *nabi'*. One is 'a person subject to possession trance', as in 1 Samuel; the other is 'a seer, a diviner, a medium, a prophet'. It is certainly true that the term 'prophet' covers a wide variety of characters, and we must not assume that the prophets whose oracles we read in the later prophetic literature of the Old Testament were in all respects identical with the prophets of the eleventh and tenth century BC, at the time of Samuel and Saul. Yet the use of the same word *nabi'* for both must mean that there was some connection between them. It seems more likely that the one developed from the other and that, whether or not the later prophets were subject to possession trance, their predecessors were – and this knowledge of the history of the institution of prophecy led them to some embarrassment, and to a desire to dissociate themselves from the kind of behaviour their predecessors had indulged in. It would not be the only time in history that that sort of thing had happened. We shall see later that this is a matter of some importance when assessing the attitude of the later prophets to mediumistic behaviour, and to the way in which Christians have reacted towards the woman of En-dor.

And it is to the woman of En-dor that we must return, or we will never finish the story. We had got as far as the medium entering her altered state of consciousness, and 'when the woman saw Samuel appear'. Up till then, King Saul had preserved his incognito; but when the woman goes into trance, it looks as if she is then able to produce extrasensory material (telepathically or clairvoyantly from the sitter), because it is only then that she shrieks out, 'Why have you deceived me? You are Saul!' The king replies, 'Don't be afraid. What do you see?' 'I see a ghostly form coming up from the earth.' 'What is it like?' 'Like an old man, coming up, wrapped in a cloak'.

The narrative continues with a dialogue between the ghost and King Saul. We presume that the words attributed to the spirit of Samuel were uttered by the medium. The prophet Isaiah (8:19) refers to 'controls and mediums (*'oboth* and *yidde' onim*) who squeak and gibber'. Probably the medium's speech when entranced was not her normal voice. Was it a kind of ritual intonation, like that of the New Zealand Maori when they say their incantatory prayers? The Greek translation of the Old Testament calls the woman of En-dor an *engastrimuthos*, a belly-speaker, a ventriloquist. Lindblom draws our attention to the so-called 'Sleeping Preachers' of Finland, who went into a trance, then 'with a terribly distended chest, and in a voice loud enough to fill a medium-sized church ... began to speak'.[8] If the Israelite medium had a standard intonation when in trance (and this is indicated by the fact that Isaiah 29:4 can speak of a person's voice sounding 'like a ghost's from the ground', assuming that people would know what kind of a voice he was referring to), then maybe the account of En-dor does not imply what present-day parapsychologists refer to as 'direct voice communication', but the standard Israelite form of trance speech, which Saul assumed was the speech of Samuel because that was the person he had asked for, and because the woman had told him that she was seeing an old man in a long cloak.

The séance continues. Saul asks advice of the shade of Samuel, and is given a sharp answer. This is not the kind of sitting where the client gets nothing but saccharine platitudes. Saul is told flatly that the Lord has deserted him and that by the very next day he will be in the land of the shades with Samuel. At this, he is overcome, falls terrified to the ground, and has no further strength left in him.

It all comes true. At Gilboa, Saul engages in battle and is killed. Whether this is because a prophecy came true or because he had no stomach for the fight after an experience like that, is a moot point. As in so much of the interpretation of paranormal phenomena, 'you pays your money and you takes your choice'.

The general assumption amongst Christians, with whom the woman of En-dor has enjoyed a consistently bad press, is that Saul did ill to enquire of the medium and that that was why God deserted him. In fact, the account in 1 Samuel 28 is much more favourably disposed to the medium than many commentators notice. She only performed under protest and to help Saul. When he was prostrate she helped him up, and fed him from her own fatted calf and with bread she had baked herself. Saul's sin was not that he enquired of a medium, but that he had not been ruthless enough in exterminating the Amalekites (see verse 18). The fact that Saul had put the mediums out of the land is stated as pure fact, for which neither praise nor blame attaches. It was necessary to state this in order to explain why Saul went in secret and with a disguise. It is only in later accounts that the anti-mediumistic bias of the writers of subsequent centuries comes to the fore. For instance, in the re-written (and much later) account of the death of Saul in 1 Chronicles, the writer states that 'Saul died for that he transgressed . . . because Saul enquired of a medium to seek, and he sought not the Lord'. This is a deliberate smear – the original account makes it clear that Saul *did* enquire of the Lord, and that the normal divinatory methods gave him no clear reply, so that he went to the medium instead. And not even the writer of the books of the Chronicles can make stick the suggestion that the medium was fraudulent. The Septuagint (Greek translation) of this verse adds explicitly, after the words about Saul enquiring of a medium, the phrase 'and Samuel answered him' (1 Chronicles 10:13).

The books of the Chronicles, however, are far from being alone in their dislike of mediumship. Anti-mediumistic texts are not hard to find in the Old Testament. Isaiah 8:19ff. reads, 'Men will say to you, "Seek guidance of *'oboth* and *yidde'onim*, who squeak and gibber; a nation may surely seek guidance of its gods, of the dead on behalf of the living, for an oracle or a message?" They will surely say some such things as this; but what they say is futile'. Or look at Leviticus 19: 31 or 20: 6 and 17, or 2 Kings 23:24, or Deuteronomy 18:9 ff. – 'Do not learn to imitate the abominable customs of those other nations. Let no one be found among you . . . who casts spells, or traffics with controls or mediums, and no necromancer. Those who do these things are abominable to the LORD.'

These attacks come as a result of the teachings of the prophets. Why were the prophets so dead set against mediumship? They knew the same kinds of altered states of consciousness – could they not recognise the mediums as their allies rather than their enemies?

The answer may be that prophecy had developed in the interven-ing centuries and that the mediums were too akin for comfort to the type of character out of whom the later prophets had developed, and with whom they were not very happy to remain identified. 'Prophecy' is a blanket term, but prophets of different centuries behaved very differently. 'He who is now called a prophet was formerly called a seer', we are told in 1 Samuel 9:9, in a marginal note which a later scribe added as explanation to his day for an ancient story which might otherwise mislead his readers – and the marginal note became incorporated into the text. It is the 'seers' of old rather than the writing prophets who seem more akin in their altered states of consciousness to Lindblom's shamans, *kahin*, and dervishes. Look, for example, at the way in which Saul as a young man (1 Samuel 10:10) meets a band of prophets or seers and catches their corybantic ecstasy. Look at Balaam the son of Beor (Numbers 22-24), the soothsayer (Joshua 13:22). He is employed to bless or curse one's friends or enemies, though he can only act as the hand of God comes on him, when (Numbers 24:16) 'with staring eyes [he] sees in a trance the vision from the Almighty'.

He receives his mysterious knowledge by means of dreams and omens of different kinds. He lies prostrate on the ground and sees secret things by his inward eyes, opened towards the hidden world . . . A seer is a man or a woman who claims to possess the faculty of knowing things that are concealed from ordinary men. The chief methods used by the seer are dreams, extraordinary perspicacity, clairvoyance, communications from ghosts and spirits, and finally, external signs and omens. Sometimes the seers also obtain their extraordinary knowledge in a psychic state of ecstasy or trance.[9]

Divining was an acceptable way of discerning the will of God in Israel. Joseph (Genesis 44: 5, 15) had his divining-cup. Divination by means of the sacred lot, the Urim and Thummim, was the standard method of the priests of Jahweh — indeed, we have already seen that it was only because the Urim failed that King Saul went to the medium at En-dor. Samuel was able to see where Saul's asses had got to, and he gave his divination for a fee. Elisha was able to see what his servant Gehazi did when he was away from him (2 Kings 5:26, which sounds like an out-of-the-body experience).

Thus, we see, the seer and the diviner are closely akin, with the same kind of paranormal abilities. What is more, the seer and the medium both have similar altered states of consciousness. When to this we add that 'he who was called a seer is now called a prophet', we want to know why it is that the prophets have nothing but scorn for the mediums and the diviners. Why, when ostensibly they have so much in common? Why, when phenomenologically they are so hard to distinguish?

It rather looks as though the seers and the mediums had more in common with the popular religion of the common folk than the prophets (as successors of the seers) liked to acknowledge. The later prophets were concerned with differentiating the religion of Jahweh from the popular beliefs of the Canaanites, but they were not entirely successful in eliminating those beliefs from the written records which eventually formed the canonical books of the Old Testament. Their dislike of mediumistic practice was because it was too redolent of folk-belief, and folk-belief was as tenacious in ancient Israel as the old paganism is in our own country, despite the veneer of Christianity which covers it in many members of our congregations even today.

One of the folk-beliefs was the belief that the departed, when they die, become as gods, with vast stores of knowledge which can be used for the benefit of the living. The professionals in the religion of Jahweh stamped on this belief, and replaced it with the conception of She'ol,[10] but the old belief did not completely die out, and traces of it can still be seen in the Old Testament where the censorship has not been totally effective — for instance, in the En-dor story, where the woman says she sees 'gods' (*elohim*) coming up out of the earth. The She'ol concept was very far from this one, and it maintained that the dead were helpless, and in a place where the writ of Jahweh did not run. Hence, the practitioners of the religion of Jahweh poured scorn on the activities of the mediums, because they needed to persuade the people that mediums were consulting, not gods, but powerless shades.

She'ol, the abode of the dead, like the Greek Hades, was deep below the ground. There is no doctrine of resurrection in the Old Testament, nor (except in a very few texts, and those the latest in the whole of the Old Testament) no doctrine of the presence of God in She'ol. 'As Yahwism developed, death came to be thought of as total extinction . . . She'ol was never regarded as offering any kind of worthwhile, significant, or personal life, and in developed Yahwism death came to be equated with cessation of being.'[11] This concept comes out clearly in such texts as Job 14: 7-12, or Ecclesiastes 3: 19f., or 9:5f.; or Isaiah 14:10 or 40:6.

Small wonder, then, at Isaiah's sarcasm about those who consult the spirits of the departed (8:19). Should one seek the dead on behalf of the living? If the dead are so weak and helpless, what good can they be to us? If we want help, let us get it from the living, and supremely from the living God. Indeed, if the dead are cut off from God's hand (Psalm 88:5), we are being disloyal to God by looking for help outside the realms of his competence or influence.

Remember, too, that at this stage there was no developed Israelite doctrine of the devil. It was not that mediums were supping with the devil, because no such person was at that time conceived of as the great adversary of Jahweh. Surrounding nations had their beliefs in demons, but – however much they may have been a part of popular superstition – they do not come into the pages of the Old Testament. Only in the latest parts of the Old Testament do we begin to see the first glimmers of the idea of Satan as God's supreme adversary, and the doctrine was not fully developed until the inter-testamental period.

As far as the prophets were concerned, therefore, the dead were powerless in She'ol, though they could be called back for a while by women who had controls. These women had links with an older view, which still had some following amongst the populace, but which the prophets were trying to discredit, because it was too close to the religion of the surrounding nations, who did not worship Jahweh. The prophets knew how easily the people would backslide away from Jahwism, and used all their powers of rhetoric and invective to prevent this from happening. In relation to the mediums, they laid great stress on a belief in She'ol as a place where the undead shades drag out a grey existence, and on the belief that She'ol is beyond the reach of Israel's God.

Christians have the New Testament for their scripture as well as the Old, so they do not need to be bound by Old Testament beliefs in this regard. The New Testament reverses the Old on this matter. Its message is a message of resurrection. The writ of God, say Christians, *does* run in the world of the departed, for Jesus in his resurrection has harrowed She'ol and enabled even that dreadful place to be fertile for a harvest of redeemed souls. God in Christ has power to resurrect from She'ol to a state of eternal life with him. Therefore, those who are communicating with the departed are *not* thereby communicating outside God's realm, or going where he is not, or seeking the help of another god.

In fact, the matter is more complicated, because the dead are as mixed a bunch as the living. We need, therefore, to ask *what* departed we are communicating with, and what spiritual influences they are under, and what influence they can have on us – malign or benign. As we are warned by 1 John 4:1, we must 'not trust any and every spirit', but 'test the spirits, to see whether they are of God'. The communications we receive – like the people we meet on this present earth – *can* be good, holy, orthodox, helpful, god-fearing. Alternatively, they *can* be malevolent, blasphemous, sly, or intent on our destruction. They can be (and they often are!) just plain silly. Death does not transform Aunt Ada into Saint Augustine. She may be just as infuriatingly cretinous in the spirit

world as she was in the flesh. In that case, her communications will
be as vapid as her earthly conversation was. Test the spirits. Don't
think that because they are departed spirits they are either
necessarily demonic, necessarily heavenly, or necessarily profound.
Apply to them the same criteria of spiritual value as you would
apply to communications from earthly friends or spiritual gurus.

Test the spirits. That also means we need to ask whether the
messages that come are brought from the spirits, or whether there
may be a more mundane explanation behind them. There is no
Christian virtue in credulity, any more than there is scientific or
parapsychological virtue in accepting everything at its face valua-
tion. In this regard, our patron saint might well be Daniel, who was
not easily fooled. King Cyrus (I take the story from the books of the
Apocrypha, from that addition to the book of Daniel called *Bel and
the Dragon*) had a great idol called Bel, which had the most colossal
appetite. It consumed twelve bushels of fine flour a day, forty sheep,
and fifty gallons of wine. The food and drink was put before it
every night and had gone by the morning. Daniel mocked, and the
king did not like it, so the seventy priests of Bel submitted to a test.
The king, like a bad parapsychologist, thought it was good enough
to seal the door of the temple so that nobody could come in. He did
not know that the priests had a secret entrance under the table, for
themselves, their wives, and their children to come in night by night
and feast themselves. The door was sealed with the king's signet and
the next morning his majesty arrived, saw the seals had not been
tampered with, and had the doors opened. King Cyrus saw the
empty table and exclaimed 'Great art thou, O Bel!' But Daniel, like
a good ghost-hunter, had gone one cleverer. He had brought in
ashes and sifted them over the floor before the doors were sealed. So
he laughed, and held back the king. 'Just look at the floor', he said,
'and tell me whose footprints these are'. And that was the end of
Bel.

Answers to parapsychological teasers will be found only by
rigorous examination of the data, rigorous closing of possible loop-
holes, and an almost boundless scepticism. Parapsychology is part of
man's attempt to find out what sort of a world God's world is. We
don't find the answer by metaphysics but by observation and experiment. It is not for us to have *a priori* theological criteria by which
we decide in advance what are or are not the powers possessed by
man, or the state of the departed, or the truth or falsehood of the
statements they purport to make. It is the genius of the scientific

revolution which distinguishes us from the medieval world that such questions are solved not by philosophy but by the experimental method.

There are so many questions we would like to ask about human capabilities. Is it humanly possible to be aware of another person's thoughts or actions by non-sensory means? Is it possible to bend spoons, or start clocks, by an act of will? Is it possible to heal diseases by a word, or contact or prayer? Is it possible to speak with unknown tongues, or foretell the future, or to survive death? Can the departed contact us? If so, are their messages distorted or undistorted? These are some of the questions of psychical research. The Christian parapsychologist also regards them as questions about God's world and about the way he made it — just like such questions as 'What causes cancer?' or 'Why do radioactive elements decay?' or 'What did a Brontosaurus eat for dinner?'

We need our wits about us to answer any of these questions. There have been many promising blind alleys and many attractive false turnings in research into oncology, or atomic physics, or palaeontology. Sometimes this is because the data themselves have had more than one possible interpretation. Sometimes it is because of such practical jokes as the Piltdown Man. Parapsychology has more than its fair share of multiple interpretations, and more than its fair share of practical jokers. That is part of its fascination. That is why the parapsychologist has to be tough-minded, always looking for possible alternative interpretations of the data, almost boundlessly sceptical.

Biblical scholars are often like that, too. They have as great a horror of credulity as the psychical researcher. They seem to prefer to cast doubt on almost every verse of the Bible. It is all done with the best possible motives — so that when the scholars *do* build, it is upon a firm and assured foundation, with all possibility of misinterpretation done away. Yet there are times when I suspect that Biblical critics are being unnecessarily sceptical, and that if they knew something about the parapsychological possibilities behind their Biblical texts, they might judge otherwise than they sometimes do on the reliability of the account they are studying. To put it plainly, some Biblical incidents make sense on a parapsychological reading of the data.[12] That still does not *entail* a particular interpretation of the incident in question , but it does mean that the account as received has a fairer chance of being true, and that if we disbelieve it, it must be on better grounds than that we don't like the sound of it, or that nothing like it has happened outside the pages of the Bible. We still have to ask whether we can put credence on reports that come, often, a very long time after the events they purport to describe; but (to quote Boyce Bennett of the General Theological Seminary New York), we need 'to see if some of the parapsychological categories which are currently being investigated can shed any light upon our understanding of the biblical material'.[13]

For example. When the King of Aram (2 Kings 6:11f.) complains that the King of Israel knows more about his battle-plans than he ought to, and asks who is the secret agent in his camp, one of his staff replies, 'None of us, my lord king; but Elisha, the prophet in Israel, tells the king of Israel the very words you speak in your bedchamber.' What does that mean? That Elisha's intelligence work was exceptionally good? Or that he was a telepathic sensitive? Is it an Old Testament foretaste of Ingo Swann's novel *Star Fire*, where psychic intelligence and counter-intelligence direct the course of the war? If we take our parapsychology seriously, we shall not thereby solve the question. It will, however, mean that we have to keep the question open. We cannot automatically take the sceptical view that it was nothing more than normal intelligence work or intuition.

The same goes for John 2:24, where we are told that Jesus did not need evidence from others about men, because he knew what was in them; or Matthew 9:4, where Jesus knows what the lawyers are thinking. Do these texts mean that Jesus was astute and a good judge of character? Or was he a sensitive, able to read thoughts? Or are all good judges of character telepathic, and is it that which makes them good judges?[14] The question stays open.

Or what about the Synoptic apocalypses? Matthew 24 and Luke 21 claim to be sayings of Jesus, but they refer – somewhat obliquely, it is true, but still they refer – to the sack of Jerusalem, which happened about thirty-five years after his death. Do we *have* to say, therefore, that the accounts were improved by the Church's scribes after AD 70, or may we allow that Jesus was able to foretell the future?

Is the account of the Transfiguration purely symbolical, or is it as literal an account as is possible in human language of an actual mystical experience? Boyce Bennett has analyzed altered states of consciousness in terms of lateralization of function between the two hemispheres of the human brain.[15] Recent scientific studies of brain functioning make it likely that the left hemisphere, the normally dominant one, is characterized by logical and abstract thought, single definitions of meaning, and analytical linear reasoning, whilst the right hemisphere is characterized by analogical thought, puns and double meanings, visual and verbal imagery and poetic symbols. The left hemisphere is the philosopher's, the right is the poet's, the visionary's, and the prophet's. When we try to translate left-hemisphere experiences in right-hemisphere terms, language fails us, for the two sets of concepts are incompatible. Has this happened as we try to express the experience of the Transfiguration in human language? Is it verbally incommunicable?

If so, then the truth of the Transfiguration is like the experience of the numinous – it can only be evoked, it cannot be described. And we may be attempting the impossible if we ask such apparently straightforward questions as 'Were the figures that were seen with Jesus symbolic figures, Moses standing for the Law and Elijah for the prophets, which passed away whilst Jesus remained? Or is it conceivable that in some way Moses and Elijah themselves were present on the mountain and conversing with Jesus?' What looks like a simple question to which parapsychology could enable us to frame a simple answer is by no means so susceptible of a single response. All the same, the data of parapsychology help to keep the question of the objective presence of the departed lawgiver and the departed prophet on the mountain-top, an open question. We cannot simply state that it could be nothing but a subjective vision.

The same is true of other accounts of visions which scatter the pages of the Bible. Consider, for example, the angels of 2 Kings 6:17, where Elisha's servant-lad was terrified at the sight of the enemy and, when the prophet had prayed for his eyes to be opened, the lad saw the hills covered with horses and chariots of fire. Or trance visions like those of Paul (Acts 22:17) or Peter (Acts 10: 10ff.); the vision of Daniel 10:7 which was not shared with the bystanders; the auditory hallucination of John 12.28 when a voice sounded from heaven with a message which was intelligible to Jesus, but the crowd said it was thunder and others said an angel had spoken; to say nothing of the post-mortem appearances of Jesus to the disciples, which some writers have compared with veridical hallucinations of the departed.[16] What are they? Veridical, subjective, or the invention of the Biblical authors? The question is at least open.

We have undertaken no more than an exploratory lightning-tour of some of the more obvious biblical passages dealing with paranormal events. In the light of it, is it possible to affirm anything about the Christian attitude to psychic investigation? I believe paranormal phenomena to be no less part of God's creation than other natural phenomena, and research into them to be no less legitimate for Christians. Yet it is possible to give the psychic dimension too great an importance and too central a place in one's religion. It can become a fixation and prevent real spiritual growth. The great 'writing' prophets of the Old Testament seem to have grown up, whereas the seers of earlier centuries and the *yidde'onim* or mediums belong more to the popular religion of Israel and not to the developed lasting and central tradition, from which growth in spiritual stature can spring. If, as I believe, it is not only possible, but fatally easy, to get stuck on the psychic level and never to grow up into the spiritual level, the Christian who engages in psychical research needs to do so responsibly. Over some investigations he will remember that he is not only a scientific researcher, but also a human being dealing with human beings. Just as some experiments with bacteria are too dangerous to carry out (ought we to store smallpox virus under any conditions whatever?), so are some experiments with some sensitives. Just as some people have allergies and are not able to cope with certain substances, so some sensitives may not be able emotionally or spiritually to cope with certain experimental situations.

In Acts 16:16-19 there was a sensitive with an oracular spirit, a slave girl who earned her owners a good living by telling fortunes. Paul was pestered by her so much that he banished the oracular spirit from her. She lost her psychic gifts and the owners raised a riot. That does not mean that the Christian attitude to psychic powers is to go round exorcising everything within sight. It *does* mean that we should exercise discrimination. The girl of Acts 16 had clearly lost her balance and needed to be rescued from a psychic life that had become an obsession. In that case, there was nothing to be done but to rescue her from her addiction. Because there are some alcoholics, does not mean that all Christians should become teetotallers. It *does* mean that they should responsibly handle what could become a danger – and take drastic action if it becomes so! *Mutatis mutandis* with the psychic.

Psychic sensitivity is a marvellous thing, but it can also be a dangerous thing. There is need for pastoral care and spiritual guidance and constant monitoring so that the sensitivity of the medium can be rightly used to the good of her sitters, her own growth into spiritual maturity, and the greater glory of almighty God. Nobody ought to engage in psychical research without spiritual guidance – a father confessor or a guru who can help the researcher see where his studies are tending, who can warn him when he sees the danger signals, help him keep his balance, and encourage him in dry patches.[17]

If that could be the case in psychical research, I have a vision! That we could be at the end of our long period of ignorance, suspicion, or hostility between the Church and psychical research, and at the beginning of a fruitful period in which parapsychology and theological reflection can work together for their mutual enrichment and understanding.

Do you think that could happen? Is that a vision of mine the wild disorder of a sickly mind? Or is it precognitive, and could it even be prophetic?

We'll have to see.

References

1. But not for that reason. He went in disguise and at night because he did not want to arouse other people's suspicions, and because he was about unlawful business.

2. H.W. Hertzberg, *I and II Samuel: A Commentary* (translated by J.S. Bowden from the German edition of 1960), London, SCM Press, 1964, *ad loc.*

3. K. Thomas, *Religion and the Decline of Magic: Studies in Popular Beliefs in Sixteenth- and Seventeenth-Century England* (1971; Penguin edition 1973), pp. 517-8.

4. In a comment on the original form of this paper, in the *Parapsychology Review* for November 1979 (Vol. 10, No. 6), p. 26. I am grateful to him for taking issue with me on this point.

5. S.B. Parker, 'Possession Trance and Prophecy in Pre-Exilic Israel', in *Vetus Testamentum* Vol. 28, No. 3 (July 1978), pp. 271-285.

6. J.B. Pritchard, *Ancient Near Eastern Texts* (New Jersey, Princeton University Press, 1955), pp. 25f; or in *The Report of Wenamun* (Baltimore 1975) by H. Goedicke, pp. 53-55.

7. J. Lindblom, *Prophecy in Ancient Israel* (Basil Blackwell, 1962), p. 8.

8. *ibid.*, p. 15.

9. *ibid.*, pp. 92, 94.

10. See D.J. Bretherton, 'A Clergyman's View of the Afterlife', *Light*, Vol. 102, No. 1 (Spring 1982), pp. 10-27.

11. Paul Badham, *Christian Beliefs about Life after Death* (Macmillan, 1976), p. 4.

12. See Michael Perry, 'Parapsychology in Apologetics', *Church Quarterly Review* Vol. 160 (1959), pp. 77-84.

13. 'Vision and Audition in Biblical Prophecy as Illuminated by Recent Research on Human Consciousness', in *Psi and States of Awareness*,

edited by Betty Shapin and Lisette Coly (New York, Parapsychology Foundation, Inc., 1978), p. 112.

14. In a similar way, E.D. Dean and J. Mihalasky believe that successful executives are successful because they are better than the average at precognition tests. They explore this hypothesis in their book *Executive ESP* (New Jersey, Prentice Hall, 1974).

15. Boyce Bennett, article cited in note 13 above, pp. 104-6.

16. For example, George Zorab, *Het Opstandingsverhaal in het Licht der Parapsychologie* (den Haag, H.P. Leopolds, 1949); Michael C. Perry, *The Easter Enigma* (Faber, 1959); Leslie D. Weatherhead, *The Resurrection of Christ* (Hodder and Stoughton, 1959).

17. See the suggestion of C.E.J. Fryer of a mutually supportive 'Order of Christian Sensitives' in his *A Hand in Dialogue* (James Clarke, 1982), p.114.

Part 3
Death and dying

When the Reverend David Goodacre invited me to present a paper to the Sunderland group of the Institute of Religion and Medicine in 1975, and suggested that I should speak on the theology of death, I was anxious to accept the invitation. Most of my writings and interests until then had concentrated on the gospel of resurrection or on the possibility of continued experiences beyond death, and I had only thought of death as a preliminary, not as a subject in its own right. Oliver Edwards once said to Dr Samuel Johnson that he had tried to be a philosopher, but that, try as he might, cheerfulness kept breaking in. Readers of what follows will observe that I have had similar difficulty in keeping my convictions about resurrection out of my consideration of death, but I hope they will consider it worth while trying to examine 'Death from a Theological Viewpoint', which was the original title of the paper when it was subsequently published in *Contact* No. 55 (1976: 4), pages 21-27. *Contact* is a journal founded by the Scottish Pastoral Association and now sponsored by the Clinical Theology Association, the Institute of Religion and Medicine, the Association for Pastoral Care and Counselling, the Westminster Pastoral Association, and the Irish Pastoral Association. It publishes articles on topics of common concern to doctors, the clergy, social workers, nurses, teachers and others in similar professions.

The experience of dying leapt into public prominence in the late 1970s as the result of a number of convergent lines of research, so I tried in an article in the *Expository Times* (Vol. 91, No. 7, April 1980, pp. 199-203) to open this subject up for the consideration of the clergy and ministers. The article was reprinted in the *Journal* of the Academy of Religion and Psychical Research, Vol. 3, No. 3 (July 1980), pp. 161-9, and translated into Dutch in *Bres* No. 79 (November/December 1979) as 'Sterven, hoe ervaar de jat?', pp. 13-25. An abbreviated version was published in *Catholic Digest* for November 1980 (pp. 107-111). There have been so many advances in this subject, and so much published on it, even in the two-and-a-half years between the publication of the original article and the preparation of the present volume for press, that it has had to be considerably supplemented to take more recent writing into consideration. The subject seems to be a major growing-point in parapsychology at this time.

7
Death

The experience of death

Death is like sex used to be — everybody does it, but nobody talks about it. And yet in some respects we cannot leave the subject alone. We see so much death in our newspapers and our television viewing, and it is so much more explicit than it used to be. We get horrifying pictures of deaths, and they have become the subjects of journalistic titillation. The pornographers of death realize that their pictures exert a kind of fascination (a revulsion, yet a horrified attraction) over those who are 'hooked' on them. And, as with sexual pornography, there is the law of diminishing returns. The stimulus has to be progressively greater in order to achieve the same level of response.

Perhaps the voyeurism about death is akin to voyeurism about sex, in that in both cases we know it is happening but we also know that we are not normally allowed to see it, or to know what it looks like. Gone is the Victorian death-bed, the death at home, surrounded by familiar furniture and familiar faces. Death now takes place in featureless wards, with gloss paint from floor to ceiling and screens round the bed lest the scene distress those who might otherwise catch a glimpse of what they must not be allowed to see. Death is now even more dreadfully lonely than it has ever been before.

Why does death embarrass us? I suspect that the embarrassment is a presenting symptom rather than the underlying one. It hides the fact that death is too painful to contemplate. It is absolutely inevitable yet absolutely mysterious. It will come to all of us, but none of us knows what it will be like. We can observe the dying, we can converse with them, we can ask them what they feel like; but the moment of death is something about which we can question no one. And yet it is going to happen to *me*. Over it I shall have absolutely no power. Argument, struggle, terror, asphyxia – whatever I do, death cannot be avoided. My death is too terrifying to think about, and I shall make sure that the conversation is never allowed to get too close to the bone. My embarrassment hides my terror.

On the one side, terror; on the other, a horrified fascination. That is an attitude of ambivalence we have met elsewhere. Rudolf Otto, in that famous analysis of the primitive religious awareness which he published over sixty years ago under the title of *The Idea of the Holy*, coined the word 'numinous' to characterize man's awareness of the Wholly Other. When the numinous moment passes over a man, he is aware of a vast transcendent mystery which surpasses human description. Before it, he can but cower in awe. And yet he feels he cannot keep away from it – try as he might. Like a moth before a candle, he must needs draw near, even if its bright fire consumes him to a cinder. The apprehension of the Holy has those two poles of *mysterium tremendum* and *mysterium fascinans*. If our attitude towards death contains that same combination of the *tremendum* and the *fascinans*, perhaps that is because death is a mystery in its own way as numinous as the mystery of God. If, then, there is something about death which brings it into the same category as divinity, there is good hope that by articulating a *theology* of death, it could make wider sense than we might at first have supposed.

The necessity of death

First, let us ask whether death is a bad thing or a good thing. Surprisingly enough, there are many reasons for seeing death as good, even necessary. Some of these are biological, some psychological, some philosophical, some religious. Let us look at them in turn.

Biologically, death is essential for sheer survival, let alone for evolution. Except for those primitive forms which subsist upon inanimate matter, every form of life is dependent upon the death of other forms of life for its food. Furthermore, if it were not for death, the world would become over-populated within an astonishingly short space of time. If they all survived, the progeny of a single bacterium could populate the entire surface of the earth in less than two days. Flies would take a little longer — say, a year. Even the elephant, if all his progeny survived and multiplied, could do it within the century. We can conceive of the absence of death only in an entirely static universe where a pre-determined number of members of different species had been created in the beginning and remained constant for ever. No eating or drinking, no marriage and procreation, no growing up for the children, no hope that students should ever become professors, or junior doctors turn into senior consultants. That (thank God) is not our universe. In an evolutionary world, death is a necessity of life.

Psychologically, a life without the boundary of death would be a very different one from the one we now know. If there were an infinity of time available, no one would take it seriously. If opportunities were endless, no one would bother to grasp them. It is only death which challenges man to a proper use of life, to a proper realization of the urgency of opportunities and of the transience of relationships.

Some philosophers have seen death as a necessary good. It speaks to them of release from the physical body, of which the soul or spirit could be well rid. In that form, the philosophy is Socratic or Platonic, and we shall have more to say of it shortly. To such a philosophy, death brings a release from all that constricts us as bodily creatures.

In religion, death can be welcomed as the gateway to a new and fuller life. Many religions ritualize death as a ceremony of initiation, or (to use the term of the anthropologists) a 'rite of passage'. Conversely, many rituals of initiation involve a quasi-death. The rite symbolizes the dying to an old state of life and the embracing of a new one. Initiation rites are about change, and about the terrors and uncertainties which must be accepted if change is to come about. They are about a man's fear of novelty, when he must launch himself out into the unknown. If he is to live the new life, he must first die to the old. There is no womb without a tomb.

In the Christian religion, this is ritually accomplished in the intiatory rite of baptism. The catechumen descends into the choking waters to drown his old man, so that the new man may be born. 'We were buried therefore with [Christ Jesus] by baptism into death, so that as Christ was raised from the dead by the glory of the Father, we too might walk in newness of life' (Romans 6: 4).

The Christian believes, however (and in this he is not alone

amongst men of religion), that just as there is no womb without a
tomb, so the tomb can itself be a womb: 'through the grave and gate
of death we may pass to our joyful resurrection' (the Burial Service
in the Book of Common Prayer). Death initiates into a newer and
fuller life. Moreover, the initiand knows that every rite of passage
has its moments of terror and trauma. It would not be a proper
initiation if the subject could pass through it unmoved. That is true
of lesser rites of passage; it is even more true of the greatest and
most terrible rite of passage, death itself. But the initiation is worth
the trauma. If there were no death, there would be no life beyond it,
and we should be condemned to the imperfections and limitations of
this earth to all eternity. It is in this sense that St Paul can say 'my
desire is to depart and be with Christ, which is far better' (Phil. 1:
23). There was a telling line in a radio play about Lazarus, whom
Jesus brought back from the dead. He comes back into this life of
transience and impermanence and imperfection, and in the end he is
constrained to cry out, 'Give me back my death!'

There are, therefore, biological, psychological, philosophical, and
religious reasons why death is a necessary thing. Yet our instinct for
survival is so strong, our love of living so ingrained, that we cannot
but feel we should fight against death with all our power. What is
there about death which compels us to shrink from it? Three aspects
in particular: death is powerlessness, separation, and alienation.

Powerlessness, separation, alienation
Death is powerlessness. To be human is to wield power. As a child
grows into a man, he learns how to manipulate his environment to
his advantage. His powers extend and mature. But then comes the
time when the adult passes his peak of physical maturity. There
comes upon him the agony of diminishment, as his powers wane.
'When you were young you girded yourself and walked where you
would; but when you are old, you will stretch out your hands, and
another will gird you and carry you where you do not wish to go'
(John 21: 28). The ultimate in powerlessness is the powerlessness of
death. In it, the active verb has been entirely replaced by the
passive. There is absolutely nothing a man can *do*; he can only be
done to.

Death is separation. Those who are left behind feel the pangs of
being separated from those who have gone through death. The com-
panionship, the love, the advice, the support we relied upon is no
longer available simply by turning towards that person who means
so much to us. But the road to death, for the dying person, is also a

road of separation and solitariness. On it, every one of a man's companions and every one of his possessions is ruthlessly stripped from him. 'Naked I came from my mother's womb, and naked I shall return' (Job 1: 21). All the things we have surrounded ourselves with, to make life comfortable and tolerable, are taken from us. We are even deprived of the very air we breathe. Death is separation.

Death is alienation. There is a connection in the Bible between sin, death, and judgement. Sin is alienation from God, the source of life, and is therefore a death more radical than physical death. Sin is the reason why death came into the world, and it is the devil who has the power over death (Hebrews 2:14). Death, therefore, is the outward symbol of man's rebellion against God. Both sin and death lead to judgement. Death brings us in our sin face to face with the God with whom we have through that sin been estranged and alienated.

For all these reasons, therefore, death is to be feared. Not for nothing did Paul (1 Cor. 15:26) term it the 'last enemy' of Christ. We are right to regard it with that ambivalent attitude we noticed at the first. Some things about it we recognize as necessary and inevitable, and yet we cannot be human and at the same time regard death as a purely neutral biological phenomenon. It poses us with a theological problem. The province of theology is to give us a context within which to set our perplexities, ambivalences, and ambiguities of attitude. Perhaps we can best do this by first setting out a pre-Christian and non-Christian philosophy of death, in order that the Biblical doctrine can be the more clearly and distinctively seen against it. It is the more necessary to do this since that non-Christian philosophy has often been mistaken for a Christian theology.

Philosophies of death

Socrates died in 399 BC. We know his thought through the writings of his pupil Plato. He taught that soul and body belong to different worlds. Life holds them together in uneasy harness, but death − the supreme liberator − can be welcomed since it allows them to do what is natural, and go their separate ways. For the philosopher who has kept his soul pure from the defilements of the body by a lifelong pursuit of wisdom, in which bodily desires are an encumbrance that the wise man would do well to be rid of, death is the object or goal of knowledge. It sets the philosopher free at last for self-fulfilment. It liberates the essential self, the true or real Socrates, from the body with which it has been temporarily and fortuitously associated during its earthly life, and which has made the pursuit of wisdom so hard. At the time of Socrates, there was a custom of offering up a cockerel to the god Asclepius as a thanksgiving for recovery from illness. Socrates asks his friend Crito to observe this custom after his death. The soul has, as it were, been cured by death of its disease of association with a mortal body. Death has no very great significance. Man's soul or spirit is inherently immortal and indestructible. Thus it is that Socrates, like the dying swan, can sing most sweetly as the hemlock takes its effect.

This is not the Christian nor the Biblical view. Jesus in Gethsemane regarded death with horror, so that his sweat stood out like great drops of blood (Luke 22:44). Jesus on Calvary met his death with a terrifying cry of 'My God, my God, why hast thou forsaken me?' (Mark 15:34). This is poles apart from Socrates calmly discoursing of immortality over a cup of hemlock. If, therefore, we want to articulate a Christian theology of death, we need first to rescue the Biblical view by looking at death in the pages of the Old Testament, and then considering the radical sea-change which came over it through the fact of Jesus.

The Old Testament is about God, and God is about life, not death. He is the fountain and cause of life. Life is his gift, and not man's inalienable possession. A man's prayer to God, therefore, is for long life and a ripe old age. He lives on in his descendants, and one of the greatest blessings bestowed upon the patriarchs was that they lived long and were promised progeny as numerous as the grains of sand on the sea-shore. What was evil, terrifying, repugnant, about death was that it was isolation from God. 'The slain that lie in the grave' are 'those whom thou dost remember no more [O God], for they are cut off from thy hand' (Psalm 88:5). Death breaks up in She'ol (the place of the shadows) that relationship between human and divine which is the glory of man's life. It is not a return of the soul to him who made it, but a return to the dust where all things are forgotten.

Any doctrine of resurrection, or of the power of God over She'ol, or of his presence there, is read from the Old Testament only uncertainly and in very late texts (such as Psalm 139:8 — 'If I make my bed in She'ol, behold, thou art there also'). By the time of Jesus, the new-fangled doctrine of resurrection was becoming a subject of considerable speculation and debate. But what was peripheral to the Old Testament comes out fully into the open in the New. Christianity, in the words of Professor Christopher Evans[1], is 'a precise, confident and articulate faith in which resurrection has moved from the circumference to the centre'. And it is a faith in resurrection, not immortality.

In the terms of the New Testament, God and death are opponents. There is a victory, but it is one for which God had to fight. Its outcome was not an affirmation of human immortality, but a declaration of divine power — a power great enough to achieve resurrection. It is in this power that Paul exults (Phil. 3:10). What happened to Jesus was not an illustration of the inherent immortality of the human soul (after the doctrine of Socrates), but a decisive victory by God over the forces of death whereby resurrection was achieved. For Jesus, his death was a matter for terror, beyond which nothing seemed certain. It was a real death, no sham. But in it, there was contact between God and death — and God did not die!

Death, therefore, still has its terrors, but it cannot isolate man from God. And within the Godhead there is the experience of death. In death we are no longer absent from God. He has entered the realm of death and by so doing has ensured the death of death; but the new man of the resurrection is created, not in spite of death, not by doing away with death, but *through* death and *out of* death. The resurrection does not annul the death of Christ, it gives it its meaning. By the victory won in the death of Christ, the sting of death is left behind, like the sting of a noxious insect which dies as the last of its poison is exuded. We are still left with the sting of death; it is still painful; but in the life of God, it can no longer do what it once could.

The Christian therefore confronts death in the knowledge that it is still real and it still has power and that when he is in its grip he is in a position of absolute powerlessness; *yet* the powerlessness of man is a precondition of the exercise of the power of God, and his power is greater than any power of death. It is in this kind of understanding of the meaning and significance of death that we can go on to say something about the *ars moriendi*—the art of Christian dying.

The *ars moriendi*

How should the Christian approach his own death? With confidence. Not without anxiety, nor without fear, for we are men. The Christian claim is that what is required is not the bravado which makes light of death, but the confidence that all its terrors (genuine though they be) are of no *real* account to one who knows who will be his companion. 'I said to the man who stood at the gate of the year, "Give me a light that I may tread safely into the unknown." And he replied, "Go out into the darkness, and put your hand into the hand of God. That shall be to you better than light, and safer than a known way.'"[2]

Put your hand into the hand of God. In death we are absolutely in the grip of something we are absolutely unable to control. But this hopelessness and inescapability is the prior condition for exercising Christian faith and trust, because the Christian's confidence is grounded one hundred per cent in God and not at all in himself. When Carlyle met a particularly vapid young woman who said, 'I accept the Universe', his immediate comment was, 'By Gad, she'd better!'[3] The same is true of death. What matters is not *that* we accept it — we have no choice — but *how* we accept it. Most of us have terrors of 'letting go' and submitting to the inevitable. Falling in love requires a similar willingness to lose control and relax in giving one's-self to the trusted partner. Christian dying is a consummation of the act of falling in love with him whom we have learnt to trust during a life-time's courtship; and just as the act which consummates human love may be terrifying in its very loss of control, so may the act of dying. Yet it may be joyfully accepted as the climax of a life of self-abandonment to the divine providence, a life-time in which we have become so used to giving ourselves into the care of God that we have at this final stage no hesitation in letting him take complete control of us and of what is to happen to us.[4] That man dies in peace who knows that in death he is surrounded by the love of a gracious God, who in our total powerlessness will never abuse his power.

That does not come easily. John Donne once confessed that he was afraid of death:

> I have a sin of fear, that when I've spun
> My last thread, I shall perish on the shore.[5]

But in the end he won through to a Christian confidence, as he was finally able to say with ringing assurance —

> Death, be not proud, though some have called thee
> Mighty and dreadful, for thou art not so,
> For those whom thou think'st thou dost overthrow,
> Die not, poor death, nor yet canst thou kill me . . .
> One short sleep past, we wake eternally,
> And death shall be no more; death, thou shalt die![6]

References

1. C.F. Evans, *Resurrection and the New Testament* (SCM Press, Studies in Biblical Theology, Second Series No. 12, 1970), p. 40.
2. M.L. Haskins, 'The Gate of the Year', quoted in *King George VI to his Peoples* (John Murray, 1952), p.21 – a broadcast on Christmas Day, 1939.
3. The poor woman was Margaret Fuller.
4. This last section owes much to my discussion of the subject on pp. 6-7 of *The Resurrection of Man* (Mowbray, 1975).
5. *Divine Poems*: 'To Christ', verse 3.
6. *Holy Sonnets*, X.

8
What is dying like?

Most of us assume that while we can observe and question the dying, the moment of death itself is something about which we can have no reliable information. Whilst that may have been true a few years ago, there have recently been real advances in charting the last few moments of earthly life, and there is something approaching an explosion in what is becoming known as 'thanatology'. Michael Simpson, in his book *The Facts of Death*, has a splendid give-away line at the head of his bibliography, as he casually mentions the fact that he has read and reviewed over eight hundred books in the area of death and dying.[1] There is already in America an International Association for Near-Death Studies with its own Newsletter and twice-yearly academic publication *Anabiosis*.[2]

Whether what is being charted is the first phase of a life after death is a point to which we must return at a later stage in this essay. It is a matter for a deal of controversy. Christians will not necessarily all take the same side on this, but they ought to know something of the data on which the arguments are based.

We had better (for our immediate purposes) leave aside the notoriously ambivalent data of hypnotic regression experiments and of psychical mediumship. Perhaps the dead may return to, or communicate with, this earth and tell us what it was like to die; perhaps under hypnosis a person may recollect details of a life in a former incarnation and of the death at the end of it, but Christians are deeply divided as to the propriety of dealing with such evidence, and there is enough to be going on with if we simply deal with what the dying themselves tell us, or what those at their bedsides observe.

Second-hand evidence

Deathbeds no longer have the same fascination for us that they did for our forebears a century ago. Perhaps that is because a death at home, surrounded by familiar sights and family friends, is now so much less frequent — though there is a welcome tendency to discharge terminal cancer patients to their own homes rather than retain them in the hospital to the very end. Despite this, death so often nowadays is institutionalized. The patient has probably been sedated, the nurse is too busy to sit with the dying patient and share the experience with him, and the relatives may visit only sporadically. The contrast between this and the practice in earlier generations is dramatic. To Victorian piety (sentimental at its worst but realistic at its best) the idea of making a 'good death' was still a goal at which to aim.

Despite all this, the dying throughout this century have continued to have visions of religious figures or of close relatives who have passed on before them, who purport to be there to receive them over the threshold of death.

The recent history of the study of such cases is documented for us by D. Scott Rogo,[3] who reminds us that discussion of them 'stretches back to the very beginnings of parapsychology in the 1880s'. The case of Daisy Dryden, an adolescent girl who saw a whole host of deathbed apparitions in the last three days of her life, was recorded as long ago as 1864. Frances Power Cobbe in her book *Peak in Darien* (1882) recounts several cases of deathbed visions, though Rogo believes that 'her reporting is purely anecdotal in the worst sense, and her accuracy was just as poor as her reporting'. Cases were discussed by the founders of the Society for Psychical Research, who were particularly impressed by collectively-perceived deathbed visions. Nowadays, researchers are more interested in finding specific and recurring patterns in their data than in verifying any individual cases. In this, they are following in the steps of James Hyslop (1907), who made a comprehensive analysis of a large number of cases and began to study their statistical aspects. But the only book solely devoted to cases of this kind was Sir William Barrett's *Death-bed Visions*. Barrett was Professor of Physics at the Royal College of Science in Dublin, and

his wife was an obstetrician. She had delivered a baby to a dying
mother. The mother suddenly

looked eagerly towards one part of the room, a radiant smile illuminating
her whole countenance. 'Oh, lovely, lovely', she said. I asked, 'What is
lovely?' 'What I *see*', she replied in low, intense tones . . . Then – seeming
to focus her attention more intently on one place for a moment – she
exclaimed, almost with a kind of joyous cry, 'Why, it's Father! Oh, he's
so glad I'm coming; he *is* so glad.' On looking at the same place again she
said with a rather puzzled expression, 'He has Vida with him'.[4]

Vida was her sister who had died three weeks previously, and,
because of her precarious health, the mother had not been told of
this. Lady Barrett's story so impressed Sir William that he set about
the task of collecting and synthesizing a vast amount of the relevant
literature and making a collection of similar cases. This was
eventually published posthumously, in 1926.

Not until the 1950s was the study of deathbed visions taken up
statistically, using modern survey methods and sophisticated
sampling techniques. The work was begun by Dr Karlis Osis, a
Latvian now resident in the USA, where he is on the staff of the
American Society for Psychical Research. In the 1970s he was
joined on this project by Dr Erlendur Haraldsson, an associate
professor of psychology in the Univeristy of Iceland at Reykjavik.

A pilot survey was carried out in the USA and reported in a
monograph entitled *Deathbed Observations by Physicians and Nurses*.[5]
Dr Osis mailed a questionnaire to 5,000 physicians and 5,000
nurses practising in the USA. He received 640 replies, reporting a
total of over 35,000 observations of dying patients. Of these, 1 in
27 saw apparitions, 1 in 40 reported visions, and 1 in 47
experienced what Osis terms 'mood elevation shortly before death'.
190 cases were followed up in detail and analysed.

The pilot survey was sufficiently encouraging for Osis to carry
out a second US survey in 1961-64 and for Osis and Haraldsson to
do a third survey in India in 1972-73. India was chosen because the
researchers wanted to know whether the phenomena were artefacts
of religious or cultural expectation in America or whether the same
sort of results could be obtained in a totally different society.
Statistical analyses were carried out to see what correlations there
were between the various aspects of the reported experiences and the
personal details (and beliefs) of the dying patients concerned. All
three surveys are reported in *At the Hour of Death*.[6]

Dr Osis found two distinct types of deathbed hallucination. One was rambling and confused, and tended to re-live the this-world concerns of the dying patient. This type of vision characterized particularly the persons with brain damage, brain disease, high fever, or heavy medication affecting the patient's brain processes. Such hallucinations tended to recur, and were usually of strangers, bizarre figures, or symbolic characters whose importance to the patient was compensatory either for the deprivation and loneliness of hospital life or for his lowly status in society. The other kind of vision, which tended to be much briefer in duration, was coherent and consistent and purported to be a vision of a loved one or of a religious figure (Mary, Jesus, an angel, Krishna, a *yamdoot* or Hindu messenger of death) coming to take the dying patient away. This kind of vision was reported by the patient who was clear-brained at the time of death. Five out of six hallucinations of this type in the pilot study were of close relatives and seven out of ten were of the departed. This contrasts sharply with the incidence of hallucinations seen by persons in a normal state of health, where 67 to 87 per cent are of *living* persons; or with the hallucinations of the mentally ill, which are commonly not of relatives but of strangers or bizarre figures.

On the whole, the American experience is of a former member of the immediate family who meets the dying person, whilst in India, religious personages are more frequently seen. This may be an artefact of religious belief or pre-expectation. More Indians than Americans believe in reincarnation, so that many of the Indians would not believe that their departed relatives were still about in a post-mortem world to be available to help them over the barrier of death. Another factor which may have been culturally conditioned was that although three-quarters of the patients who saw a 'take-away' figure were happy to go with him or her, more Indians than Americans reacted negatively to the sight of this figure. This may be because a *yamdoot* is traditionally a frightening personage, or it may be because Indians die younger (on average) than Americans so that more dying Indians are in what we would have called the prime of life. The actual identification of the religious figure — as Jesus, Mary, an angel, or Krishna — obviously mirrors the religious beliefs of the patient concerned, who will interpret an ineffable experience in terms sufficiently familiar to him as to admit of verbalizing what he perceives. Those who were actively involved in their religion were slightly more disposed to see a 'take-away' figure, though the visions did not conform either to Christian or Hindu religious pre-expectations. As Osis and Haraldsson remark, 'Christian ideas of "judgement", "salvation", and "redemption" were not mirrored in the visions of our American patients. Furthermore, while we had many reports about visions of Heaven, visions of Hell and Devils were almost totally absent'[7] (we shall return to this last point later). Dr Osis concludes that statistical analysis shows that the visions were not due to wish-fulfilment, inner conflict, religious or cultural expectations, or the effects of hallucinogenic medication. It very much looks to him as if we have to believe what we are told – that when our time comes to die, we shall be helped over the threshold by our friends, and we may be able to tell those around our death-beds what we see happening.

At first hand

So far, we have been relying on secondhand evidence, from people at the bedside. Can the dying themselves tell us anything? Since it is now becoming increasingly common to resuscitate a patient from a state of clinical death, we can question a growing number of people who have either had a very close brush with death or who may even have passed through the experience and yet returned to tell us. The subject of what the growing literature on the subject refers to as the 'near-death experience' (NDE) leapt into public prominence in the late 1970s, first with the publication of Raymond Moody's *Life After Life*, and then with Johann Christoph Hampe's *Sterben ist doch ganz anders*. Both were first published in 1975, quite independently of each other, but Hampe's did not appear in English until 1979, under the title *To Die is Gain*.[8] Hampe is a German Lutheran minister who was clinically 'dead' during a dangerous illness from which he recovered, Moody an American with a background in philosophy, medicine, and psychiatry who had heard the stories of several patients who had recovered from clinical death and realized they had many elements in common. Both rely extensively on first-hand accounts, but apply no statistical analyses to the material they use.

Hampe discovered that there is 'an extraordinarily increased activity on the part of the consciousness in the moments before death' and that three elements recur persistently in the accounts. They are the escape of the self (or out-of-the-body experience, for which see below), the account rendered by the self (a flashback panorama of one's past life), and the expansion of the self after passing through a dark tunnel into openness and light. Moody's scheme is more ambitious. He found fifteen separate elements which recurred in the accounts and built up a composite description of the 'perfect case', though all these elements have never yet been present together in one single instance.

In Moody's composite description, a man hears himself pronounced dead by the medical personnel surrounding him. He hears a loud uncomfortable noise and seems to be moving very rapidly through a long dark tunnel. Then he suddenly finds himself outside his physical body, looking at it from a distance, as though he were a spectator of the resuscitation attempt he is witnessing. Then, other things begin to happen. He glimpses the forms of relatives and friends who come to meet him and help him in the new and strange environment to which he is slowly becoming acuustomed. This is succeeded by a vision of 'a loving, warm spirit of a kind he has never encountered before' who asks him a question which is perceived non-verbally. This question makes him evaluate his past life, in which he is assisted by a 'panoramic, instantaneous playback' of its major events. Eventually he comes up against some kind of barrier or border which he is unable to pass, because it represents the irreversible border of no return. His time for death has not yet come, so regretfully he fails to cross the border. He is filled with intense feelings of love and joy and peace, which make him want to remain in his present state; but this is not to be, and he suddenly finds himself reunited with his physical body and back in the 'normal' world once more.[9] *Life after Life* is dedicated to George Ritchie, who had a similar experience in 1943 whilst in the US Army Medical School. A recent re-telling of his story appears as *Return from Tomorrow*.[10] He was in a coma for four days, during which he was resuscitated from a near-death experience. During this time he appeared to himself to be sitting on the edge of the bed, surveying with some distaste an inert body which remained there. He dressed, began to make his way out of the hospital, and was disturbed to find himself walking through an orderly carrying a tray of instruments. He then appeared to fly at tremendous speed to a town (which he later recognized as Vicksburg) and back. His subsequent out-of-the-body experiences were more dream-like but included a judgemental review of his life in the presence of a being of light whom he took to be Jesus Christ. The experience (not surprisingly) changed his life.

The purely anecdotal material so far reviewed was enough to interest many researchers in this new field, and more statistical studies are now being undertaken, akin to those which transformed the study of the deathbed experience from the era of Sir William Barrett's anecdotal collection of cases to that of Osis and Haraldsson's examination of correlations, percentages, and cross-cultural analyses. The subject is very new, the data-base on which conclusions are reached is still very narrow, and cross-cultural checks on any large scale are still not available, so any theorizing has to be tentative in the extreme; but we are at the beginning of an exciting period of research and analysis, and he would be a bold man who ventured to prophesy what will and what will not be established within the next ten years. The most important single study to date is Kenneth Ring's *Life at Death*.[11] He examines the records of 102 people who went through the near-death experience either as the result of illness (50 per cent), accident (25 per cent), or a failed suicide attempt (25 per cent). About half of these retained some memory of an experience, and Dr Moody's composite description was (broadly speaking, but not in every detail) found to fit their reports. What was particularly interesting was that the further one went into the experience, the rarer were the accounts. Thus 60 per cent of respondents experienced a feeling of peace, 37 per cent experienced body separation, 23 per cent the entry into darkness, 16 per cent saw the light at the end of the 'tunnel', and only 10 per cent reported actually entering into that light. The suicides' experience was truncated in that none of them went beyond the third of these five stages, but that group may not be statistically typical in that almost all of them were drug-induced suicide attempts, and the drugs may have affected the experience.

The state of being 'out of the body' is not at all unusual and has been variously estimated as being known to between 10 and 33 per cent of the population. Sometimes (as in the cases we are considering at the moment) it is associated with a near-death experience, sometimes it is the result of a psychological trauma, sometimes it can be eenetered at will as a means of escaping from intolerable conditions. The doyen of researchers into the state was the late Dr Robert Crookall, a retired geologist who remained active and writing well into his nineties. In a long series of books culminating in *What Happens when you Die*[12] he has presented us with a veritable descriptive geography of the world of the life to come. His books do not make easy reading because of their staccato style and their liberal use of parentheses, and the conceptual scheme he adopts is a far from simple one; but he believes that mediumistic statements tally with those of people who have recovered from a near-death experience and with those who can have out-of-the-body experiences at will, and he finds it possible to describe, almost hour by hour, the post-mortem experiences that all of us are to expect.

Interpretation

What are we to make of all this evidence? Not every reader will take it at its face value, and we are not short of reductionistic explanations. It is possible to explain the data away in terms of the psychodynamics of the process of dying. The patient cannot bear to admit to himself that he is *in extremis* and the thought of his own extinction is too painful for his conscious mind to accept; so his subconscious produces a scenario whereby death's finality is denied. This may even have some value for the physical system, because it prevents the unhelpful panics which might otherwise ensue and enables the body's resources to be concentrated on fighting the infection or lesion or whatever, instead of being wasted in useless terror. Part of the scenario may be a re-living of the birth experience – both birth and the NDE involve passing through an unpleasantly restricting tunnel into an ambience of unwonted light and expansion, in which one is received by a white-robed creature of immense majesty.

That is a psychodynamic explanation of the NDE. Another reductionist explanation is the psychopharmacological. Dr J.F. McHarg, consultant psychiatrist, writing about the Osis findings, tells us that when the brain is starved of oxygen, hallucinations and mood changes may occur. In his opinion, this is the real reason for what the dying see and how they react in their final moments. Moreover, epileptiform seizures are often associated with emotions of transcendental 'awareness'.

The striking mood changes are simply *assumed* by the authors to have been *caused* by the apparitions and they show no awareness of the medical facts that such mood changes, in the direction of ecstasy, with a religious, 'other-worldly', colouring, have long been recognised as being rather typical of temporal lobe paroxysms.[13]

As for the out-of-the-body experience, Susan Blackmore[14] believes it is simply 'an altered state of consciousness in which the powers of imagination and memory are used to construct a particularly convincing "other world"'. The experience is readily induced by progressive relaxation followed by monotonous auditory and visual stimulation. Some years ago, the late Sir Cyril Burt pointed out[15] that a change in blood pressure in the inner ear evokes the experience of rising, hovering, or floating in space. Persons who possess vivid powers of optical imagery may have this feeling and visualize a 'duplicate' body moving away from their physical body in agreement with this sensation. 'Flying' dreams are frequent and have a ready psycho-physiological explanation.

Accounts of the out-of-the-body experience often include the fact that the patient, in his 'other' body, saw what the nurses and doctors were doing to him, and surprised them on recovery by telling them so. This could be no more than a visual dramatization of what has been subconsciously perceived as happing to and around the patient, and therefore have no paranormal content at all. The fact that the experience ceases precisely as the resuscitating injection is given by the doctor may indicate that it is an artefact of lack of blood oxygen to the brain, and stops as soon as the blood supply recovers.

As for the feeling of travelling down a long tunnel and subsequent 'expansion of the self', this need not betoken anything objective. I myself remember, when I had my tonsils out in 1945, zooming rapidly down a rotating purple tunnel into unconsciousness under the anaesthetic. Not only the delirious, but those who have experimented with psychedelic drugs, may have had great inexpressible intimations of cosmic significance which proved quite irretrievable in a normal state. We do not necessarily believe that they have any objective referent. May not the same be true of Hampe's 'expansion of the self'? Hampe himself surmises that the flash-back of one's former life may occur because 'fear of death causes the adrenal gland to produce and excrete hormones which have a similar effect to certain poisons, for instance hashish and LSD'[16]. Deathbed visions may simply be archetypal images, psychologically explicable, or a compensatory method of bolstering up our failing self-confidence in a desperate situation.

And what is 'clinical death'? It need not imply that the patient has actually moved across a real boundary and back again. It could be a synonym for a state close to death but assuredly on this side of it. That is why students of the subject prefer to talk of the 'near-death experience' rather than an 'experience of clinical death'. It is a moot point whether we are being told true descriptions of life shortly after death, and seeing what consciousness might be like if it were not tied to the physical body. We could just be logging the coincidental artefacts of the thought-processes of a brain close to collapse.

The fact that the reported experiences are almost universally pleasant may simply indicate how ready we all are to hope for the best in untheological optimism. Dr Maurice Rawlings is a specialist in cardiovascular disease who has not only performed many resuscitations but listened to the patients during the process. He believes that bad experiences are as numerous as good ones, but that the bad ones are so terrifying and impossible to face up to that they are almost immediately repressed into the unconsciousness and lost to memory. Researchers like Osis and Ring, therefore, who rely on secondhand reports or on interviews with patients who have had time to repress their bad experiences, will paint a tolerantly rosy picture of death because they believe all NDEs are pleasant. Dr Rawlings suggests that the whole process may be a Satanic ruse to lull us into a false sense of security.[17] Zola Levitt and John Weldon come to a similar conclusion. They review Moody's cases, and compare the anodyne nature of the reports with the scriptural expectations of judgement and punishment, and the mild nature of the 'review of life' with the Christian view of the gravity of sin. They conclude that the father of lies is not far in the background. The task of the devil is

to undercut and counterfeit what God has established . . . If there is a way to relax people away from a natural fear of death, the enemy will find and use it . . . The biblical explanation of death is very clear . . . Each man dies once, with one of two possible results. Either the individual is forgiven and taken to be with God or he is not forgiven and is taken to the future home of the devil.[18]

This eschatology would not satisfy every Christian theologian; but it is nevertheless disturbingly true that many Spiritualists (and Weldon and Levitt chronicle a good many spiritualistic leanings in researchers whom we might otherwise assume to be purely scientifically motivated) have not so much as begun to consider the gravity of sin.

It seems, therefore, as if the study of the experience of dying is as tantalizing as any part of parapsychology. We may interpret the accounts as if they afford us glimpses of a life beyond the grave, or we may read them through purely this-worldly spectacles, as the last wild fantasies of wish-fulfilment in a deluded brain, or the last wild paroxysms of a brain starved of oxygen. Dr Grosso has recently[19] analysed the present 'state of play' on all this, and rejects the reductionist explanations. The experience is not induced by drugs, sensory deprivation, lack of blood oxygen to the brain, epileptiform seizures, religious pre-expectation, depersonalization, schizoid defensive belief-systems, or a psychodynamic denial of the reality of approaching death. For him, three things make NDEs significant:

1. They are self-consistent over a wide variety of experiments and cultures in a way we would not expect delusional hallucinations to be.

2. They include parapsychological aspects which have to be explained either on a survival hypothesis or on a hypothesis which argues such fantastic powers in the living mind that human survival is thereby made more rather than less credible.

3. Near-death experiences lead to changes in outlook and behaviour on the part of those who have been through them which seem incongruous if they are illusory or pathological.

We are yet far from proof, however suggestive the evidence may be. The significant thing is that the question is still open, and we may be on the threshold of new discoveries about the process of dying and the progress beyond it. If the present writer inclines more to the positive and less to the reductionistic reading of the evidence so far to hand, he would urge that the accounts be treated critically, and not used as correctives of a supposedly-mistaken theology. After all, they can at the most tell us of the first few moments of the life to come, and Christians have traditionally seen death only as the first of the Four Last Things – there are still judgement, hell, and heaven to be reckoned with.

Practicalities

Experience is still experience, whatever its interpretation. These accounts at which we have been looking show us what it feels like to die, and at the very least they should help us to treat the dying as persons, not as objects. Medical science should not retreat embarrassed at the onset of death; it is our duty to help people make as human and dignified a last journey as possible.

In 1969 Walter Pahnke was reporting[20] his experiments in preparing patients for death. Terminal cancer sufferers were given, under carefully regulated conditions and within the context of brief but intensive psychotherapy, a dose of the psychedelic agent LSD. The psychological effect of lysergic acid derivatives depends greatly on the context within which they are administered. Dr Pahnke's aim was to induce a sense of mystical awareness, and he claimed that he was able to do this so that death was accepted and welcomed positively. Christians do not normally welcome attempts at the chemical manufacture of religious awareness without ascetic discipline, but death is an ascetic discipline of supreme rigour, and when there is no time left, one cannot go the long way round. After all, a penitent thief on a cross was granted a short cut.

LSD research of this kind has also been carried out by the Czech-American Stanislav Grof and his wife Joan Halifax, who have issued five volumes on their researches and methods. The second of these (though the first to appear in the UK) is *The Human Encounter with Death* (1978) where they demonstrate the power of the drug, appropriately administered as part of an overall regimen of psychedelic therapy, to transform dying into an experience of reconciliation and repose.

Dr Elisabeth Kübler-Ross is another American who has made outstanding inroads into the problem of caring for the dying patient. Over the years, originally as assistant professor of psychiatry at the University of Chicago, she has sought to deepen her own empathy and that of the medical students in her care so that they can provide a positive care for the dying in which they can be encouraged to grow in stature through their experience. Of her many books, perhaps the best known is *On Death and Dying*.[21] In the UK we have reason to be grateful for the pioneering work of Dr Cicely Saunders, who believes that a person should be enabled to die with human dignity and Christian hope. In St Christopher's Hospice, pain control is made a major part of total care, so that the person is in relative ease yet not so heavily sedated as to have to die in a coma. Her work and that of the increasing number of hospices on both sides of the Atlantic has been recently described by Sandol Stoddard in *The Hospice Movement* (1979).

All this is a welcome step back towards the recovery of that mediaeval art, the *ars moriendi*, the knowledge by Christians that death is something to be prepared for. Long ago, that fourteenth-century mystic the Blessed Henry Suso had the following dialogue in his *Büchlein der ewigen Weisheit*:

Lord, what wilt thou teach me?
I will teach thee to die and I will teach thee to live . . .
What need have I, Lord, of being taught how to die bodily? Surely it teaches itself when it comes.
He who puts his teaching off till then, will find it too late.

The Litany in the Alternative Service Book 1980 points us in the right direction, therefore, when it bids us pray: 'from violence, murder, and *dying unprepared*, good Lord, deliver us'.

References

1. Michael A. Simpson, *The Facts of Death* (Englewood Cliffs, NJ and Hemel Hempstead, Prentice-Hall International, 1979), p.264.
2. Editor, Kenneth Ring. Enquiries to IAN-DS, Box U-20, University of Connecticut, Storrs, CT 06268, USA.
3. D. Scott Rogo, 'Deathbed Experiences: Some Contemporary and Historical Perspectives', *Parapsychology Review* Vol. 9, No. 1, (January – February 1978), pp. 20-27.
4. W.F. Barrett *Death-Bed Visions* (1926), pp. 11-14.
5. New York, Parapsychology Foundation, Inc., 1961.
6. New York, Avon Books, 1977.
7. *At the Hour of Death* (Avon, 1977), p. 190.
8. Raymond A. Moody *Life after Life* was first published by Mockingbird Books of Atlanta, Georgia in November 1975, and taken over by Bantam Books, after four Mockingbird printings, in November 1976. Bantam's nineteenth printing appeared in August 1977, since when I have not kept track. A sequel, *Reflections on Life after Life* (1977) appeared as a Bantam book in the USA and a Corgi in the UK in the following year. J.C. Hampe *To Die is Gain: the Experience of One's Own Death* (Darton, Longman, and Todd 1979) is a translation of *Sterben ist doch ganz anders* (Kreuz Verlag, Stuttgart, 1975), made by Margaret Kohl.
9. See Raymond A. Moody, *Life after Life*, pp. 21f.
10. *Return from Tomorrow* by George Ritchie with Elizabeth Sherrill (Kingsway, 1978).
11. Kenneth Ring, *Life at Death: A Scientific Investigation of the Near-Death Experience* (New York, Coward, McCann and Geoghegan, 1980). See also Michael B Sabom, *Recollections of Death* (Corgi, 1982), for an analysis of a further 116 cases.
12. Robert Crookall *What Happens When You Die* (Colin Smythe, 1978).
13. *Journal* of the Society for Psychical Research, Vol. 49, No. 777 (September 1978), p. 887 (in a review of *At the Hour of Death* – see note 6 above).
14. Susan J. Blackmore, *Parapsychology and Out-of-the-body Experiences* (SPR and Transpersonal Books, 1979); see now her much more substantial examination of the phenomena in *Beyond the Body* (Heinemann, 1982).
15. Cyril Burt, *Psychology and Psychical Research* (SPR, the Myers Memorial Lecture for 1968), esp. pp. 79 ff.
16. J.C. Hampe *op. cit* (n. 8 *supra*), p. 54.
17. Maurice Rawlings *Beyond Death's Door* (Nashville, Tennessee,

Nelson 1978; London, Sheldon Press 1979).

18. Zola Levitt and John Weldon *Is there Life after Death?* (Kingsway, 1978), p. 77.
19. Michael Grosso, 'Toward an Explanation of Near-Death Phenomena', *Journal* of the American Society for Psychical Research, Vol. 75, No. 1 (January 1981), pp. 37-60.
20. In his Ingersoll Lecture on the Immortality of Man, printed in the *Harvard Theological Review*, Vol. 62 (1969), pp. 1-21.
21. Elisabeth Kübler-Ross, *On Death and Dying* (Tavistock Publications, 1970).

Part 4
Survival

Christianity, Spiritualism and psychical research all have an interest in whether anything lies beyond death. The interest of the psychical researcher is that of an exploratory investigator; Christians and Spiritualists have emotional, theological, and spiritual capital invested in their various answers to the question. The three pieces which follow are attempts at building bridges of understanding between those whose approach to the questions about survival is differently motivated.

The Survival Joint Research Committee Trust was founded in 1963, to investigate survival of bodily death by gathering together a limited number of leading Spiritualists and knowledgeable parapsychologists interested in the survival problem. It has been instrumental in bringing down the barriers of suspicion and distrust between these two groups. One of its day conferences, organized in London on 21 April 1979, was chaired by the late Maurice Barbanell, editor of *Psychic News*. Paul Beard, who was then President of the College of Psychic Studies, spoke on how we were to judge the evidence for survival. I was asked to open the conference with a paper on 'The Theological Approach to Survival'. Extracts from this were reported in *Psychic News* for 26 May 1979, and the whole paper was printed in the *Journal* of the Academy of Religion and Psychical Research for January 1980 (Vol. 3, No. 1, pp. 31-36).

Spiritual Frontiers Fellowship is another 'bridge' organization, involving Christians of many different kinds of persuasion as well as 'New Age' thinkers and those interested in psychic studies, unorthodox healing, and similar aspects. A good introduction to its concerns and attitudes was given by Leslie Price in an article entitled 'American Perspectives on Christian Parapsychology' in *The Christian Parapsychologist* for December 1982 (Vol. 4, No. 8, pp. 252-6). Frank Tribbe, the Editor of *Spiritual Frontiers* (SFF's quarterly) asked me to write for him and his readers a statement of what I believed to be the case about the future life – not the reasons on which I held my beliefs, but what they amounted to. In the end, what I wrote turned out to be more of a discussion about the nature of analogy than a straight description of what I expected would happen to me after death; but that did not stop him from publishing it in the Fall 1981 number of *Spiritual Frontiers* (Vol. 13, No. 2, pp. 67-76) under the title 'The Hereafter – How Will You Survive?' It has also been translated into Dutch for *Bres* (102 September/October 1983), pp. 14-26. In the present volume it is entitled 'Life after death—what will it be like?'

Finally in this section, but first in time, Paul Beard had invited me to the College of Psychic Studies in London to deliver the annual Beard Memorial Lecture on 29 March 1977. The College was formed in 1884 by scientists and churchmen to foster a spirit of free enquiry into the psychic and psychological fields, and now maintains a centre in London where there are library and meeting facilities for lectures, workshops, courses, counselling, and healing. Paul Beard established the Beard Memorial Lecture in the late 1960s in memory of his father Ernest and his two uncles Sydney and Percy Beard. Its general theme is 'The Spiritual Implications of Survival'. The 1977 Lecture was printed in the College's quarterly, *Light*, for Summer 1977 (Vol. 97, No. 2, pp. 50-64). It was translated into Dutch for *Bres* (No. 70, May/June 1978, pp. 15-25, as 'De dood te vrezen is erger dan te sterven'). A slightly abbreviated version was published in pamphlet form by the Churches' Fellowship for Psychical and Spiritual Studies and Transpersonal Books as No. 2 of *Christian Parapsychology Papers* (1979). At the time of writing, that reprint is still available from CFPSS or Transpersonal Books.

9
The theological approach to survival

I have a great respect and admiration for Ian Ramsey, the Bishop of Durham, who died on 6 October 1972. He believed it was the job of the theologian first to find out the facts of the case, and only then to start thinking about what ought to be made of them. He was writing once about Christian moral decisions, and held up as an example the report prepared for the 1958 Lambeth Conference on *The Family in Contemporary Society* (SPCK, 1957). It was a water-shed in method. Instead of starting by telling people what they ought to be doing, it began its work by gathering together experts in as many relevant disciplines as possible – sociologists, economists, theologians, social workers – and listening to what they had to say. 'In this way', wrote Bishop Ramsey

it was acknowledged that Christian moral decisions can only be made reliably when full justice is done to the empirical situation on which a moral judgement is made. No longer can we think of theology dispensing the answers; no longer is it a question of 'applying theology in a rule-of-thumb fashion'. The first condition for reaching a Christian moral decision is that we shall do as much justice as possible to the empirical details of the actual situation.[1]

What goes for moral decisions should go also for pronouncements about survival. Facts first, theology follows.

I wish it were as simple as that for the subject of survival. We all know it just is not so. If the facts could establish survival, then every reasonable, thinking human being would have accepted survival long ago. But – as we all know – the facts are incredibly ambiguous of interpretation. I cannot, therefore, agree with Ian Currie whose book *You Cannot Die* presents it as though all reasonable folk who look at the evidence will agree about how to read it. He writes of

a host of fascinating discoveries which lead to four inescapable conclusions:
*human beings do survive physical death
*they continue to exist after death at varying levels of awareness and creativity, in a realm that embodied human beings cannot normally perceive
*this realm is periodically left when the individual takes on a new body . . .
*successive re-embodiments do not occur at random.

'These conclusions', he writes, 'are solidly based on scientific research'.[2]

Others of us feel less sure about it – and not through ignorance of the data. The fact is, that whatever we consider – apparitions or out-of-the-body experiences, mediumistic statements or death-bed visions, automatic writing or 'drop-in' communicators – we can always find a reason for them which does not involve survival.

Sue Blackmore tells us that out-of-the-body experiences are constructs from memory compounded with imagination, eked out at times with a little extra-sensory perception.[3] James McHarg believes that the Osis kind of death-bed vision is an artefact of a brain starved of oxygen and that the elevation of mood often observed in a dying patient is something that frequently accompanies a paroxysm of the temporal lobe (e.g. in an epileptic fit).[4] We all know about the 'super-ESP' hypothesis, which reckons that mediums get all their information by means of telepathy from the living or clairvoyance from objects in this world. It may not be likely, say its supporters, but it's a deal more likely than communication from the dead. Yes, I am afraid that things are not what they seem – and don't the parapsychologists know it!

If theology has to start with the position as it is, then it must start with this ambiguity. Perhaps the acceptance of the survival hypothesis *can* never be a matter of knock-down certainty, inescapably and logically following from incontrovertible facts of which only one interpretation is possible? It is certainly the case that some people are persuaded of the truth of survival by looking at the evidence, and others can look at the evidence just as carefully and know it just as well, but remain *un*-persuaded of survival. So it cannot be a matter of pure, logical reason. The survivalist, whether Christian or not, has made a leap beyond what the evidence unequivocally demands. And the theological word for such an attitude is 'faith'. The survivalist *believes* in survival.

Why does he so believe? I ask 'why?' because when we are dealing with faith, we must know what the grounds are on which that faith is held. It *is* possible to hold a belief on no grounds at all. The Queen told Alice in *Through the Looking Glass* that it only needed practice. When she was Alice's age, she used to practise believing impossible things for half-an-hour a day. 'Sometimes', she said, 'I've believed as many as six impossible things before breakfast'.

That way does not appeal to us. Belief is not *created* as a result of a logical argument, but there must be *some* grounds of reason for holding a particular belief. Faith is not created by reason, but it must take off from where reason leads, and when it takes off, it must do so in the same direction in which reason has pointed. In the case of the survival hypothesis, the evidence points to survival as a reasonable inference and we are prepared to jump the gap between reasonable inference and logical proof. Some people jump the gap because they are not sufficiently philosophically sophisticated, and they are not even aware that there is a gap to jump. Some people jump it because their general view of human personality and their general value-system makes them believe that something as inherently valuable as human personality cannot just cease to exist. Some people jump the gap because they are Christians and they believe that God created the human race, that he loves each individual within it, and that his love could not bear that any human being should perish. But in all these cases, a gap has been jumped, and we ought to realize that we are in the realm of faith. We are arguing for our particular interpretation of ambiguous facts, and we are arguing by means of philosophical or theological speculation. We ought to be honest enough to realize that there is nothing like theological speculation for getting a man airborne in the shortest possible time!

So far, I have said that theology has to react to empirical facts, and that the most notorious empirical fact on the survival scene is the ambiguity of the evidence. But what if that no longer held?

After all, there is an awful lot of research going on into survival. Maybe, one day, it will decide the issue one way or the other. What would theology say then?

Suppose it proves negative. Suppose we discover that all out-of-the-body experiences *are* memory plus imagination plus mundane extra-sensory perception, all death-bed visions cerebral anoxia or temporal lobe seizures, all mediumistic statements are ESP from the living?

Dr R.H. Thouless wrote an important article for the *Journal* of the Society for Psychical Research[5] entitled 'Theories about Survival'. He discusses eight possible kinds of survival theory, and points out that, even with eight theories, he is still a long way from exhausting the possibilities. So far, I have been speaking as if 'survival' means what Dr Thouless calls 'continual survival' – i.e., the stream of consciousness going on indefinitely after death without cessation. But that is only one possibility. There could be what Dr Thouless calls 'intermittent revival', or there could be what he calls 'terminal revival'.

'Intermittent revival' is what we generally call 'reincarnation' – the consciousness reviving after an interval, in a different physical frame from the one it occupied before. The person could be conscious in the interim between incarnations, as he is believed to be in (for example) the Tibetan *Book of the Dead*; or he could be completely unconscious until he was revived in the new body.

'Terminal revival' is the Christian idea (or, perhaps, we ought to say, '*a* Christian idea', or 'one of the Christian ideas') of a long sleep through the rest of human history, with the consciousness coming to life again on the Great Last Day, the Day of the Lord, the Day of General Resurrection. And, again, the person could be unconscious during the interval between death and the general resurrection (the idea of the 'long sleep'), or he could be conscious, which approximates more closely to the ideas expressed in the imagery of Revelation 6:9, where the souls of the martyrs are continually crying out to God and asking how long it will be before their blood is avenged.

Any of these ideas could mean that there is no communication between the departed and ourselves; but they are not theories of non-survival. For that matter, it is perfectly possible to hold that the theory of 'continued survival' in the Thouless sense is true but that the surviving personality is unable to make contact with this earth. That is what Dr Thouless calls 'continuous survival in another time dimension'. The two dimensions of time – our time and the time of the life of the world to come – would intersect at the moment of death only. At all other points they would be incommunicado to each other.

None of these positions would be at all embarrassing to Christian theology. Although Christianity includes a belief in the life of the world to come, it is not necessary to Christianity to hold that this new life begins consciously the moment the old one ceases, or that in this new life we can communicate with people on earth. So, if our research into survival came up with a clear negative, it would not necessarily mean that there is no such thing as a life of the world to come. It could be that the life was to be postponed beyond human history, or it could be that that life and ours are for ever incommunicado to each other.

What, however, if continuing survival were proved? There are many people for whom – to all practical purposes – it is proved. The evidence has convinced them and they have made what I called the jump over the logical gap. And, indeed, I must number myself among such people. As a logical scientist I can see that the proof is far from absolute; but as a Christian parapsychologist I hold to the personal belief that the dead do survive and that they may on occasion communicate with us.

If we hold that belief in that form, then what (theologically) flows from it?

In theological terms, we are within the doctrine of creation, not of salvation or redemption. In other words, we are talking about how God made the world and how he made the men and women within it. We are saying nothing about any redemptive act of God upon those men and women, nothing about their salvation from sin, decay, pointlessness, or futility. Again, using theological terms, survival has to do with immortality rather than with resurrection – Ian Currie's *You Cannot Die* as a fact of creation, an objective statement about human nature, about the way we are made. So, theologically, we say that if God has made us in such a way that our consciousness continues relatively unimpaired after physical death, that is a fact – a fact of creation. It is a theological fact in that God is the creator, but it is not a theological fact of the greatest significance. If men survive, they are not thereby any the more spiritual, any nearer to God.

We could guess as much from the communications we receive. Most of the surviving communicators think no more of God or of Jesus than they did when they were on earth. That is to say, if God was at the periphery of their earthly lives, he remains at the periphery of their post-mortem existence. If he was central, if the person was a converted Christian whose whole life was directed by a sense of conscious communion with God, then God will be as central to that person's post-mortem life as he was on this earth, and his pilgrimage after death is going to be even more deeply and religiously significant than his pilgrimage before it. Death by itself makes no miraculous transformations.

Now, whether these two categories of people – the converted and the non-converted – can change over after death, is a matter in the realm of theological speculation. There are theologians who believe that 'where the tree falls, there it lies' (Ecclesiastes 11:3). I am not one of them. Briefly, I maintain that the doctrine of salvation or redemption can apply after this life as it applies within this life, and that the hopeless futility of a life without God can be reversed in the life to come, just as it can be reversed in our present life. That seems to me to be consonant with our doctrine of God and our knowledge of his ways with man. It requires conversion on the part of the human being, and resurrection as God's response to human conversion.

Resurrection is the act whereby God brings a human being out of the sin-bound futility of the purely natural life – whether the purely natural life of this earth or the purely natural life of a post-mortem existence – and into the glorious liberty of the sons of God to partake in eternal life. Immortality is man's natural possession – a matter of creation, of how we have been made. We could be bored to death with immortality. Indeed, the contents of some mediumistic communications are so trite and banal that one wonders whether the surviving entities would prefer to be dead rather than immortal. Resurrection, on the other hand, is the individual act of God on the individual soul, the touch of God on to the personality, and it brings life abundant in the knowledge and love of God as movement towards fulfilment and maturity. Resurrection is God's act whereby man is liberated from immortality. It can happen either side of death.

Finally, what does theology have to say about survival research? There are theologians who look at it very askance. The fact that the data are so inescapably ambiguous shows, they say, that we are *intended* not to know. What happens after death must be held on faith, and if you try to buttress faith by research into survival, the text to use against you is :Thou shalt not put the Lord thy God to the test' (Matt. 4:7, quoting Deut. 6:16). That, you will remember, was the reply of Jesus to Satan when Satan suggested that he ought to carry out an experiment to prove that God really was taking care of him. The experiment was that of jumping off the temple pinnacle in order to see whether the angels really would bear him up. Survival research is a temptation like the temptation of Jesus to put God's promises to the test. The being who tempts us to survival research is the devil. Parapsychologists are supping with the black gentleman and not using a long enough spoon. If we trusted God enough, there would be no need for survival research, as God's promises would do for us. If we fall prey to temptation, and undertake survival research, we find no certainty. We should not expect to, because Satan is the father of lies and is not going to lead us to the truth about life after death.

That is an ingenious theological argument, but I cannot share it. I could not edit a journal called *The Christian Parapsychologist* if I did. For some of the reasons, read the full report of the 1939 Committee on Spiritualism which reported to the Archbishop of Canterbury.[6] The majority of the members of that Committee were far from uncritical of Spiritualism – indeed, they gave it some hard knocks – but they saw no reason to doubt the legitimacy of the search which both Spiritualists and survival researchers are engaged in – the search for truth about part of the doctrine of creation. Did God create man mortal or immortal?

I hope we are in for an era of dialogue between Christians and Spiritualists. Dialogue does not mean soft speaking; it means being honest with each other, and each telling the other what it sees wrong in the other's attitude. It also means a critical reassessment of one's own beliefs and attitudes, and a willingness to concede that one may have been mistaken both in one's own beliefs and in one's attitude to (and assessment of) those who do not appear to share them. And it means getting together, seeing what each other believes (as contrasted with what one imagines the other believes), and seeing how far it is possible to move towards a consensus.

Christians and Spiritualists both believe in survival. As a Christian I would say that survival research is legitimate, but it needs to be carried out in the right frame of mind. If you embark on the quest for evidence in a self-centred frame of mind, to prove your own immortality or to snatch evidence of the continued existence of a dead relative and evidence of his continued interest in you, and if God has no part in your quest, then that quest is not of a very high spiritual order, and maybe your soul will suffer as you pursue it. But if your quest is the disinterested quest for knowledge of the way God has made the universe and the men and women in it, then I cannot believe that your quest will be unrewarding. You do not set out to 'prove' survival. You do not set out to 'prove' anything. You set out to find the truth; and it is my deepest conviction that the person who is seeking the truth is looking for God, and that every true scientist is also a theologian.

As to what you will find in that search — that is another matter! The ideas we currently have, the theories and hypotheses about survival that we are testing, are probably too unadventurous by half. As Dr Thouless writes, 'lateral thinking on the subject may well be a necessary pre-condition for the final solution';[7] or, to quote Professor C.T.K. Chari, 'our first semi-scientific guesses at the truth may have to begin by steering clear of the tranquillizing myths of *homo sapiens* whose pilgrimage to find out his destiny has hardly begun'.[8] In other words — and this the theologian will insist on — we will be in for surprises when we find out the truth. God is nothing if not inventive, and he has in mind for us things that will amaze us.

References

1. *The Church Quarterly* Vol. 2 (1970), p. 221.
2. Ian Currie, *You Cannot Die* (Hamlyn, 1979), pp. 8 f.
3. S.J. Blackmore, *Beyond the Body* (Heinemann, 1982). Dr Blackmore now no longer believes ESP is necessary to explain out-of-body experiences.
4. See Dr McHarg's review of Osis and Haraldsson *At The Hour of Death* in the *Journal* of the SPR, Vol. 49 (1978), pp. 885-7.
5. Vol. 50 (1979), pp. 1-8.
6. The report was not released until 1979, after a forty-year embargo. The full text is given in *The Christian Parapsychologist* Vol. 3 (1979), pp. 40-73.
7. *art. cit.*, p. 2.
8. *Spiritual Frontiers*, Vol. 10 (1976), p. 26.

10
Life after death – what will it be like?

Over thirty years ago, when I was still a schoolboy, I picked up a copy of G.N.M. Tyrrell's book *The Personality of Man* and realized that I was going to get hooked on parapsychology. True enough, it has been an interest of mine ever since.

Five years later, I had just graduated in natural sciences at Cambridge University and was about to start my ministerial training at theological college. There you can see another couple of strands in my personal make-up – a commitment to the search for truth through scientific method, and a belief in the Christian God; a commitment and a belief so strong that my whole life and career has been built around them.

'But surely,' you say, 'you can't expect an objective assessment of what parapsychology says about how you will survive death, from a person with a history like that? He can't help letting his beliefs cloud his judgement.'

That's as may be; but one thing I have learnt, over the years, is that if there is one thing that is certain about the interpretation of parapsychological data, it is that the interpretation is *not* certain. It always seems that it is logically possible to hold more than one opinion on the basis of the facts alleged. What you cannot do is to take those data and use them to *compel* another person to your own way of thinking. 'Compulsion' is not a word in the intellectual vocabulary of parapsychology. Facts are sacred, but interpretation is free. *I* may see the facts one way, but that does not prevent *you* from seeing them in a different way.

So let me give you my interpretation of the data on survival. As you read it, I ask you – on the one hand – to realize that it is one man's interpretation, coloured by his background and his beliefs, but – on the other hand – to accept that that one man's beliefs have been tested out and seem to him to be both a logical and a reasonable inference from the data. I will not rehearse the evidence here, or argue the pros and cons of alternative explanations of the evidence. All I will say is that, having sifted through a mass of parapsychological data over the years, with that scientific turn of mind which prefers a normal explanation to a paranormal one, I have come across a lot of evidence which satisfies me as to its paranormal nature. (I have also come across even more which does *not* satisfy me, but you won't want to hear about that: 'Tell me your certainties; I have doubts enough of my own.') The evidence that has satisfied me, has tied in with my theological convictions as a Christian believer. That is no *proof*; but it is a comforting indication that there is some consistency between this interpretation of empirical data, and beliefs which have characterized Christianity. So it is that – for me – the discoveries of parapsychology have reinforced Christian faith and helped illuminate Christian doctrines. They have fitted naturally in to a Christian framework of thought (sometimes in unexpected detail) and have not led me to desert or compromise my Christianity.

What, then, do I believe about the hereafter? How will you survive? Where? In what kind of body? And what sort of things will you be doing?

Where will we be?

As soon as we start thinking about *where* we survive death, it is all but impossible to do other than think of that 'where' as a place which can be described in terms of its relation to the 'where' of this physical universe in which we are now alive. At one time, people thought of the next world as being up in the sky, or on another planet, or on a planet of some other sun in the physical universe. But that would not do. How would we get there if we did not get there in our physical bodies? And if we were not in our physical bodies, what would be the point of being somewhere else in physical space-time? In any case, if we *were* somewhere else in physical space-time, then the conditions under which we would be living would be the same as (or at least analogous to) the conditions of life here on this earth. There would still be physical bodies, and they would still be subject to physical laws. They would still age, and decay, and rot. But that is not what we are led to expect. The life to which we will survive (if Christian theology and parapsychological indications are anything to go by) is a life where the limitations of this earth-bound existence do not apply. So it cannot be in this space-time.

Yet, even though the next world is not a place within our present space-time, it must in some way interpenetrate it. The two worlds link at the moment of the death of the individual, so that he is then leaving one and entering the other. There are other times when this interpenetration can be experienced. Not continuously, and not for every person. But certain people at certain moments or in certain mental, psychic, and spiritual states can be aware of both worlds, or can alternate between the two, and can act as intermediaries for messages between them. We call them sensitives, or mediums.

How can there be two worlds like this – one in space and time and one not in our space or our time; separate, answering to different natural laws, in which bodies have very different kinds of properties? How can they be so distinct and yet interpenetrate?

On earth our minds are attuned to physical space-time, so they begin to boggle when they try to explain or visualize what is involved in thinking of other worlds which are not a part of space-time and yet which interpenetrate it. The best they can do is to evolve parables or analogies or metaphors; verbal and mental devices designed to make the incomprehensible idea more acceptable to our space-time understanding. Beware when you are using analogies, however. They are useful as an aid to conceptualization, but they become dangerous when they are mistaken for 'the truth, the whole truth, and nothing but the truth'.

Some communicators talk about different 'planes' of existence, so that we are now on 'earth-plane' but transfer at death to 'astral-plane' or whatever. They cannot be talking literally, but in analogy. If we took them literally, it would imply that the world of the life to come is some kind of a celestial Sears Tower which we enter at ground level and where we can take the elevator to whatever floor suits us best. Most of us will only make the intermediate stations, but the super-spiritual will get to the viewing platform on the one hundred and third floor and get a real God's-eye view of the rest of humanity in the Loop below.

The ancients used the same kind of analogy when they spoke of surviving in She'ol or Hades or in paradise. If pressed, they would talk of She'ol as the *under*-world, or of paradise as '*above* the bright blue sky', but the spatial aspect was not the primary consideration. It is only we folk of the Western twentieth century, with the superiority which comes of having read *Honest to God*, who foist that literal idea upon them. The essence of She'ol is not that it is underground, but that it is away from Jehovah. The essence of heaven is not that it is vertically above the surface of the earth, but that it is the 'where' in which God is to be found. 'Heaven' is a place of quite a different character from this earth, and in order to emphasize this point, the imagery which is developed in talking about it (for instance, in the prophecy of Ezekiel or in the visions of the Book of the Revelation) is imagery which says, 'You can see from the way we are talking that we are not speaking about events which could possibly happen in this earth, but of a "where" in which earthly constraints do not apply.'

When we use the language of 'up' and 'down', it is easy to see that we are talking metaphorically. The same is true of the language of 'planes of existence', which is only a slightly more sophisticated way of using the 'up' and 'down' metaphor. So we don't try to press the analogy too far. We don't, for example, ask how many miles the astral plane is from the surface of earth – or if we do, the very foolishness of the question immediately shows us that we are asking a literal question about a metaphorical statement, and warns us against pressing the analogy farther than it can usefully go.

There are other kinds of metaphor which are a bit closer to reality. That is good in one way, because they help our minds to grasp reality a little bit less inadequately. But in another way it is more dangerous, because if the metaphor is closer, it is easier to mistake metaphor for literal reality. That is what some people do with the metaphor of 'vibrations'.

We have been familiar from childhood with the idea of radio waves. We know they are invisible modulations of the electromagnetic continuum (though most of us would be hard put to it to explain what we actually *meant* by using that high-sounding phrase). We know that a multiplicity of messages can cross the same space without interfering with each other. We know that is because they are carried on different wavelengths. We know, too, that they can only be detected by a receiver tuned in to the wavelength in question. What is more, we know that this too, too solid flesh (and the solid earth it stands on) is nothing like as solid as Hamlet thought, but that it thaws and resolves itself into a whirling dance of wave-forms no more solid than light itself. We are as much a conglomeration of vibrations as our favourite television programme.

When, therefore, we talk of our present bodies as being on a particular wavelength, or composed of particular vibrations appropriate to physical conditions, and when we talk of changing our wavelength or frequency or rate of vibration as we change from this world to the world to come, it is easy to forget that we are still only using pictures or metaphors or images or analogies. We are using a form of words to try and convince ourselves that it is possible to imagine our selves ceasing to exist in this world but continuing to exist in an interpenetrating world which is not subject to rules of space and time. We have not explained anything. We have only used a helpful mental device to show that survival in 'another world' is thinkable. The language of 'heavens' satisfied the ancients; the language of 'planes' satisfied our fathers; the language of 'vibrations' is one to which this generation resonates (and notice the use of the same language in 'vibration' and 'resonate'). In the next century, no doubt another term will gain currency. There is some evidence that it maybe the language of 'dimensions', in which this world and the next are thought of as being multi-dimensional spaces which intersect under certain conditions. The mystical novels of Charles Williams (particularly *Many Dimensions*) are a foretaste of what may well become fashionable in the next few decades. But all these terms are simply semantic devices which enable us to speak with integrity of things which are by definition beyond our experience and our comprehension, and which our present language-systems were not designed to express.

Perhaps the best thing to do is simply to come back to the plain term 'the hereafter'. Why, I wonder, do we speak of the '*here*after' rather than the *there*after? Surely the essential thing about another world is that it is *there* and not *here*? No. If we talk about 'thereafter' we might be tempted to point to a 'there' where it is taking place. 'Here', on the other hand, is where we are, the point of view from which we experience the world. In the now, we experience the world from a physical point of view and our bodies are subject to the laws of physics. After death, our 'here' will be elsewhere and we will experience a continuing life from a non-physical point of view, in a set of co-ordinates which allow things to happen in a very different way from that in which they happen on this earth. We shall still be aware, and therefore we shall still speak of our own 'here'; but it will be another 'here' – the hereafter.

I think there is a deal of mileage to be got out of the suggestions of Professor H.H. Price in a lecture he gave to the Society for Psychical Research in London thirty years ago, which he entitled 'Survival and the Idea of "Another World"'. He suggested that the 'next' world could be one where the laws of psychology replaced those of physics and where communication was by means of telepathy. But as to 'where' it was, he remained coyly imprecise. If I dream of a tiger, he said, I don't ask whether it is three feet from the end of the bed or three hundred. It is in my dream world, which is its own 'where'. So my surviving self is not three miles or three light-years from the surface of the earth. It is in its own 'where', which can interpenetrate our physical earth simply because it is a non-physical world, and space and time are irrelevant to it. So surviving entities can communicate simultaneously to friends in New York and in Paris – the interpenetration takes no more account of physical distance than telepathy does.

As to whether there is one 'next world' or a host of them, I do not know. There is much in Christian tradition and in psychic communication to suggest that there may be more than one 'next world' and that life after death is as much a pilgrimage as life before death. The statement in John 14:2 about 'many mansions' is compatible with the account in Paul Beard's remarkable essay *Living On* (Allen and Unwin, 1980) in which he gives his own reading of the mediumistic and other evidence for what he terms 'altering consciousness after death' in a series of extra-terrestrial existences. Whether all these possible 'next worlds' interpenetrate with each other and with this world, again I do not know. The story of Dives and Lazarus (but remember, it is only a parable, and its details may not have been intended to be taken literally) suggests that between certain of the possible next worlds there is 'a great gulf fixed: so that they which would pass from hence to you cannot; neither can they pass to us, that would come from thence' (Luke 16:26). There is much parapsychological evidence to suggest that some next worlds are closer to our own and interpenetrate more easily. Paul Beard's book gives some of it. As souls progress, so they can become less earth-bound. But even the greatest of the saints can manifest here on earth if need be. In the Communion of Saints, no member is out of touch with the rest.

What kind of body?

Words like 'planes' and 'vibrations', then, are used as analogies rather than as exact descriptions. The same goes for that word 'body'. I believe we shall survive in a body. But I do not believe that this means I shall carry my present flesh and bones into the next

world. A straightforwardly literal hope like this was expressed by
some writers in Biblical times. In the second century BC, the writer
of the second book of the Maccabees expressed it forcefully (if
somewhat crudely) in two passages in particular. One of seven
brothers tortured for his faith showed his tongue and held out his
hands and said, 'The God of heaven gave me these. His laws mean
far more to me than they do, and it is from him that I trust to
receive them back.' Razis, who preferred to die by his own hand
rather than surrender to the infidels, turned his sword upon himself,
'took his entrails in both hands and flung them at the crowd. And
thus, invoking the Lord of life and breath to give these entrails back
to him again, he died' (2 Macc. 7:11, 14:46).

St Paul's talk was far more subtle than that. He writes of the
resurrection of the body, but he also states categorically that 'flesh
and blood cannot inherit the Kingdom of God' (1 Cor. 15:50).
This is because he makes a clear distinction between the words for
'flesh' (*sarx*, in Greek) and 'body' (*soma*). In neither case is the stress
on individuality, as if what mattered was *my* body. The stress is,
rather, on solidarity, corporateness, incorporation (as those last two
words, with their roots in the Latin *corpus*, indicate). The classic
exploration of these concepts in St Paul's thought is the exploration
which J.A.T. Robinson carried out in his book *The Body*, published
by the SCM Press in 1952. He writes:

Paul starts, as we do, from the fact that man is bound up in a vast
solidarity of historical existence which denies him freedom to control his
own destiny or achieve his true end. This is the 'body' of sin and death, in
which he is involved at every level of his being . . . The resurrection body
signifies . . . the *solidarity* of the recreated universe in Christ. It is none
other than the Body of Christ in which we have a share [*op. cit.*, pp. 8,
79].

Both the word *sarx* and the word *soma* are used to designate the
whole man in his various relationships, but whilst *sarx* ('flesh')
emphasizes the solidarity of man with the creation in Adam, the
word *soma* ('body') is a word which can be used in a context of
solidarity either with Adam or with God. Man is made of the seed
of Adam, yet he can be redeemed from the futility of Adam and
resurrected into the glory of Christ.

This all shows us that when St Paul uses the term 'body', he uses
it in a highly analogical and metaphorical way. When he speaks of
'the resurrection of the body', he is not primarily referring to the bag

of blood and bones which we carry round with us on our earthly pilgrimage. The more we explore that word 'body', the more we realize that it is being used – as we moderns use the words 'plane' or 'vibrations' – as a parable, a shorthand word. We have to ask, therefore, what the function of 'body' language is. What truths about the life of the world to come is the use of this term 'body' in that context designed to safeguard?

Two, in particular: that, in that world, I shall be aware of myself as myself; and that I shall be aware of (and able to communicate with) others.

For present-day thinkers (though not, as we have seen, necessarily for St Paul), the use of the term 'body' indicates primarily that I shall be aware of myself as myself. My body is what distinguishes me from other people, and me from the external world. My body and the bodies of others can get very close. They can touch and they can intertwine. But they cannot coalesce. My skin is the envelope of myself. It is that which defines me as myself and others as not myself. Because I have a body I know myself as a unique individual.

Yet it is the body, and bodily senses, which enable me to be recognized by other people and to communicate with other people; and we have seen that for St Paul, this corporate rather than individualistic *nuance* is the more important. If I were bodiless, others would not be able to know who I was; and I would have no tongue with which to talk, or ear to hear, or fingers to write to those others (I am not referring to exceptional methods like extra-sensory perception, but to normal self-awareness and normal communication).

When Christians use the term 'resurrection of the body', one thing they want to do is to safeguard the truth that in the next world we shall still be aware of ourselves and of others. We shall not be merged into some group soul, or spread out like a drop in an ocean. Frank Tribbe will know himself as Frank Tribbe and Michael Perry as Michael Perry. Yet the limitations put upon Frank Tribbe and Michael Perry by their present bodies of flesh and blood, which age and which wear out and decay, will be transcended. H.H. Price (in the lecture we have already referred to) imagines a 'next world' whose laws are those of psychology rather than of physics. In this present world, where we live in physical bodies, if we want to go to to a sun-drenched beach in the South Pacific, we have (with great labour and expense) to transport our bodies there. In the next, desire would be king, and the wish would create the environment. Similarly, in this world, when we wish to communicate with our friends, we have to use physical instruments – i.e. our physical bodies (except for those rare and sporadic occasions when telepathy 'works'). In the next world, the physical limitations of sensory perception and sensory communication will go. Telepathy and mind-to-mind contact will replace speech and print.

Our first unthinking reaction when we hear of a world where desire is king and the earthly limitations of communication are lifted is 'this is too good to be true'. Our second thoughts may well be 'this is too true to be good'. How terrifying a prospect! The thoughts of all hearts will be revealed; they will know what we are *really* like! Could we *bear* to be in a world where everyone would know the secret thoughts of everyone else? Could we bear to be in a world where our *own* secret thoughts and desires came to reality? Could we bear the truth about ourselves? The thought is more terrifying than comforting. But the terror of self-knowledge is part of what we must expect in the world to come. It is expressed in one way in the imagery of the Tibetan *Book of the Dead*, and in another way (the imagery is different, but the fundamental message is the same) by the Christian doctrine of judgement. Not that some external judge will look at the evidence, decide on the verdict, and pass sentence; but that we shall become aware of what we have made ourselves, because we shall be in a situation where the external physical constraints are lifted, the lid is off, and we will know ourselves as we really are. I don't know *you*, but I do know *myself* well enough to be afraid that it will not be a pretty sight in my own case.

There is a ray of hope. We shall have bodies. We shall not be left to rot in self-encapsulated loneliness. We shall be able to communicate with others (human, angelic, and divine) and they with us. We can get help. And the others – at any rate, those human others – will know what it is like because they will have gone through the same experience of judgement.

And we shall know God. The Buddhist insists that if we are not able to save ourselves, nobody else will be able to do it for us, and we shall find ourselves chained again to the terrible wheel of rebirth. The Christian insists that we cannot save ourselves, and that it is only by the divine assistance that we can arise after the experience of judgement to the continuing pilgrimage of the next world. We shall know God, and he will help us to know ourselves and purge our desires until we *want* to go forward, until the confusions of our present whirl of contradictory desires – desires for God, for goodness, for revenge, for lust, for cruelty, for self-aggrandisement, for spite, for self — are stilled into a single desire, or a coherent pattern of desires, and our hearts have been purified.

I said that we would know God. Even that word 'know' is an analogy. Will the knowing be in terms of visual awareness, or of personal speech, or of mystical realization? What will God look like? We cannot say. He must bear *some* relation to what we have experienced of him here, or we would not recognize that it was him with whom we were having to do; but it ought to go without saying that we are in for mind-boggling surprises that we on this earth can hardly conceive of.

What shall we do?

If we survive into a world which is other than this physical one, but which can interpenetrate it; and if we continue to be aware (though in a new and fuller way) of our selves, of others, and of God, what then shall we *do* with our time (or with what replaces time in that world)?

We have outgrown the ancient imagery of harps and crowns. In a way that is a pity, because — by using it — we would realize at once that it cannot be taken literally. The trouble with so many mediumistic communications, on the other hand, is that they sound so credible that we *are* likely to mistake them for literal truths. The better communicators, however, insist that what they tell us about themselves and their world is only figurative. It is told in earthly terms because these are the only terms we can understand while we remain in our earthly bodies.

In the first moments of entry into the next world, there is bound to be the sheer bewilderment — the culture shock — of an environment which reacts to our wills in so different a way from the one we have spent a lifetime getting used to. But, once we have got used to it, what sort of things shall we be doing?

There will be self-development and self-awareness. There will be things to learn and knowledge to be gained. There will be social intercourse. There will be friendships to be taken up once more — friendships which were interrupted by death. There will be people to help; those, in particular, who have passed over more recently, and who need assistance as they adjust to their new situation, or who need help as they face up to the horrors of self-knowledge that their judgement brings. There will be (for many, though not for all; and possibly for a limited time only) the continuing contacts with the earth that we have left behind. There will be messages to get across, help to be given, inspiration to be fed. There will be non-human spiritual beings to get to know – the whole wonder of the angelic creation, of which we are so blindly unaware here on this earth. There will be sheer relaxation and enjoyment. And, above all for the Christian, there will be the continuation in another environment of his exploration into God – a new realization of the length and breadth and depth and height of the love of God in Christ Jesus, to know whom passes all human knowledge.

Not only will the limitations of our physical bodies be transcended, but also the limitations which our physical brains put upon our souls and minds. How often in this world do our real selves express themselves so poorly because they only have our physical brains through which to express themselves! In this world, we cannot express the ineffable, but can only steal glimpses or give hints. In the hereafter we shall be conscious of a life lived within a great weight of glory which has never been seen by human eye and which can never be expressed through earthly brain. Perhaps that is what the mystics know when they feel 'a wink of heaven, a tremour of bliss'. Perhaps that is what the cardiac arrest patients who tell their experiences to Raymond Moody or Ken Ring or Pastor Hampe are at the threshold of experiencing, as the human psyche, untrammelled by the limitations of the physical brain, expands into a world of inexpressible splendour.

If all this is true, then the thought of reincarnation back to this earth is a thin and unsatisfying prospect. The Buddhists who regard reincarnation as a possibility to be avoided are far nearer the truth than those shallow optimists who are so incapable of imagining anything better than this world that they think reincarnation is a fate preferable to that of extra-mundane exploration. And if all this is true, then what survives death is not a fragment or 'psi-factor', nor a husk of disintegrating personality which can communicate with this earth only for a brief while before it falls to pieces, but a total human being. Where it survives, what its new surroundings are like, what sort of a body it has, what sort of things it does – these can only be hinted at, by using analogies based on our experiences on this earth. In these pages, I have tried to utter the unutterable, taking my hints from the points where parapsychological findings seem to chime in with Christian doctrines. In so short a space, there is much that I cannot touch upon, and what I have expressed, I may have done so with an appearance of specific certainty or an attitude of dogmatism which is far from what I really feel. What I have written is personal speculation, not dogmatic assertion, though I

have tried to curb my speculation by reference to the findings of
present-day research and the ancient body of Christian truth. What
needs to be said in conclusion is that when we actually begin to
experience the hereafter and see how we survive, we shall be in for
surprises — and there will be none more surprised than those who
were most specific beforehand what was going to happen to them.
In the words of a veteran psychiatrist and parapsychologist, written
at the end of a long and distinguished career, 'We see in a glass
darkly, and dogmatism is the only unpardonable sin'.[1]

[1]Gardner Murphy, *The Paranormal and the Normal* (New Jersey,
Scarecrow Press, 1980), p. 71.

11
The spiritual implications of survival

If the College of Psychic Studies asks a Christian minister to lecture it on 'The Spiritual Implications of Survival', it must expect him to give a Christian slant to what he says. So let me do my best to show you how the subject you have set me looks to a Christian who has an interest in parapsychology and a smattering of knowledge about it.

'Spiritual Implications of Survival'. There are two opposite reactions which Christians might have to that title. One is to say that survival is a matter for God alone and that therefore the spiritual implications are the only implications. The other is to say that survival as such is a purely natural matter – every human being survives death – and that therefore there are *no* spiritual implications, any more than there are spiritual implications of breathing or of the circulation of the blood. I hope that by the time I have finished, you will agree with me, not that those reactions are necessarily wrong, but that they are both over-simplifications.

For a start, even if anything is natural and a universal human possession, it certainly has spiritual implications. Every one of us is alive, and *that* is a fact with enormous spiritual implications, for it is in this world that we must begin to shape our eternal destiny. Every one of us has a physical body, and that too has a tremendous effect on our spiritual life. We cannot neglect, or play down, or deny the fact that we are bodily creatures with a spiritual element.

Every one of us is going to die; and death is a fact with spiritual implications. Death is something *more than* a physical fact. Raymond Fletcher, the MP for Ilkeston, wrote an article in *The Times* in which he claimed that 'the business of dying is not, and cannot be, a serious one to me. It is a change of biochemical condition to be seen through with as little fuss as possible, no more'.[1] It was a brave article, because it was written as a result of Mr Fletcher's surviving a serious heart attack; but though it was brave, I think it was too shallow to be of real help to those of us who are going to die. Death *is* a change of biochemical condition, but it is more. The Christian tradition – almost lost even amongst Christians nowadays – tells us that our death is a great spiritual experience, and we shall not make the best of that experience if we come to it unprepared.

We learn *that* much from the communications we so often get through sensitives. How tragic it is when messages from the other side speak of those who have died without learning to do so, and who refuse to acknowledge that they have passed over! They are locked in this life and they cannot believe there is anything beyond it. When they wake up, it is sometmes a long and an arduous business to get them to readjust to their new state, and to get them to begin their spiritual pilgrimage, Often, they have not seen *life* as a spiritual pilgrimage, so it is not surprising that they are unable to see *death* as a crucial element in that pilgrimage, or to treat the life after death as anything other than 'the mixture as before'.

On the other hand, the man who has treated every new venture into the unknown as an opportunity to put his hand into the hand of God and to go forth as a pilgrim, will do the same on his journey into the unknown through death. The man who has not done so, and who has had no inkling of the spiritual implications of living, will find no spiritual implications of dying and will miss the spiritual implications of survival.

If I am to go on to discuss what those spiritual implications might be, I must first say something about what *kind* of survival I think we can reasonably expect.

Bodies and images

The first point to make is that I believe it will be an *embodied* and not a disembodied existence. There has been a deal of discussion amongst the philosophers on this point recently – I cite particularly Terence Penelhum's *Survival and Disembodied Existence* (Routledge and Kegan Paul, 1970) and H.D. Lewis' *The Self and Immortality* (Macmillan, 1973). The discussion has been taken up by the theologians – Paul Badham's *Christian Beliefs about Life after Death* (Macmillan, 1976) and John Hick, whose *Death and Eternal Life* (Collins, 1976) is the best thing I know on the subject and which integrates philosophical, parapsychological, Christian, Hindu, and Buddhist thought into an impressive synthesis. The general conclusion of the philosophers is that disembodied surivival is not a concept which can be made logically coherent. To quote Professor Penelhum, 'the notion of a persistence through time of a disembodied being and of its identification with a pre-mortem being, does not seem intelligible' (*op. cit.,* p. 77).

We shall survive with a body. But it will not be this present body of flesh and blood. See what happens as we try to work with the theory that what survives is a body identical to that which we now inhabit, only in some other place within this universe. Dr Badham explores the notion (with some help from Professor Hick) and soon shows what kinds of difficulties are in store for it. For a start, it cannot be an exact replica of the body which has just died, because 'an exact replica of a dying man at the last moment of life would be a dying man at his last moment of life! In other words the first thing that the resurrection body would do would be to expire'.[2] So we have to suppose that 'in its new environment it is subjected to processes of healing and repair which bring it into a state of health and activity'.[3]

No good, says Dr Badham. A body to which this could happen 'would have to be composed of some type of matter so unlike the material of which our bodies are at present composed that such a body could not be described as an exact replica'. The problems 'magnify as we consider them: presumably my heart pacemaker and artificial knee-joint are replicated with me, but what about my glasses and false teeth? Do limbs amputated years ago grow again during the process of healing?' Clearly we cannot posit an exact replica. We could, however, reasonably posit that what survives is 'the complete man, not subject to the . . . maiming or disease which the deceased actually endured'. Even so, is it reasonable to suppose that such a replica comes into being in some other place in the Universe as each of us dies? What would be the *point* of a resurrection like this? We would have to think of the resurrection-life as being lived on another planet of some distant star, where there would be a vast population-explosion (for the resurrected would not die, and unless they were reproductive and sexually active they would not be human in an identical way to that in which *we* are human). At each step the hypothesis grows more and more bizarre.

For reasons like this, John Hick finds difficulties in 'the divine creation in another place of an exact psycho-physical replica of the deceased person', even if he is to accept Dr Badham's modification of 'another space' for 'another place', and the omission of the word 'exact'. Right at the end of his chapter (pp. 294f.) he states that this kind of imagined resurrection 'represents the simplest model' but that

this model is only the most accessible of a range of possibilities. It is conceivable that in the resurrection world we shall have bodies which are the outward reflection of our inner nature but which reflect it in ways quite different from that in which our present bodies reflect our personality.

And, just as it looks as if he is going to get on to something interesting, he continues, 'In supposing this we have already begun a process of speculation which we cannot profitably pursue.' That disappointed me considerably, because I think his process of speculation might well have led him to something really significant – the idea that the bodies of the life of the world to come might be the outward reflection of our inward nature, but that they might reflect it in ways very different from our present bodies. And here I must turn to the speculations of Professor H.H. Price (which both Dr Badham and Professor Hick also discuss) because I think they contain the right clue for us as we try to discern the spiritual implications of survival.

Professor Price's lecture was originally given in 1952, as part of the seventieth anniversary celebrations of the Society for Psychical Research, but it has been much discussed and reprinted since.[4] He wants us to think of the next world as a world of mental images. That does not mean it is an imaginary world, only that it is – like this world – a world in which we have sensations. In this world, sensations are the result of physical objects and physical sources. I can see you because you are a physical object and because physical light-waves pass from your body to my eye. In the next world, the sensations would be generated by something non-physical, because the next world is not a physical world; but it is still true that I could have sensations, and it could be quite possible that those sensations should be indistinguishable from the sensations caused in this world by physical objects.

That is not so crazy as it sounds. After all, we know that there can be sensations like that in this world. We know of people who have had hallucinations – some of them veridical hallucinations. For instance, Canon J.B. Phillips (the man whose New Testament translation has sold millions of copies) tells us of an occasion after the death of C.S. Lewis when he was sitting at home ready to watch a television programme, and looked towards a chair in his room, and there was C.S. Lewis sitting in it, looking 'ruddier in complexion than ever, grinning all over his face, and, as the old-fashioned saying has it, positively glowing with health'.[5] Of course, the body of Lewis was not there – it was a mental image which resulted in a sensation identical with what would have been received had Lewis been sitting in the chair physically. In my opinion either Phillips was self-deceived (at a time when he was suffering from clinical depression) by a subjective hallucination reminding him of the robust faith of C.S. Lewis, or he had received what we might term a telepathic message from the surviving Lewis, and the sensation of seeing his figure was then built up around the message as a form of authentication, to assure Canon Phillips that it really *was* Jack Lewis speaking to him.

So then, to return from example to argument, the next world could be a world of mental images. Not an imaginary world, but a world of sensations generated by non-physical means, rather like the sensation of the appearance of C.S. Lewis which was non-physically generated.

In the original form of his paper, Professor Price spoke of the next world as being peopled by 'discarnate human personalities'. The word, note, was 'discarnate', not 'disembodied', and he went on to suggest that 'there is no reason at all why there should not be *visual* images resembling the body which one had in this present world' which

might form the continuing centre or nucleus of one's image world, remaining more or less constant while other images altered. If this were so, we should have an additional reason for expecting that recently-dead people would find it difficult to realize that they were dead, that is, disembodied. To all appearances they *would* have bodies just as they had before, and pretty much the same ones [p. 7].

And, if there could be communication between discarnate human personalities in the next world, it would be reasonable to suppose that the telepathic communications would be authenticated by visual images corresponding to the incarnate body of the person who was communicating, just as the message from the post-mortem C.S. Lewis was authenticated by a visual image corresponding to what his earthly body had looked like.

Now, once we start using this kind of language, it is difficult to use the term 'disembodied' (you notice it slipped in to the passage we have just quoted). 'Discarnate', yes; because it is not the fleshly, carnal body which is being perceived – but hardly 'disembodied', because there are mental percepts which perform in the life of the next world a good many of the functions which the flesh-and-blood body performs in *this* world. That is, the mental percepts provide a means by which we are aware of our selves as continuing objects as well as self-aware subjects, and whereby we are recognized by other people when we communicate with them. They are not the same as our earthly flesh-and-blood bodies, and their properties are going to be remarkably different, but their function is similar.

Perhaps it is for this reason that in a later article Professor Price called this body a 'dream body or image body' and suggested that there was not perhaps quite so radical a difference between an 'image body' and an 'etheric body' as might as first appear. 'There may be realities in the universe which are intermediate between the physical and the psychological realms as these are ordinarily conceived', he wrote.

The contents of the other world, if there is one, may be in this intermediate position, more material than ordinary dream-images, more image-like or dream-like than ordinary material objects; like material objects in possessing spatial properties of some sort, and some degree at any rate of permanence; like mental images in that the causal laws they obey are the laws of psychology rather than the laws of physics.[6]

If there is anything in what Professor Price is saying, and the next world is a world of mental images, but also a world of inter-related persons who have these mental images and who can know each other as if they were sufficently embodied to be visible and to communicate with each other, what does this say about our likely experiences in the next world?

Desires and purgation

First of all, let us consider the next world as if it were a world entirely made up of our own private mental images. If this is what the next world is like, then it is a world in which desire is king, because I am the master of my own mental images, and I can do with them what I will. The life of the world to come would be one long superb day-dream; except that in this present world when I day-dream of sunning myself on a palm-girt beach in Tahiti, I remain obdurately in a wet grey wintry day in this septentrional island. In the next world, I could have all the sensations appropriate actually to *being* in Tahiti, with no danger either of insect-bites or of sun-stroke. Would it not be marvellous to be in a world where our desires were automatically granted?

Not necessarily. There are conflicting desires within the same person. Few (if any) of us are completely integrated personalities, and if we came to a next world where we were completely left to ourselves, then all those bits of incongruity would well up to the surface, and we might easily find ourselves not in paradise but in purgatory.

For example, a man may appear (yes, even to himself, and even to his introspective self) to have a fairly harmonious set of desires. But appearances are deceptive, and harmony has often only been achieved at the cost of repression. We have all heard bloodcurdling stories about the sort of things that sweet old ladies have said under anaesthetic. To speak of the human being I know best, I cannot help feeling that *I* am a pretty un-integrated personality, with many conflicting desires – some towards God, some towards self, or cruelty, or sensuality – and the unconscious desires battle with the neatly organized pattern of my conscious life. After death, if there is to be no other influence on me except my own desires and character, and if the repressive effect that my conscious has upon my unconscious is relaxed, then the lid will be off. All the things that have been seething below the surface come out, in the form of appropriate images, and the harmony and integrity of my personality is destroyed. Those formerly-repressed desires will manifest themselves by appropriate images, and the dreadful thing is that I will both want them and not want them. I will discover that my wish-fulfilments are mutually incompatible. Yet I cannot believe that I can remain myself without being *this* myself, and so I foresee a time ahead in which I live in a nightmare world where I realize how much of a warring battleground my personality is. But this will be a nightmare from which there is no waking up.

There is much in common between the picture I have just been drawing and the description of the state of the soul after death as given in the *Bardo Thödol*, or Tibetan *Book of the Dead*. This dates from about the eighth century AD and is a text from the tantric branch of mahayana Buddhism in Tibet. The soul after death passes through the intense and blinding light of Pure Reality, after which the majority (those who do not wish to become one with that light) encounter a series of karmic illusions. Clothed in a body constituted of his own past thoughts and deeds, the soul sees successive Buddhas and Boddhisatvas of awesome aspect, and is invited to respond to them in trust, and so enter paradise. The impure soul shrinks back, afraid to lose his self-hood, and therefore meets again that same reality, but now as wrath and terror rather than as light and glory.

Dense darkness, terrifying and unbearable, will go before you, with terrible cries of 'Strike!' and 'Kill!'. Do not be afraid of them. In the case of others who have done great evil, many flesh-eating demons will appear as a result of their karma, bearing various weapons, yelling warcries, shouting 'Kill! Strike!' and so on. You will feel that you are being chased by various terrifying wild animals and pursued by a great army in snow, rain, storms and darkness. There will be sounds of mountains crumbling, of lakes flooding, of fire spreading, and of fierce winds springing up. In fear you will escape wherever you can, but you will be cut off by three pre-cipices in front of you, white, red and black, deep and dreadful, and you will be on the point of falling down them.[7]

But the significant thing about these experiences is that the initiate has to realize that he is not being pursued by external forces or forced over actual precipices. All these are to be recognized as nothing more than projections of his own mind:

O son of noble family . . . do not be afraid of it; it is your own confused projection . . . They are not really precipices, they are aggression, passion and ignorance.[8]

I will recognise whatever appears as my projection
and know it to be a vision of the bardo;
now that I have reached this crucial point
I will not fear the peaceful and wrathful deities, my own projections.[9]

Is this not saying in religious and poetic form what I have just been saying in psychological language, in terms of desires and repression and the effect upon desire in the life of the world to come of the lifting of repressions? It is not a pretty sight, but then we are not pretty people.

If this is what is likely to be happening to us in the next world (and the teaching of the Tibetan *Book of the Dead* is astonishingly like the Christian teaching about Judgement and Purgatory) are there not some very practical spiritual implications of survival – practical in that we may begin to practise them here in this world, before we find ourselves in the next one? Ought we not to be so turning ourselves towards the light of goodness in this world that the darkness of evil becomes unattractive to us, not only consciously unattractive but unattractive to our unconscious also? Ought we not to be seeking the integration and harmony of character here and now?

And, if there is to be a body in the next life which bears some degree of continuity with the body we have in this one, then what we do in and with our bodies here has a great deal of bearing on what we may expect to experience in the life of the world to come. I am taking a wedding shortly, and one of the hymns the bride and groom have chosen is a hymn which is normally used for the dedication festival of a church:

> To this temple, where we call thee,
> Come, O Lord of Hosts, today.[10]

It is, in fact, a hymn remarkably apposite to a wedding, for St Paul taught (in 1 Cor. 3:16) that our bodies were the temples of God, where the Holy Spirit dwells. Survival has spiritual implications for our bodily life.

All this illustrates the importance of that 'trick question' in moral theology: 'Who is the better – a man who does good naturally and because he enjoys it, or a man who would really much rather do the bad thing, but who disciplines himself to do the good and manages it even if he sometimes has regrets about what he has missed?' Being Englishmen, heirs to the Puritan tradition, and believers in stern moral fibre, our instinct is to say that the man who had to struggle to do good was much better than the man who did good naturally. St Augustine would never have agreed. It was he who said, 'Love God, and do as you like!' He would want the man who so loved God that he did the right thing naturally. And Augustine is right. The man who has to struggle continuously to do good, against the constant promptings of his lower nature, is not the perfectly converted man. We must aim to be so turned towards good, that evil does not interest us. Only so can we be sure that when the lid is off, there will be nothing to crawl out of it and make life hell for us. Only so can we contemplate survival with equanimity.

Help

But wait. When I started on the previous section of this lecture, I said, 'Let us consider the next world as if it were a world entirely made up of our own private mental images'. I do not believe it is. I believe that, besides our own self-generated mental images, we also have to reckon with a world of inter-related persons who have these mental images, who know each other, and who communicate with each other. We are not left to rot, each in our own private self-encapsulated hell. There are other folk with us; and they can help us, right from the moment of our entry into the other world.

If there is any truth at all in the stories of deathbed visions (and I believe there is a great deal of truth in them) then we shall not be alone as we make our first steps in that new world. We owe a great deal to Dr Karlis Osis for our understanding of the significance of deathbed visions. In his studies of dying patients in America and India, he and Dr Erlendur Haraldsson interviewed nurses and doctors who had attended dying patients who had acted as though they were seeing a figure or figures at the hour of death. Their computerized studies of the results showed that there were two kinds of deathbed hallucination. One was rambling and confused, and tended to re-live the this-world concerns of the dying person. The other was brief and coherent, and the details of the vision were consistent. The rambling and incoherent type of vision characterized the patients with brain damage, brain disease, high fever, or medication affecting the mentality. People who were clear-brained at the time of death saw more of the purposeful apparition which purported to be a vision of a loved one coming to take the dying patient away.[11]

The sort of thing which Dr Osis reports is a case like this one. A woman of sixty was dying painfully of intestinal cancer. The doctor reported that

all of a sudden she opened her eyes. She called her [deceased] husband by name and said she was coming to him. She had the most peaceful, nicest smile, just as if she were going to the arms of someone she thought a great deal of. She said, 'Guy, I am coming'. She didn't seem to realize I was there. It was almost as if she were in another world. It was as if something beautiful had opened up to her; she was experiencing something so wonderful and beautiful.

Or, from an older source than Dr Osis, how about this one? Two brothers died on successive days, fourteen miles away from each other. The death of the one child was kept from the other, but about an hour before the second child died, he sat up in bed, and pointed to the bottom of the bed, saying, 'Harry's calling for me'. The child knew neither that his brother Harry had died the day before, nor that he himself was expected to die shortly.[12]

Dr Osis' computer print-outs and statistical analysis shows that deathbed visions of loved ones coming to call the dying patient over the threshold of death are not explicable as wish-fulfilment, inner conflict, religious expectation, or the result of hallucinogenic drugs. It looks very much as if we have to believe what we are told – that when our time comes to die, we shall be helped by our friends, and that we may be able to tell those around our deathbed that we can see it happening.

There are other indications that the departed work for, and help, each other. Let me simply give one example from a mediumistic source. It comes from Bishop Pike's book *The Other Side*, in which he told us of the tragic suicide of his son Jim and the way in which he was eventually persuaded that Jim was alive in the next world, communicating with his father, and engaged in helping souls with whom he was coming into contact. 'I have been given the job', he said through Ena Twigg about a couple of years after his death, 'of helping those who come over after having committed suicide – it's because I understand.'[13]

So the next world does not need to be one in which the surviving soul is encapsulated in its own self-created world of disintegrating horror. It can be; and members of the College of Psychic Studies will be well aware of the kind of communication which occasionally comes through a sensitive in which we seem to be in touch with lost souls, or souls which are tied to earth, or souls which are confused and unhappy and want to escape into a world of greater meaning, but seem quite incapable of doing so. It is sometimes that kind of spirit which is responsible for poltergeist activity or hauntings – sometimes as a way of drawing attention to itself and its needs, as the newly-dead Jim Pike used poltergeist manifestations to alert his father to the need to consult a psychic sensitive. (More often, I believe, poltergeist activity is the physical externalization of psychic energy in a house where there is tension between the occupants;[14] but that does not affect the fact that it can sometimes be the result of the activity of departed spirits.)

When we come across cases where the spirits of the departed are causing disturbances of a psychic or poltergeist nature, we may have the privilege of helping to give rest to the spirit which is using this method to signal its need to us. I am sorry when I hear of the kind of person who, if ever he comes across such a case, can think of nothing better to do with the disturbed house than to exorcise it, as though it is possessed with an evil spirit which needs to be banished to hell. Can people not realize that poltergeist phenomena can be caused by human spirits which want love and understanding and pastoral care – which need to be set upon their road of pilgrimage and helped towards spiritual harmony and integration? When he comes across a case like this, and once he is certain of his diagnosis, the Christian priest will want to seek his bishop's permission to use the Requiem Eucharist in the disturbed house with the special intention towards the reconciliation of the departed soul with the loving purposes of almighty God – 'Rest eternal grant unto him, O Lord: and let light perpetual shine upon him.'[15] Yes, the dead help each other; they can help us (do not many Christians ask the saints to pray for them?); and we can often help them.

So there is hope in the life of the world to come. We are not left there alone. We do not have to learn to live for all eternity with what we have made ourselves. The Christian is clear as to the nature and the source of that help. He believes that character *can* change; desires *can* be modified. We are not stuck for all eternity with the character and desires we now have. It is perfectly possible to have what Professor Price called 'second-order desire, a desire that some of one's own desires should be altered'.[16] These 'second-order' desires do not work rapidly. They require a long period over which they can become gradually more and more effective, if they are sufficiently frequently exercised. But it *is* possible, I believe, even for a man's habitual and 'permanent' desires to be modified, exchanged, made harmonious. As a Christian, however, I am bound to say that I only believe such desires to be alterable if the natural man is confronted by, and given the assistance of, God.

The Christian knows the hopelessness of 'second-order' desires when made by the natural man. St Paul knew that. 'What I do is not what I want to do, but what I detest. The good which I want to do, I fail to do, but what I do is the wrong which is against my will' (Rom. 7: 18-19). Thank God, however, that Paul also knew that what was impossible in human strength *was* possible in the power of God: 'Who is there to rescue me out of this body doomed to death? God alone, through Jesus Christ our Lord!' (Rom. 7:25). With the help of God, in the solidarity of Jesus the Christ, the natural man can be converted. The Christian believes, not in a continuance in the next life of the helpless moral struggle of unassisted man, but in the assistance which Christ can bring even to the most hardened character – both in this life and in the life to come. He has seen it happen on earth (he may even have known it happen to himself) and he will not therefore expect it to be impossible for any man. He will not expect it to be either instantaneous or painless; but he will know that it *can* be done.

That is my hope of heaven – a hope that my character will in the end be so purified that it will be congruous with the presence of God, that my good desires will in the end be so strengthened that my evil desires will simply wilt away, that in the end I shall be able to be with God without a feeling of shame or a shudder of incongruity – that I shall be pure.

It is the pure in heart who see God and rejoice; and purity is not the simpering milk-and-water kind of repulsive niceness – it is something *positive*. Purity means being one hundred per cent what one is supposed to be, like the pot of honey on my breakfast table which is proudly advertised as one hundred per cent pure honey – no other admixture. When I am pure in my desires, when I want nothing but God and nobody but God, then I shall have him and he will have me and I shall be utterly and completely happy – because there will be no remaining taint, no remaining admixture, of those base desires which make me want to escape God and which cause the conflict in my life. I shall have what I want: I shall have whom I want: I shall love God, and do as I like. That is heaven.

The transformation cannot be an instant one, or it would not be credible. Roland Smith tells the story of the old tramp and his dog, wandering aimlessly round the lanes near where he used to live, and 'usually connected by a length of dirty string, and by a mutual disregard for hygiene'. Eventually the old man was taken into care and looked after in a geriatric hospital; and his dog was also groomed and accepted into civilized society. Then the two of them were reunited. It was not a success. The poor dog did not recognize his old master – the place, the clean-shaven face, the fresh pyjamas, held nothing familiar, and there was certainly nothing to recognize in the smell. 'I am bothered', admits Roland Smith, 'lest the same sort of thing could happen to me. If I ever get to heaven I may find myself so cleaned up that even my best friend won't know me.'[17]

That would be a credible fear if the soul's transformation at or after death were instantaneous. There are Christians who believe that it will be so, but I cannot follow them. God's way is more usually one which respects our individuality and our characters. The act of God in purifying a human being needs to be individually applied to the individual intricacies of every individual soul, at that soul's own natural pace. That is what the Christian means by resurrection. The Christian – like the Spiritualist – believes that every human being survives death; but he does not see that, necessarily, as good news. He sees it as part of the natural order of things – ordained by God in so far as God is creator, but not part of the order of redemption and therefore, as it were, part of God's impersonal work. The Old Testament believed in survival, but it was survival into the kind of world where God's writ did not run,[18] and the departed were in a kind of grey, colourless existence that could hardly be called 'life' because 'the dead know nothing, they have no more reward; but the memory of them is lost' (Eccles. 9:5-6); 'thou rememberest them no more [O God], because they are cut off from thy care' (Psalm 88:5). When the psychic sensitive from En-dor called back the shade of Samuel for King Saul (1 Sam 28:3-20), it was from the realms of the shades – the colourless existence of the place the Hebrews called She'ol – that she called him. I feel that many of the departed spirits with whom sensitives are in touch, are in like case. We need, not to keep them earth-bound, but to guide them towards the resurrecting power of God the Father of Jesus. What distinguishes the New Testament from the Old is the power of Christ's resurrection. 'All I care for', says St Paul, 'is to know Christ, to experience the power of his resurrection, and to share his sufferings, in growing conformity with his death, if only I may finally arrive at the resurrection from the dead' (Phil. 3:10-11). If there are spiritual implications of survival, the important thing is to realize the way in which God enters into the whole business. We look forward to seeing God resurrect each individual, because without God the individual is doomed to an eternity of mere survival – in the Bardo world of illusion when he could be savouring the resurrected world of reality.

So survival does have spiritual implications, because we want to escape survival and experience resurrection. To do so, we need to know God. Today, we are in *this* world. What has talk of a next world to do with the Monday mornings of life? It has this to do, that we live in a world of choice, and our choice has momentous consequences. In Christian parlance, the Four Last Things are death, judgement, hell, and heaven. Our question should be, 'What about me? Am I living so as to make my life in the world to come heaven? or hell? or purgatory?' If we ask that question, we shall be putting last things first; but when the last things are the Four Last Things of death and judgement, hell and heaven, then the first place is the only place to put them, and when we do so we shall find that survival after death will have immense spiritual implications for us before death.

References

1. *The Times*, 17 January 1977, p. 12.
2. Paul Badham, *Christian Beliefs about Life after Death* (Macmillan, 1976), p. 75, quoting John Hick, *Death and Eternal Life* (Collins, 1976), p. 294.
3. Hick, *op. cit.*, p. 294.
4. 'Survival and the Idea of "Another World"', in *Proceedings* of the Society for Psychical Research, Vol. 50 (1953), pp. 1-23. Reprinted in *Brain and Mind* (edited by J.R. Smythies, Routledge and Kegan Paul, 1965). The same arguments are presented in different and briefer form in an article by Price in *Man's Concern with Death* (A. Toynbee and others, Hodder and Stoughton, 1968), pp. 251-6. The original paper was read to the SPR on 16 July 1952.
5. J.B. Phillips, *Ring of Truth* (Hodder and Stoughton, 1967), p. 89.
6. *Man's Concern with Death* (see Note 4 above), p. 256. Also in *Tomorrow* (New York, Parapsychology Foundation), Autumn 1956.
7. *The Tibetan Book of the Dead* (edited by W.Y. Evans-Wentz, Oxford University Press, third edition 1957), p. 162; or (edited by Francesca Fremantle and Chögyam Trungpa, Shambhala, 1975), p. 75. The Fremantle-Trungpa translation is followed here.
8. *Tibetan Book of the Dead*, Evans-Wentz, p. 162, Fremantle and Trungpa, p. 75.
9. *ibid.*, Evans-Wentz, p. 103, Fremantle and Trungpa, p. 40.
10. *Hymns Ancient and Modern Revised*, No. 474, verse 3, or No. 620 verse 7. Probably seventh or eighth century in its Latin original, translated by J.M. Neale, 1851.
11. An interim and non-technical report of this research is given in the Winter, 1975, *Newsletter* of the American Society for Psychical Research, under the title *What did the Dying See?* For a full report with technical detail, see Karlis Osis and Erlendur Haraldsson, *At the Hour of Death* (New York, Avon Books, 1977).
12. Quoted by Michael Perry, *The Resurrection of Man* (Mowbray, 1975), p. 99.
13. James A. Pike with Diane Kennedy, *The Other Side* (Allen, 1969), p. 300. (Though see below, p. 189, note 17.).
14. See, e.g. D. Scott Rogo, 'Psychotherapy and the Poltergeist' in *Journal* of the Society for Psychical Research, Vol. 47 (September, 1974), pp. 433-46, and *Exorcising Devils* by Dom Robert Petitpierre, OSB (Hale, 1976), pp. 107-9.

15. For practical details of discernment and treatment, consult Douglas Howell-Everson, *A Handbook for Christian Exorcists* (available privately from Bamford Rectory, Sheffield, 1982).

16. *Proceedings* of the Society for Psychical Research, Vol. 50 (1953), p. 23.

17. G. Roland Smith, *I Suppose I shall Survive* (Seminar Books, 1982), p. 10.

18. For a good brief summary of the Old Testament position, see Paul Badham, *Christian Beliefs about Life after Death* (Macmillan, 1976), pp. 3-17.

Part 5

Resurrection and reincarnation

The resurrection of Jesus has been at the top of my theological agenda for a long time, and was the subject of my first book, *The Easter Enigma*, which Faber and Faber published in 1959. I have returned to the subject from time to time, and wrote two articles for *The Expository Times* which were published in February and March 1974 (Vol. 85, Nos. 5 and 6, pp. 136-9 and 164-7). Parts of these articles were taken up and expanded in *The Resurrection of Man* (Mowbray's Theological Library, 1975). Other parts of them have formed the basis for the first essay in this present section. It was presented to CANTESS (The Canterbury Summer School) on 27 July 1977 and to the Churches' Fellowship for Psychical and Spiritual Studies at Jordans, Beaconsfield, on 10 November 1979.

As late as 1975, when *The Resurrection of Man* appeared, I thought that the doctrine of reincarnation could be summarily dismissed in a couple of pages (96-98) of a book on 'Christian teaching on life after death'. Partly that was due to my own ignorance, but partly, I believe, because it came before the great spate of books and writings on the subject which have poured forth in the late seventies and early eighties. It is now obvious that Christians need to grapple with the issues raised in the reincarnation debate. That is why this section contains two further items – three reviews of books on reincarnation which Renée Haynes asked me to contribute to the *Journal* of the Society for Psychical Research, and a paper in which a Christian reaction to the reincarnation debate is sketched out. The reviews appeared in the SPR *Journal* for June and October 1981 (Vol. 51, Nos. 788 and 789); that of David Christie-Murray's *Reincarnation: Ancient Beliefs and Modern Evidence* on pp. 102-4, Ian Wilson's *Mind out of Time?* on pp. 167-170, and Benjamin Walker's *Masks of the Soul* on pp. 170-171.

The final paper is based on presentations given to a conference which John Walters organized on Iona from 9 to 15 May 1981 and at the Presbyterian School of Christian Education in Richmond Virginia on 17 July 1981. In an abbreviated version of its present form it was read to meetings of the Churches' Fellowship for Psychical and Spiritual Studies at York on 8 March 1983 and Chichester on 10 September 1983, and printed in *The Epworth Review*, Vol. 10, No. 2 (1983), pp. 53-62.

12
Resurrection

Did the resurrection of Jesus happen? And what does it imply if it did?

I remember, a year or two ago, listening to a performance of Bach's *B Minor Mass* in Durham Cathedral and being captivated by what is arguably the greatest piece of music ever written in the Western world. We were in the *Credo – passus et sepultus est* – calm, quiet, beautiful, and solemn music. Then, with the drama of which Bach is an absolute master, *et resurrexit!* The music sprang to life; and I looked at the conductor as he was throwing himself into his task, hopping first on one leg and then on the other, not so much conducting as dancing. Suddenly it dawned on me that the resurrection was something to *dance* about. It wasn't simply a doctrine about someone being dragged back to living after a terrible experience, but it told us about someone who came into a new kind of life together. Survival of death is not something to dance about, but when the life-giving power of God comes upon the individual, it's a different matter altogether.

In that case, the question we need to ask is, 'Is God a resurrecting God?' Is resurrection something he does or not? That sends us back to the historical question of the resurrection of Jesus. As St Paul said, 'If Christ is not raised, then our preaching is pointless' (1 Cor. 15 : 14). If Christ has been raised, then it is conceivable that we shall be raised, but if he has not been raised, it is inconceivable that we shall be. In order to affirm anything about our own future prospects, we need to look at the case of Jesus, to see whether God is a resurrecting God or not. Our verdict on the historical question is going to have a lot to say about our views on the theology and meaning of it.

Did the resurrection of Jesus happen? The old-fashioned way of answering that question was to examine the New Testament as though you were an historian trying to establish the factual bedrock of the accounts. Until relatively recently it was the Christians who attempted to turn the tables on the infidels by proving that if you took a fine enough comb to sift through the records, you came across all sorts of ways in which the narratives unexpectedly supported each other, and all sorts of ways in which apparently plausible alternatives fell to pieces in your hands as you went rigorously enough into them. The approach is the approach of the detective-story writer who treats the New Testament like a crime story in order to show that the only answer to 'who-done-it?' is 'God', and that the *modus operandi* can only have been resurrection. Perhaps the most famous attempt to do that this century was the attempt by Frank Morison, whose book *Who Moved the Stone?* is still being read and recommended, though it is now over fifty years old.

And yet — as I said — this approach is very old-fashioned. No longer is it only the infidels who argue against it, but the Christian theologians. No wonder some Christians are asking 'Who needs enemies when he has got friends like that?'

But the historical evidence is *not* completely watertight. There *are* gaps and there *are* discrepancies between the accounts, and the true, impartial, historian recognizes them and points them out. It is only the pseudo-historian with an axe to grind who gives certain of his sources the benefit of the doubt (for reasons unconnected with the general historical veracity of the document) whilst denying it to others, or introduces certain assumptions in order to derive a chronological account from sources which do not seem over-interested in chronology.

The Gospels are made up of individual units of earlier traditions which originally circulated independently. Each unit had its own theological point to make, and the synoptic evangelists only took such units as made the points they wanted to stress, or such units as could be amended to fit their own theological stance. They are not interested in proving that the resurrection happened. That is the pre-supposition, not the conclusion, of their argument. They are not interested, either, in providing an historical reconstruction. If we try to do this, we are using the narratives for a purpose which was not their original purpose, so if we fail we ought not to be surprised – and, conversely, if we look like succeeding, it is only a fluke. As Professor Christopher Evans put it,

It is not simply difficult to harmonize these traditions, but quite imposs-ible ... For what have to be combined are not a number of scattered pieces from an originally single matrix, but separate expressions of the Easter faith. Each of these is complete in itself; each has developed along its own line so as to serve in the end as a proper conclusion for an evangelist of his own particular version of the gospel ... Each evangelist gives his own version as a total version, which was not intended to stand up only if it stood alongside another, or was supplemented by another.[1]

Thus the question to ask is not 'what was the original order of events?' The material for answering that is gone for ever. We should, rather, ask 'What is the individual gospel-writer (or what were his sources) intending to get across to the reader by the anecdotes he relates and the way in which he tells them?' This is the purpose behind Dr Norman Perrin's posthumously-published book *The Resurrection Narratives: A New Approach* (SCM Press 1977). It puts us in an inescapably *theological* frame of reference, and makes us ask theological questions.

But first it is necessary to get back to the problem of what happened, and whether we can find out what happened, and why it matters to us what happened.

The narratives of the resurrection, as distinct from the sheer proclamation of the resurrection, belong to the later strata of the New Testament, and if we arrange our material chronologically, we can almost – as it were – see the stories forming under our very eyes. Professor R.H. Fuller has done this with particular care in his book *The Formation of the Resurrection Narratives.*[2] The earliest mention of the resurrection in the New Testament documents is that in 1 Corinthians 15. Professor Fuller believes that the earliest Easter message was not an account of the resurrection, but a single word in Greek – *egegertai* – 'he was raised'. This, he says, is a 'reverential passive' denoting that the real subject is God. In other words, 'he was raised' means that God raised him. By looking at the Old Testament usage of that word *egeiro*, Fuller sees that it implies a transition from one mode of existence to another. Resurrection is not a restoration to a former mode of existence. The word used about

Lazarus, or the widow's son from Nain, or the daughter of Jairus, is
not *egeiro*. They were not raised, they were simply brought back to
this life. The word *egeiro* is used, not of bringing back to this world
but of transition from one world to another. So, then, the resurrection is an event which takes place at the end of history, at the point
of exit from history, at the place where the history of this world
gives way to the realities of the next. In the Lazarus story, Jesus says
to Martha, 'Your brother will rise again', and she replies, 'I know
that he will rise again *at the resurrection on the last day*' (John 11:24).

The Jewish hope (in so far as there was a single 'Jewish' hope
rather than a whole constellation of possible scenarios) was for a
resurrection at the end of time, but the Christian Gospel is that since
God has raised this single person Jesus, then that last day has
already begun and that single person must be someone very special
because in him the time of the world to come has actually impinged
on the time of this world here and now. So the proclamation *egegertai,* 'he was raised', puts the resurrection at the border where the
historical gives way to the supra-historical. That is why – to quote
two phrases of Professor Fuller's, 'the resurrection was not access-
ible to witnesses' (because witnesses stand in history and resurrection is something beyond history; they could not see the resurrection
– all that witnesses could see would be a body disappearing, and
that is not resurrection), and 'the resurrection as such cannot be
narrated but only proclaimed'[3]. You cannot tell stories about
resurrection; you can only tell stories about a body disappearing or
about people seeing visions – and that, again, is not resurrection
because that is a story about things which are happening on this
world. When you proclaim the resurrection, you proclaim something which lies at the border of this world and the next, and you
are touching on an ineffable and inexpressible mystery. So the primitive Easter message was the single, theologically-charged word
egegertai.

But when Paul wrote to the Corinthians, he collected a number
of formulae about the Gospel, such as 'he was buried', and 'he was
raised the third day according to the Scriptures'; and to these he
added a series of lists of resurrection-appearances. This is the first
sign of something which will expand in later accounts to form full-
scale narratives. So, he appeared to Cephas, to the Twelve, to over
five hundred of our brothers at once, to James, then to all the
apostles. Paul gives this as a chronological list. In this we see the
beginning of the move from theological proclamation towards the
compilation of lists of appearances. The theological message of the

resurrection is becoming enmeshed within history.

When we move from Paul to the earliest of the Gospels, that is to Mark, the 'feel' is the same. Mark gives us no stories of resurrection-appearances, for the simple reason that he had none to draw on. Even Matthew has very little in the way of *narratives* – his account is not much more than a list, with a mention of an appearance of Jesus to the women in Jerusalem and another one to the eleven on a mountain in Galilee. It is not until we come to Luke (which Fuller takes as being later than Matthew) that we get full-blown narratives with all sorts of additional material – the long story about the walk to Emmaus, and the massively physical demonstration of 'look at my hands and feet . . . Touch me and see' (Luke 24: 39), and his taking a piece of fish they had cooked, and eating it before their eyes. This has moved right into the arena of historical fact, and is poles apart from the word of theological proclamation. The shift was made inevitable as soon as interest moved from 'he was raised' to 'he appeared to Cephas'. The fourth Gospel completes the move by adding further narrative features such as the positioning of the grave clothes and the race between Peter and the beloved disciple.

Fuller points out that the later the account, the greater the amount of detail and ends by exhorting the preacher to stick to the proclamation of the resurrection, the primitive message of 'he was raised', and to keep clear of the pseudo-historical narrative details. They are probably not factually true.

It is true that the later sources have narratives which the earlier sources do not, but it is less clear to me than to Fuller that this means the narratives are thereby less reliable. It is certainly not proven that the narratives have been dreamed up by the evangelists out of thin air. It is quite open to us to read the evidence in another way. For one thing, Fuller assumes the chronological order 1 Corinthians, Mark, Matthew, Luke, John, and he sees a fairly long period in which the compilation of the Gospels takes place. Since then, John Robinson has set the historical cat amongst the theological pigeons with his suggestion[4] that the latest book of the New Testament was completed before the sack of Jerusalem in AD 70, and (more importantly) William Farmer and others have re-opened the old hypothesis that the order of the Gospels may well have been Matthew, Luke, Mark.[5] Arguments for Markan priority are not as watertight as we had thought. If this is right, then Fuller's development looks a deal less convincing.

In any case, we have to ask, not only *whether* there are differences in the amount of narrative detail, but *why* Paul and Mark do not give us resurrection narratives and why Matthew and (to a greater extent) Luke and John do. Is it not true generally that Paul is just not interested in narratives about the incarnate Jesus, whilst the evangelists are? If we only had Paul on whom to rely for our knowledge of the historical Jesus, we would know very little indeed about him – and this does not only apply to the resurrection, but to the whole of the story. 'Jesus after the flesh' has remarkably little attraction for Paul; theological proclamations are much more his line of country. When we deal with the life of Jesus, Paul is notoriously uninterested in anecdotal details. It would be odd (and would require special explanation) if Paul were suddenly to develop a narrative interest in the resurrection which he had not had in the other details of the Gospel story.

Furthermore, the fact that it is the *later* evangelists who pick up the narrative, does not mean they may not be in touch with primitive tradition. Even Professor Fuller acknowledges that John 21, 'late though it is, seems to be in closest touch with the primitive tradition'.[6] So it could well be that what only appears late as a literary precipitate, yet may belong to an early stratum as a piece of tradition. The question of historicity is not as easily solved as that.

All this means that we are far from certainty when we talk about what happened historically on the first Easter Day. A lot depends on what we think as being antecedently probable, and a lot depends on how far we are prepared to trust the details of the accounts. We ought at least to be wary before treating them as straightforward narrative. This truth has been seized upon by some theologians as the clue to a Christian understanding of the resurrection. If God had meant us to be incontrovertibly sure of the resurrection by the use of human reasoning, they say, he would have arranged things differently. But things are as they are because belief in the resurrection is a matter of faith which is sparked off by divine revelation. The living Jesus meets us in the here and now in the preached word. We are not men of faith if we cling to the material and physical and tangible evidence of historical research. Like the body of the risen Jesus, it will slip immaterially out of our grasp if we try to hold on to it. It is not a proper basis for faith.

This appears to be the conviction behind Willi Marxsen's *The Resurrection of Jesus of Nazareth* (SCM Press 1970). He whittles down the historical evidence to conclude that the only 'more or less firm historical result' with which we are left is not resurrection itself, because that cannot be observed. But nor can we be sure that Simon

Peter saw Jesus, because he may have been mistaken. Can we prove that Simon asserted that he saw Jesus? No; all we can be sure of is that the early Church asserted that Simon said he had seen Jesus. And yet that is sufficient for Marxsen, who concludes in a moving but somewhat puzzling close to his book that:

The believer must not be modest *in his faith* ... The believer only radically believes if he believes like Jesus and thinks that, contrary to appearance, God can do *anything*. That is why Jesus makes us free for limitless faith in this world and utter confidence in God for the future.[7]

Most English reviewers of Marxsen believe he has gone too far in loosing the resurrection from its historical moorings and that we can be reasonably sure of a great deal more than he allows. This is the position of Christopher Evans, who argues that a doctrine of resurrection was a newcomer to Judaism in New Testament times, 'not a universally held belief and badge of orthodoxy, but a subject of considerable speculation and debate'.[8] Jesus has very little to say about resurrection in the Synoptics, though these are written from the standpoint of a belief in his resurrection. Mark 9:9f can even have the disciples asking among themselves 'what the resurrection from the dead should mean'. Evans' conclusion is that in view of all this, only the actual resurrection of Jesus itself, whatever that event may have been, could have created Christianity, in which resurrection is at the centre, out of late Judaism, for which it was a peripheral belief.

But however much or little we feel we can salvage as historians from the New Testament accounts of the resurrection, we must abandon the attempt to *force* people to believe in the resurrection by a knock-down historical argument. And this is not simply because the documents themselves are partial or incomplete. Even if in some miraculous way it were to be established that (for example) the account of the resurrection in the apocryphal *Gospel of Peter* was not a story based on our canonical accounts and padded out by a great deal of imaginative fiction, but sober historical truth, we would still have to ask whether it was the *resurrection* which it was describing. The resurrection may have certain historical concomitants and it may leave its mark upon history. It may be *accompanied* by the coming to life again of a dead body and its disappearance from human view. It may, for all we know, be accompanied by the scorching of a piece of linen which was left behind. But *in itself* the resurrection is other than these historical concomitants. It is a fact which belongs to the borderlands between history and what lies beyond history, and its inner essence is not amenable to historical verification.

The matter is similar to the apologist's legerdemain in 'proving God'. It is not possible to produce by a logical argument material which is not inherent in the premises, and you can therefore only end up with God if you concealed him in the jumping-off ground. The magician can only produce his rabbits out of his hat if he had them somewhere or other about him when he walked on to the stage. So with the resurrection. You cannot start with empirical, this-worldly, historical facts and end by proving the resurrection. The only thing with which you can end up is another empirical, this-worldly, historical conclusion — an empty tomb, maybe, or accounts of people who claimed to have had visions. Marxsen is right. Anything more than this is a matter of faith, not proof, of what the late Bishop Ian Ramsey would have called a 'disclosure' evoked by, but not logically dependent upon, the facts which led up to that disclosure-situation.

And yet, history matters. If the accounts cannot prove the resurrection, but only tell us about the mark left by the resurrection on history, it matters what kind of a mark was left, because the nature of the mark gives us some clue as to the nature of the resurrection. Was the mark an empty tomb? Or a strip of scorched linen? Or a series of visions? Or a conviction in the minds of the disciples? Different answers to this question produce different theologies of the resurrection.

Some Christians believe that there was absolutely nothing empirically observable in the physical realm, but that Jesus rose in a purely spiritual sense. His body lay a-mouldering in the tomb, but his soul goes marching on. For them, resurrection is an event in the spiritual realm only, and their theology tends to lay stress on the element of faith in the preached world and the change effected in a man's life by a changed attitude of mind. Their theology is not happy, for instance, with physical miracle of any kind. As Don Cupitt acknowledges, 'I have never looked for or believed in miracles, answers to prayer, particular providences or the "supernatural" in the popular sense.'[9] God is kept to the mental and spiritual realm. He may be creator, but he does not intervene physically in his creation. To do so would show that he had not given his creation its proper physical autonomy.

Other, more traditional, Christians believe that although it is no longer historically provable, there *was* some physical change in the universe at the moment of Christ's resurrection and that at that moment God intervened in the physical order. Clearly, that will lead to a very different theology of the resurrection.

Another way in which a judgement on a historical question is intertwined with a judgement of its theological import concerns the relation between the appearances of the risen Jesus and a belief in his resurrection. Some Christians believe that the appearances caused the disciples to believe in the resurrection, and others hold that the disciples came to a conviction that Jesus had been raised from the dead, and that this was then validated for them by visions which followed after. This is the nub of a disagreement between Don Cupitt and Professor Charlie Moule published in the pages of the journal *Theology* in 1972, and reprinted in Cupitt's book *Explorations in Theology* in 1979.[10]

Don Cupitt believes that the disciples reflected on the life of Jesus and the manner of his death, and came to a theological judgement on them. When this realization had dawned, the appearances were sent (by God) as a form of validation. Charlie Moule thinks it must have been the other way round. After so traumatic an event as the crucifixion and death of their leader, nothing less dramatic than the vision of Jesus alive from the dead could have impelled the disciples to rethink the meaning of the cross and passion, and to see in them God's saving action. Once more, the nature of the historical mark left by the resurrection determines the theology (or, in this case, the theology determines what we imagine the historical mark to have been). Do we believe in a God who sends visions in order to impel people into a way of thinking which can be begun by nothing less than a divine initiative beyond human credibility, or do we believe that men's own powers of theological reflection are great enough for them to come to belief in resurrection without need for a concomitant miraculous vision first? Do we believe in the powers of human reason (natural theology), or do we believe in the necessity for divine revelation of what unaided man can never discover?

Don Cupitt has analysed[11] the various types of theory about what happened at the resurrection, and distinguishes three main types. The 'Event' theory bases belief in the resurrection on historical statement about the empty tomb and the appearances. He cannot accept this, because of its confusion of logical categories. A theological event cannot be proved by historical reasoning. That, we have already seen. Cupitt prefers the 'Theological' theory, according to which the disciples made a theological judgement on the implications of Jesus' life and death, and came to realize that he had risen;

whereupon the appearances occured to validate their theological judgement.

Cupitt can dismiss the 'Event' theory with ease, because he formulates it in a grossly materialistic way. According to his statement of it, the body which the disciples are alleged to have seen after the resurrection was strictly continuous with the one which had lain in the grave, and its appearances were as physical as the appearance of the Conservative leader at the party conference. The New Testament does not bear witness to an Event quite like this. The body which was seen had very different properties from the one which had been buried. It could appear in Galilee or Jerusalem without walking from one place to the other, and appear and disappear with sovereign unconcern for such material barriers as locked doors. Perhaps it is for this reason that Cupitt introduces a third theory – the 'Vision' theory, or, to use the term he prefers, the 'Psi' theory.

The risen body has such 'odd' properties that we ought perhaps to think of a paranormal kind of seeing and a paranormal kind of body which is nonetheless amenable to historical investigation. Cupitt will have none of this. If we use the ordinary rules of historical evidence to establish that an extraordinary event has happened, and then go on to say that we can assent to a system of belief in the resurrection which gives this extraordinary event its context and makes it intelligible, we are guilty of two logical errors. First, we are once more confounding categories. Whether the Event which we are discussing be ordinary (a physical risen body) or extraordinary (some kind of paranormal phenomenon) we still cannot draw theological inferences from historical data. Secondly, if an event is 'odd' we cannot apply the ordinary rules of evidence to it, because we do not know how far the extraordinariness of the event has also affected the rules of evidence whereby we decide to give it credence.

I shall return to the former point in due course. For the moment, I want to concentrate on the second objection. With respect, Cupitt's way of looking at it is not how the matter appears to a student of psychical research. This discipline deals with 'odd' occurrences and attempts to begin to understand them by looking at them from a scientific, empirical, and historical point of view. Only on the basis of such an examination can we hope to begin to distinguish between true and distorted accounts. This must needs involve 'the ordinary rules of evidence', one of which is that the more unusual an event which is alleged, the stronger needs to be the evidence which asserts it. Evidence is strengthened either by the convergent testimony for a single event of independent eyewitnesses, or by building up the evidence for similar occurrences at other times and places. It is not often possible to apply the former method to paranormal occurrences – there are not that many eyewitnesses to each alleged paranormal event. Psychical researchers, therefore, have to use the second method, whereby they try to build up a general picture of what does or does not happen in the world, within which the credibility or otherwise of isolated incidents can be assessed.

The way this method might be applied in the case of the resurrection is first of all to take the accounts at face value and establish what kind of an event is being postulated. Clearly, it will not be a 'normal' event, in that the properties of the risen body are greatly different from those of the bodies we normally and physically perceive. It appears and disappears behind closed doors. It is not immediately recognized as the body of Jesus. It is seen in different places without (apparently) walking from one locale to another; and so on. But apparitions of the living and of the departed are known to psychical researchers, and it is possible to build up a picture – using 'the ordinary rules of evidence' – showing their range of observed properties. We could then check the accounts of the resurrection against this range in order to see whether it seems likely to us that the gospel accounts can be believed, not as accounts of the physical reappearances of a physical body, but as accounts of a paranormal event parallel in some respects to paranormal events known to happen today.[12] This investigation might lead us to assert, not that the gospel accounts are to be accepted *au pied de la lettre*, but that some kind of paranormal event underlay them, however much its details may have been distorted and magnified in the course of the transmission of the tradition.

(This assumes, of course, that the resurrection is a miracle in the sense of an event within the natural order which is seen as a sign of, or pointer to, God's activity in the spiritual realm. If, *per contra,* a miracle is taken to be an event transcending or reversing natural laws, and therefore a proof of God's extraordinary activity in the natural realm, the fact that the resurrection narratives include elements for which it is difficult or impossible to find a parallel in other accounts of paranormal events, need not imply that the gospel accounts have exaggerated what was actually and historically observed. But in that case, there is no point in trying to find parallels *at all*: God's sovereign freedom knows no laws, and it is impious to enquire into the *modus operandi* of the resurrection appearances. It seems to me, however, that there is value in seeing how far we can go with the former sense of 'miracle' before we invoke miracle as a *deus ex machina* to get us out of all our difficulties.)

Is the Psi theory a variant of the Event theory or of the Theological theory? That depends on the nature of an apparition of the departed. One school of parapsychologists holds that when an apparition is perceived, there is some kind of quasi-material body objectively *there* to be seen with the physical eye, and that it is composed of some sort of ectoplasmic quasi-substance. This supposition makes the Psi theory very close to the Event theory. It is, however, regarded as more respectable to think of an apparition as an externalization of an inner apprehension. In normal vision, an external body casts an image on the eye which is then perceived by the brain. But there is also a process whereby the brain creates an image which, to the beholder, is indistinguishable from the image produced by an external object, but which does not 'exist' in the space towards which he is looking, nor in the eyeball or optic nerve. The brain may project an image like this for no objective reason at all, or because it is under the influence of hypnosis, or because it is sick or drugged. In that case the apparition is delusionary. But it may (so some psychical researchers assert) project it as the result of receiving a telepathic communication from the person whose apparition is observed, in which case it is termed a telepathic or veridical apparition. If this line of argument is true, then the Psi theory of the resurrection is a variant of the Theological theory, whereby God first conveys a realization of the truth of the resurrection, and this is then externalized as a Christophany.

It is a *variant* of the Theological theory; it is not identical with it. The communication which is externalized as an apparition is subconsciously apprehended, and is only consciously known *at the moment of* the appearance. The Theological theory as expounded by Cupitt has it that the vision of the risen Christ would have had no meaning to the disciples if it had appeared to them *before* they had done their theological thinking about the plan of salvation-history and come to the conscious realization that Jesus must be alive. There is a world of difference between a conscious theological conviction which is capped by a vision and the subconscious reception of a message from God which is externalized into the conscious in apparitional form. And there is, equally, a world of difference to the beholder between a vision (whatever its psychological or parapsychological mechanism) and a 'spiritual conviction'.

It is for reasons such as these that I hold that the 'ordinary rules of historical evidence' may be applied to the Psi theory and that it may be a variant either of the Event theory or of the Theological theory but not (*pace* Cupitt[13]) 'a meaningless compromise' between them. I believe that it is along the lines of the Psi theory that the alleged facts behind the resurrection may be made intelligible to, and credible by, people to-day.

Notice that I wrote the 'facts behind the resurrection' and did not speak of the resurrection itself. This brings me back to Cupitt's first objection.

As has already been asserted, we cannot make theological deductions from historical premisses. To see Jesus' body alive after Good Friday (whether that body be normally or paranormally perceived) does not logically entail any theology of the resurrection. It is consonant with such theologies – indeed they could not be entertained if it were not so – but it is also consonant with the theory (for example) that some men – of whom Jesus was one – survive the death of their bodies for a month or two and that some of them can in this state occasionally communicate with their still embodied friends. So when Cupitt complains that 'the attempt to establish the occurrence of a miracle purely historically with a view to subsequently building a system of doctrine upon it must fail'[14], he is quite right. But the Event and Psi theories only break in his hands because he is trying to make them do too much. He gets them into trouble because he represents them as trying to make theories as to the historical facts do theologiccal and apologetic work which they cannot do. All they *can* do is to suggest theological reflections, and what they suggest theologically will always be a matter for faith rather than proof.

In his discussion of Cupitt's theory, Bruce Shorten[15] points out that Cupitt nowhere refers to Ian Ramsey. He would have done well to do so. Resurrection-faith arises out of the resurrection-narratives very much by the 'disclosure' method which Ian Ramsey made so much of a tool for his own theological apologetic. We look at the records of an Event – an odd event with some logically odd edges to it – and because we have read the gospels and wondered who this person is of whom this event is narrated, we are forced to ask theological questions of it. For some people – not for all, and never logically necessarily – the moment of disclosure comes. It does not come by straightforward inference from the events narrated, nor by logical deduction. There is an infinite qualitative difference between the disclosure and its antecedents. But some people read of the resurrection and are able to say 'My Lord and my God'. Cupitt is right to say that 'Easter faith was born by theological and existential reflection upon the completed life of Jesus'[16], but Moule is also right in insisting that nothing but a resurrection-event could have led to such reflection, or to reflection with such a conclusion. I cannot believe with Cupitt that the disciples could have been so philosophically cerebral as to have produced the resurrection theology without the resurrection appearances, but I can understand with Moule how an appearance (coupled with, and consequent upon, the kind of despairing reflection in which the disciples on the Emmaus road engaged, in the incident related in Luke 24: 19-21) could lead to the radical re-appraisal of one's whole theology inherent in resurrection faith.

But it is still resurrection-*faith*, and not proof of the resurrection, and Cupitt confuses what serves as the spring-board for faith and what could serve as a concrete foundation for proof. It is this which leads him to prefer the Theological theory rather than either of the other two which he mentions. Once remove the confusion, and we are again allowed to say that the theology of the resurrection emerges from the underlying event by way of reflection leading to a situation of disclosure.

When the theology *does* emerge, it will show us (as Cupitt points out) that the Christophany is a crystallization of the meaning of the whole Gospel story. In the words of Christopher Evans, the resurrection stories are intended, not to add to our knowledge of the earthly Jesus, but to place the rest of the stories in the gospels

in a totally new dimension. Like the plus or minus sign in an algebraical formula, they do not belong within the bracket, but outside it, determining anything there may be inside the bracket.[17]

That does not infer that the meaning was wrought out first and the vision came later, but that the vision was seen by later reflection to have this all-embracing theological content.

And the theological content of the resurrection is all-embracing indeed. The resurrection is central to, and constitutive of, all other Christian doctrines. The resurrection is not just one chapter in a book of Christian dogmatics, but the interpretative principle of every chapter. That means that the resurrection comes to us, not as a mere piece of information, but as a claim and a challenge, calling us to an obedience in the today to a still living Lord, whose will must be sought within the ever-changing demands of a secular world. The resurrection must not only be true, it must be true *for us*, and if we are Christians, we are entered into a heritage of resurrection-life. Harry Williams tries to give us the flavour of this life in *The True Resurrection*, in which he vividly pictures the old life where we are bound by the old death-dealing Adam, and the new life where we share in the exhilarating resurrected freedom.

If we have been aware of resurrection in this life, then, and only then, shall we be able or ready to receive the hope of final resurrection after physical death. Resurrection as our final and ultimate future can be known only by those who perceive resurrection with us now encompassing all we are and do. For only then will it be recognized as a country we have already entered and in whose light and warmth we have already lived.[18]

The resurrection of Jesus is not only a past event but a living reality, and our own resurrection is not only a future hope but a present possession. That is why, to return to the incident I mentioned at the beginning of this paper, the resurrection is something to dance about. He *is* risen, we *are* risen. Life after death is no good unless we also believe in life before death. This is for us the meaning of the resurrection, which we are bidden to teach and to preach with all the power and persuasiveness at our disposal. But we cannot preach it unless we have lived it first.

References

1. C.F. Evans, *Resurrection and the New Testament* (SCM Press, Studies in Biblical Theology, second series, 12 (1970)), p. 128.
2. MacMillan USA 1971, SPCK London 1972.
3. *Op. cit.,* p.22.
4. J.A.T. Robinson, *Redating the New Testament* (SCM Press, 1976).
5. W.R. Farmer's *The Synoptic Problem* originally appeared in 1964 (USA, Macmillan) and was noted in an Editorial in *The Expository Times* for October 1965 (Vol. 77, No. 1, pp 1-3). By the time his book was re-issued in 1976 by Western North Carolina Press, his radical ideas about the non-priority of Mark were being less easily shrugged off as an eccentricity – see the editorial in *Expository Times* for June 1977 (Vol. 88, No. 9, pp. 257-60)—but the most recent contribution to the debate, C.M. Tuckett's *The Revival of the Griesbach Hypothesis* (Cambridge, 1983), makes Farmer's arguments seem less likely.
6. R.H. Fuller, *The Formation of the Resurrection Narratives* (SPCK,

1972), p. 153.

7. Willi Marxsen, *The Resurrection of Jesus of Nazareth* (SCM Press, 1970), p. 188 (his italics).

8. *Op. cit.,* n. 1 *supra*, p. 27.

9. *Explorations in Theology* 6 (SCM Press, 1979).

10. 'The Resurrection: A Disagreement', *Theology* Vol. 75 (1972) pp. 507-519, and subsequent correspondence. Reprinted in *op. cit.* n. 9 *supra*.

11. *Christ and the Hiddenness of God* (Lutterworth Press, 1971), esp. pp. 133-167.

12. An attempt was made to do this in *The Easter Enigma* (Faber and Faber, 1959), by the present author.

13. *Op. cit.,* n. 11 *supra*, p. 150.

14. *ibid.,* p.149.

15. *Theology* Vol. 75 (1972) pp. 657 ff.

16. *Theology* Vol. 75 (1972) p. 509.

17. *op. cit.,* n. 1 *supra*, p. 62.

18. H.A. Williams, *The True Resurrection* (Mitchell Beazley, 1972), p. 13.

13

Reincarnation – three reviews

1

Masks of the Soul: The facts behind reincarnation, by Benjamin Walker
(Aquarian Press, 1981).

Of reincarnation, Benjamin Walker asserts that 'the testimony of
tradition is in its favour, while scientific evidence is against it'. Anyone wishing for a straightforward, no-nonsense, unemotional ampli-
fication of that statement would be well served by this volume. Its
bias is anti-reincarnationist, but the arguments on either side, the
major lines of evidence, and their various possible interpretations,
are all fairly and clearly set out, beginning with a survey of the attitudes of various religions and thinkers, and going on to the empirical
evidence – Shanti Devi, Bridey Murphy, Edgar Cayce, Arthur
Guirdham and his group of ostensibly-reincarnated medieval
Cathars, Ian Stevenson's researches into claimed memories of small
children, and the hypnotic regression tapes recorded by Arnall
Bloxham and others. Non-reincarnationist explanations of the data
are advanced (hoax, hysteria, hyperaesthesia, cryptomnesia,
retrocognitive telepathy, discarnate influence, possession, ancestral
memory, prenatal imprinting *in utero*, etc.), and the conclusion is
reached that the soul progresses extra-terrestrially rather than returning to this earth.

There is a bibliography of over two hundred titles which would have been ten times more valuable if annotated, and an index printed in six-point which can be easily read with a good magnifying glass. The treatment is unimaginative, on a subject where advances in understanding will probably only come by a bold leap of lateral thinking: but it does its task competently and clearly, and can be highly commended as a summary of the evidence and arguments so far.

2

Reincarnation – Ancient beliefs and modern evidence, by David Christie-Murray (David and Charles, 1981).

Belief in reincarnation seems to be as ancient as belief in survival of death, and that is as old as belief itself. Since researchers are bringing together an increasing body of data which ostensibly support this doctrine, and since it is being espoused by an increasing number of people in the West, it deserves a careful examination. To do the subject justice needs a polymath, equally well versed in the history of religions, philosophy, and the parapsychological evidence. Mr Christie-Murray has made a good beginning and this volume will be a useful source-book.

It needs, however, to be taken critically. Its first hundred or so pages give a survey of individuals by whom or cultures within which reincarnation has been accepted. I doubt whether this lightning Cook's tour of history, literature, and anthropology will add much to the reader's understanding. Parapsychologists may dismiss it as a mere catalogue of opinions (and in places that is what it degenerates into). The whole section seems to lean suspiciously heavily on a thoroughly tendentious anthology in which many writers and thinkers who do not believe in reincarnation are abbreviated or quoted out of context so as to make it look as if they did. If these chapters are to be of any use at all, the material needs a much more careful and detailed critical look.

Readers of the *Journal* of the Society for Psychical Research will be more interested in the review of the empirical evidence – *déjà vu*, hypnotic regression, the Christos procedure, and ostensibly reincarnationist memories of children and others (including the 'readings' of Edgar Cayce, the monumental work of Dr Ian Stevenson, and the experiences of Dr Guirdham who believes he is one of a group of reincarnated thirteenth-century Albigensian heretics). Here Mr Christie-Murray is more on his home ground, and he leads us through a mass of evidence and conflicting interpretations with a sure touch. We are given a good idea of the type of material available, the amount of it, and the difficulties in assessing it as evidence for what it *prima facie* relates to. Here and there we may cavil at some point of detail – as, for instance, when Mr Christie-Murray fails to tell us that Mrs Tighe, the subject in the 'Bridey Murphy' case, had as a near neighbour in her childhood days a friend called Bridget Murphy (see Eric Cuddon's review of Morey Bernstein's *The Search for Bridey Murphy* in the *Journal* of the Society for Psychical Research, Vol. 38 (1956), p. 377, as against p. 184 of the present book, where Mr Christie-Murray states that Mrs Tighe 'had never visited Ireland or had much to do with Irish people'). But it would be nit-picking to fasten upon such minor points. The fact is that we are here given an invaluable conspectus of all the relevant data, and helped to make up our own minds as to its bearing upon the question at issue. A longish quotation will help to show just how judicious Mr Christie-Murray is:

The many varieties of reincarnation experience illustrated above might be quoted as tending to prove that the doctrine is true. But the argument is double-edged. It might equally show a tendency in the human mind to create for itself illusory reincarnation experience. This inclination might be controlled in the ordinary personality by common sense and the mental faculty that seems to guard the mind against irrelevant intrusions of *psi* material into normal living. But when the censor is removed, by sleep, drugs, or abnormal conditions of some kind, or by deliberate acts as in techniques of mind 'training', the tendency may soar to the surface, proving only that it exists. Much is now known – how much babies in the womb can absorb of the thoughts, convictions and conversations of their parents; how much the mind can affect the embryo physically, a dream becoming a self-fulfilling prophecy . . . There is also the fact that anything remembered from a past life that can be proved from documentary or other evidence can be obtained either normally or paranormally and is therefore always suspect. [pp. 136 f.]

But, grateful as I am to Mr Christie-Murray for setting all this out so clearly, I cannot help thinking that he has made the question look a great deal simpler than it is. There is occasional acknowledgement of the fact that there can be more than one meaning of the term 'reincarnation', but it is generally tacitly assumed that everybody knows instinctively what this book is about. Such optimism I cannot share. What *is* an incarnate human being? What is the relation of his physical body to his total personality? What is the residue of the total personality after the physical body has been abstracted from it? What meaning is to be given to the claim that this residue can be associated with another physical body at a later stage in its continued existence? What is meant by the continuity of this residue through several 'incarnations', particularly if conscious memory of this continuity is at best fitful and at worst non-existent? Is it reasonable to adopt an 'all-or-nothing' approach to the question, or could it perhaps be that what is incarnated is only a part of a greater whole, and that in successive incarnations, different parts or combinations of it are returned to this earth? These are questions which remain to puzzle us, and Mr Christie-Murray's book will not help us wrestle with them. He lists John Hick's *Death and Eternal Life* in his bibliography, but gives no evidence in the text of having read it. He could have improved the usefulness of his book had he done so.

3
Mind out of Time? Reincarnation claims investigated, by Ian Wilson (Gollancz, 1981)

The opening chapters of this examination of the empirical evidence for reincarnation read like a book by a compulsive sceptic who insists on damning by innuendo. Ian Wilson starts with the case of the Pollock twins, born seventeen months after their eleven- and sixteen-year-old sisters were killed in a street accident. They bore birthmarks corresponding to their sisters' scars, they recognized places and toys known to their sisters, and they replayed their emotions as the car ran them down. The birthmarks may have been imprinted *in utero* by their grieving mother, and since the father was a fervent reincarnationist, his unsupported testimony on many of the details must be discounted.

Wilson then moves on to the demolition of the 'Rosemary' case, which claimed to have rediscovered the language of ancient Egypt, and finds this an easy matter. Next, Dr Guirdham, a retired psychiatrist who claims to belong to a group of reincarnated medieval Cathars, is dismissed because some of the group were his patients and he stoutly resists all attempts to contact any of them. Guirdham's claims, lacking any means of independent verification, must be regarded as unacceptable ... He must be said to have thrown away every chance of being taken seriously'. Was it a *folie à deux*, with patients having 'crushes' on their doctor, so that collective imagination ran riot until this whole business got out of hand?

On, then, to Ian Stevenson of the University of Virginia, whose painstaking and scholarly researches into 'cases suggestive of reincarnation' are, Wilson admits, 'slowly winning a grudging respect among the scientific community'. Most of his cases are of young children who tell their parents that they have 'really' come from a different family. Has he 'been cruelly misled by a series of tall stories and acting performances'? Wilson points out that some of Stevenson's investigators did not speak the language of the children they investigated, and others may be suspected of personal bias. There is no logical or consistent pattern to his cases, as regards length of time between incarnations or geographical or nationality links between them (perhaps the answer is, simply, that there isn't). The only consistency is that most of the Indian children claimed to have originated within a higher caste. Are they really 'rather unpleasant little boys putting on a thinly disguised act to earn themselves better food and an exemption from drudgery'? Wilson concludes that there are 'serious grounds for believing that Stevenson may have let through rather more fraudulent cases than he would care to concede'.

If this were all there were to Wilson's hatchet job on the evidence for reincarnation, it might have damaged a few details, but it would not need to be taken very seriously as evidence that the whole case were untenable. When, however, he comes on to hypnotic regression and similar cases, he becomes a great deal more convincing. The 'Bridey Murphy' case of 1952 shows every sign of a frantic exercise in American popular investigative journalism, and we shall probably never unravel truth from the surrounding razzmatazz; but in the more recent work of hypnotherapists such as Bloxham and Keeton, it is easier to check out some details. Keeton, for example, has conducted over nine thousand claimed past-life regressions and is therefore a prime candidate for inclusion in the *Guinness Book of Records.* The personalities which emerge during regressions are amazingly full-blooded, fluent, and realistic – a Roman matron from third-century Britain, a Jewess in a mediaeval *pogrom*, a Jesuit priest, gutter-urchins and serving-girls. 'All human life is there', with a wealth of circumstantial detail at once the dream and desperation of the historical researcher, who knows what an immense task of investigation lies before him. Frequently, the 'past life' is of a character totally at variance with the conscious subject – in attitudes, behaviour, beliefs, education, and even in sex. Some speak languages unknown to the waking subject.

Suspicion is aroused when we notice that the pattern of claimed former lives 'differ from each other precisely in accordance with the hypnotist's preconceived ideas', for example in the range of possible reincarnations and the intervals between them. Many of the details of former lives are proved to be historically inaccurate, and often owe more to popular mythology than to historical fact (e.g., a Viking helmet did not ordinarily have the wings and horns with which most people visualize it). These strictures do not seem to the present reviewer to be conclusive. Parapsychologists are used to less-than-perfect ESP. Perhaps what the reincarnation debate wants are sufficient statistical comparisons to show whether the degree of success in describing a former life was more than coincidentally significant.

In some cases, however, the source of the subject's information about details of his claimed 'past life' can be traced. He may have heard snatches of conversation, or looked at books, many years ago. Consciously they have been forgotten, but the details remain access-ible to the hypnotized self. These may then be mixed with invented names and details so that the resultant amalgam is not easy to unscramble. An example is the ostensible seventeenth-century Jesuit priest who produces some accurate details of his surroundings and is a convincing characterization, yet his name cannot be found in the Jesuit records and, though he can conjugate a Latin verb, he cannot say his 'Our Father' in that language. The powers of cryptomnesia have been investigated by Dr Reima Kampmann of the University of Oulu in Finland. Subjects are first regressed to give details of a former existence. On a subsequent regression they are taken less far back -- to the occasion in their childhood when they acquired the information on which that 'former existence' was based. Wilson believes that this shows that (e.g.) Keeton's subjects, anxious to please their hypnotist, are obligingly using cryptomnesia to build up a convincing 'past life'. He does not consider the possibility that Kampmann's subject may equally likely be trying to please *his* hypnotist by producing a convincing story about having read a book about that 'past life' in early childhood.

If, however, Wilson is right and cryptomnesia provides the data for the 'script' of the 'past life', how can we account for the convinc-ing way in which the subject takes that 'script' and makes of it a realistic total personality?

The answer is in the concept of multiple personality. Para-psychologists know of Jekyll and Hyde in fiction, Morton Prince's nineteenth-century cases, and the 'Three Faces of Eve' by Thigpen and Cleckley. Chris Sizemore ('Eve') alternated between 'White' and 'Black' personalities which were almost mirror images. In between, her face itself would change before her psychiatrist's amazed gaze, through an 'eerie blank', to the visage of the new character. Exactly the same phenomenon is observed between characters in hypnotic regressions. In Mrs Sizemore's case, a third, more balanced, 'Jane' personality took over, but before she reached her ultimate psychological balance, several other more fragmented and bizarre personalities came to the surface for briefer periods, and 'Jane' had to die before the cure was complete. In such cases of multiple personality, there is usually some causative stress which precedes the dissociation.

Is there sufficient parallel between these cases and past-life regressions to postulate similar aetiologies? Wilson believes so, and draws further parallels – e.g., the stigmata of Catholic devotion, and other traumatic abreactions, show that physical markings similar to those called in evidence for cases of reincarnation can be psychologically caused. He concludes that there is 'very little doubt that every single element of the acting displayed in past life regressions can be explained within the mechanism of multiple personality'. Though the subjects find it incredible that they should be capable of creating such a polished performance, and cannot believe that it is all a pure mental fabrication, it is well-established that the subconscious is quite capable of such feats. They can be demonstrated by hypnotic 'party tricks' in which subjects carry out the most astonishing dramatizations of the creative imagination which are quite impossible to them in their normal state of consciousness. The hidden part of the personality, commanded by the hypnotist to produce a 'past life' story, draws from forgotten memories of relevant information, supplements them with appropriate corroborative but fictional detail, and produces something which so amazes the subject that he cannot possibly believe it is attributable to his own capabilities.

Wilson believes that similar mechanisms may explain past-life 'memories' which occur in trance or dream rather than under hypnosis. For example, he looks at Edward Ryall's *Second Time Round* (not, incidentally, *Around*, as he consistently mis-titles it) and finds that the subject took his childhood memries of imaginative writing (such as *Lorna Doone*) and wove around them a likely tale about a seventeenth-century Somerset yeoman farmer named John Fletcher. Fletcher and his farm cannot be traced in any historical record, because they are as fictional as any character of Blackmore's. In some cases, we can actually see cryptomnesia at work. Keeton regressed a subject to become Joan Waterhouse, the Chelmsford witch. The 'past-life' character faithfully reproduced the one historical error in the only readily-available account of the relevant trial.

Ian Wilson is an historian, not a psychologist, though he has the professional help of his wife and of other specialists. On the showing of the evidence carefully built up in this book, the reviewer must perforce agree with him that if the case for reincarnation is to be sustained, it must be built on data other than those of hypnotic regression cases.

14
Reincarnation – a Christian option?

My children were playing a kind of 'space invaders' game on the computer the other day. If they got it right, they scored, but if they didn't, they got shot down and the programme collapsed. When that happened, the message flashed on the screen – 'Unfortunately you have been killed. Would you like another go?'

That seems as good a text as any with which to begin talking about reincarnation. After you have been killed, would you like another go? The idea of reincarnation has been familiar in the East for very many years. Only recently has it thrust itself upon the minds of large numbers in the West who are heirs to a long Christian tradition. Nonetheless, it is enjoying a remarkable popularity at present. Recent opinion polls have shown that about one person in three or four in the UK now holds such a belief. It rose from an average of 18 per cent in 1968 to 28 per cent in 1979, and the highest proportion of believers in reincarnation was that in women aged between 25 and 34.[1]

On a more intellectual level, a number of Christian theologians has recently examined this belief. Probably the most substantial treatment still remains that of John Hick in his *Death and Eternal Life*[2] but the most recent known to me is Geddes MacGregor's *Reincarnation as a Christian Hope.*[3] Two issues of *The Christian Parapsychologist* in the last two or three years have carried symposia on the subject.[4] Studies and discussions on the empirical evidence pour out of the presses. Of them, the most significant are the researches of Ian Stevenson, Carlson Professor of Psychiatry at the University of Virginia Medical School,[5] and the evaluative volumes by Benjamin Walker, David Christie-Murray, and Ian Wilson, all of which were first published in 1981.[6]

How should Christians react to this situation? And how should they evaluate the evidence which is being set before them? The first requisite is that they should be aware of the empirical evidence and the interpretations that have been put upon it. As with any aspect of parapsychology, that puts us at once into an ambiguous position. Not only is it desperately hard to establish the facts, because of the human propensity for believing hearsay and gossip, and the human difficulty in telling the difference between truth and welcome fantasy, and because of the human willingness to fabricate evidence to accord with one's own beliefs; but, even when the facts have been reasonably well established, there is then the problem of agreeing on their interpretation. It seems as if it is possible to argue till the end of time about whether parapsychological facts necessarily entail any particular way of interpreting them.

There are four main strands of evidence being used in modern arguments in favour of reincarnation:

1. Child geniuses. The mathematical or musical marvel children – the Mozarts of this world who have skills that no normal child has, and do not seem to have to learn them. Reincarnationists claim that such children must have carried their skills over from a previous life.

2. The sense of *déjà vu*. People come to a house or a place they have never seen before, and feel and know that they are already familiar with it. Before turning the corner, or going into the next room, they know what they are going to find there – and they are proved right. Have they been there in a previous incarnation, and is the visit stirring memories of what happened before they were born?

3. Dr Ian Stevenson has done extensive research on children who begin to talk about their 'former' homes or families and repudiate their present ones. Some adults, also, claim 'memories' of former lives, such as Dr Guirdham and his group of friends who believe they are reincarnations of medieval Cathars from Languedoc,[7] or Edward Ryall who identified himself with John Fletcher, a seventeenth-century Somerset yeoman farmer who died at the battle of Sedgemoor.[8]

4. Under hypnotic regression, some people not only remember incidents from their youth and childhood, or even the very birth trauma itself, but events which 'happened' to them before then. Mrs Tighe believed herself to be a reincarnation of the nineteenth-century Irish girl Bridey Murphy,[9] and hundreds of patients have been regressed to former lives under the hypnotic influence of Joe Keeton.[10]

In all of these cases, reincarnation is a *prima facie* explanation, but it is by no means unambiguously necessary as an inference from the data. In all four groups, other possible readings of the evidence are worth considering. Thus:

1. Child geniuses are as good an argument for pre-existence as for reincarnation. The soul may have existed in some other form or dimension or world before coming to this earth, and some few rare souls may bring them skills from their pre-mundane life. I think that less likely, however, than the supposition that the brain is a poor instrument for the mind to work through. It only works at a very small percentage of its theoretically available potential. May it not be that the occasional and exceptional genius is the person whose brain allows his mind to operate – in some one particular way, whether mathematical or musical – at well over the normal percentage of efficiency? These genuises are, on this supposition, not reincarnated beings, but examples of what human beings can be if their potential is more efficiently exploited.

2. There are several other possible alternative explanations of *déjà vu* besides that which involves reincarnation. One such is that there may be a temporal displacement within the brain, possibly involving the two hemispheres, so that the same material comes to conscious awareness by two different routes at two slightly different times, and this gives the impression that what is being perceived has been known in consciousness beforehand. For myself, I would prefer a parapsychological explanation – perhaps that there had been a sub-consciously perceived precognition of the scene beforehand, or even a contemporaneous clairvoyance of the room or scene just around the corner, which never came fully into the conscious mind. When the person comes to the place which had been precognized, or clairvoyantly perceived a moment or two previously, it says 'I have seen this before'.

3. Many alleged cases of memories of former lives turn out on closer inspection to be less impressive than they have been claimed. An often-quoted example is Shanti Devi, from Delhi, who claimed to be a reincarnation of Ludgi, who lived about a hundred miles away. When Ludgi's widower came to see Shanti, she immediately recognized him. What the books which cite this case do not often say is that he often visited Delhi and frequently stopped at a place within a few yards of Shanti's house, so that she could quite easily have picked up information about him by normal means. 'The manner of investigation', claims Benjamin Walker in his study of the case, was 'amateurish and wide-eyed, and tending to sensationalism'.[11] By the time Dr Ian Stevenson came to make his investigation of the circumstances, it was already twenty-five years old. That is far too late for a scientific study which depends for its strength on the accuracy of reporting of events.

Arthur Guirdham's books about reincarnations of a group of mediaeval Cathars all depend upon his own unsupported word, and he has resolutely refused to allow the names of the other members of his group to be disclosed, let alone for them to be interviewed or questioned. The case bears many of the marks of the classical *folie à deux* in which two or more people collude in their fantasies as the psychological temperature builds up. Guirdham's books about the Cathars are riddled with amateurish historical errors.[12]

Edward Ryall's book claims that he was John Fletcher, who died at the Battle of Sedgemoor in the seventeenth century. On careful examination[13] it is seen that many of the correct historical details come from books which Ryall would have known of as a child, or from such historical romances as *Lorna Doone*. Details which did *not* occur in such sources – such as names and places – prove, when examined, to be fictitious.

4. Finally, the hypnotic regression cases. These have been examined in some detail by Ian Wilson.[14] As in the case of Ryall/Fletcher, many of these accounts can be explained in terms of unconscious recall of the details of historical books or historical romances which the subject had read many years beforehand. These buried memories formed the base on which the subjects had then, under hypnosis, woven a fictitious narrative in which they play a leading part. In case after case, historical research verifies details of the 'reincarnated personality' as having arisen from statements in books which the subject had read, and fails to verify, or positively falsifies, statements which cannot be shown to have their origin in

such a source. It is particularly damning to the reincarnationist view when the hypnotized subject reproduces the historical errors of the source-material. What is more, we now know a great deal about the psychology of secondary personalities, and – point for point – the behaviour of subjects undergoing hypnotic regression has been shown to be identical with the behaviour-pattern of subjects who manifest secondary personalities. It looks as if the subject under hypnosis determined to produce the kind of story the hypnotist wanted to hear, and obligingly did so. The material for this dramatic presentation came from early memories of books read long ago, and the method of presentation was by the splitting off of a secondary personality under hypnosis, which claimed to be an earlier incarnation of the subject.

As with so many aspects of parapsychology, presently available evidence does not allow us to come to a firm decision one way or the other, but it does show us that the case may be argued in more than one direction. We need a lot more empirical data yet, but indications are that it will not be wanting, as the subject is a very lively one, and investigations are proceeding apace on a number of fronts. When we have a greater body of evidence and have subjected it to the most rigorous examination, and have devised ways of deciding between the various alternative explanations of the data, we may be in a position to see whether reincarnation is as natural an explanation as its proponents claim. We will probably be in for an interesting few years ahead, and at this stage I would not like to forecast a verdict.

That being so, are there other considerations which might help us make up our minds? Let me speak alliteratively. Christians look for a truth which will satisfy their intellects, their intuitions, and their incorporation. Their intellects, because God has given them their minds, to examine evidence and explore its implications. That is the way of the logician and the philosopher, the way of the brain's left hemisphere. But it is not the only way of arriving at the kind of understanding which satisfies the whole man. The way of intuition is a more personal approach. It is the way of the poet or the artist or the musician, the way of the right hemisphere of the brain. If it becomes obvious, as perhaps it has to the reader of the last few pages, that there is more than one tolerable way of interpreting the reincarnation evidence, then we have to ask to what interpretation we personally resonate. What seems to make sense to us as a total interpretation of our world? If we use only our intellect, we may for ever sit astride a very uncomfortable fence. If we have to declare ourselves, one way or the other, then it is our intuition which decides which explanation is most satisfying. Our judgement will depend on what we think reasonable. Each of us has his own set of axioms which make sense of the world for him, and from which he constructs his world-picture. It is in the light of these that he decides how to interpret ambiguous evidence.

That sounds (as it is) a very subjective business. How can we get beyond the position in which every individual has his own peculiar set of presuppositions within which he intuits his idiosyncratic answer to the conundrums of life? To a large extent, it will depend on the beliefs of the community within which he has been formed. That brings me to the third way in which a truth may satisfy the person who apprehends it – the way I have characterized by the word 'incorporation'. Incorporation implies a body or a community of which we are a part, and which has its own tradition or orthodoxy.

The authority of tradition is not absolute, and it can always be challenged; but tradition creates a mental predisposition and needs to be taken seriously. We do not settle an empirical question by seeing what Biblical texts bear upon it, or whether it was taught in the early Church, or what Origen really wrote, or how or on what grounds the Council of Constantinople declared his doctrines anathema; nor do we settle the question by producing a catena of passages from thinkers who have taken the doctrine of reincarnation on board. But tradition has its weight in that, if the main stream of Christian theology has found no place for a particular doctrine, even if there are a few texts which can be argued into line with it and a few thinkers scattered through the centuries who have been brave enough (or rash enough) to challenge the otherwise universal tradition, then Christians will begin by being predisposed against it. If the evidence forces them to take an opposite view, they must always be ready to have to do so; but it will not happen readily and easily. In the face of ambiguous evidence, the weight of presumption is necessarily in favour of retaining the traditional understanding. It means something, to be incorporate within the Church and an heir of its continuing traditions.

Let us therefore look at the Christian tradition in respect of reincarnation, to see how the idea sits with Biblical religion and subsequent theology.

It must be admitted that the evidence is sparse. A number of Old Testament texts have been adduced to show that reincarnation was a permissible option in late Judaism, but they can all be given alternative and entirely convincing interpretations. Several texts which have been pressed into service refer not to reincarnation but to the pre-existence of the soul in some non-earthly pre-mundane realm: such being the meaning of Jeremiah 1: 4-5 or Wisdom 8: 19-20 ('Before I formed you in the womb I knew you for my own; before you were born I consecrated you, I appointed you a prophet to the nations'; 'As a child I was born to excellence, and a noble soul fell to my lot; or rather, I myself was noble, and I entered into an unblemished body'). If the passage in Proverbs 8:22-31 is intended to refer to King Solomon, the same is true – it speaks of pre-existence, not of reincarnation. In fact, it is not Solomon who is in view here, but Wisdom, which is being spoken of in quasi-human terms and is being made to say that 'The LORD possessed me in the beginning of his works, before all else that he made'. Job 14:14 is speculating on the possibility of a man in She'ol (the abode of the dead) being able to live again, not the possibility of his being reincarnated. Psalm 90:3 ('Thou turnest man into dust, saying, Return again, you children of men') does not mean that when men have been turned to dust they can expect to return again to this earth. It is Hebrew poetic parallelism whereby the same thought is repeated a second time. Man is not expecting to return to another incarnation, but to return to the dust of the earth from which he was made. The relevance of Ecclesiastes 1: 9-11 is doubtful. Admittedly it tells us that 'What has happened will happen again . . . Is there anything of which one can say, "Look, this is new"? No, it has already existed, long ago before our time'. The statement is an expression of the doctrine of the cyclical nature of history, uncharacteristic of the rest of Jewish orthodoxy. It does not say that the individual soul has existed on earth previously in another body. Finally, Malachi 4:4-5, 'Behold, I send you Elijah the prophet before the great and terrible day of the LORD, speaks of something which is to happen once only, as history gives way to the end of time itself. It has nothing to do with the normal expectations of normal Israelites.

During the inter-testamental period, there was a great deal of speculation and development of doctrine regarding the afterlife, so that it is not surprising that reincarnation was one of the possibilities to be canvassed. Josephus tells us that the Pharisees 'say that all souls are incorruptible: but that the souls of good men are only removed into other bodies, but that the souls of bad men are subject to eternal punishment'.[15] Whether those 'other bodies' were earthly bodies of a subsequent incarnation, or whether they were heavenly bodies given to the souls of good men in order that they could enjoy the delights of their new existence, is not stated. If there was any substantial body of belief in reincarnation within the Judaism of the time of Jesus, it has left precious few literary remains. Perhaps this was what was in mind when Jesus was asked (John 9:2) whether a man born blind was being punished for his own sin or for that of his parents. Jesus gives no support to any possible reincarnationist overtones of this question, but simply answers that being born blind was not for anything like that reason.

There was speculation going round that Jesus himself might have been a reincarnation of Elijah (fulfilling the Malachi passage to which we have already referred), or Jeremiah (Matthew 16:13f); and he himself, according to Matthew 11:14, taught that John the Baptist was 'Elijah who was to come', though John himself is said to have denied this (John 1:21). As we have seen, however, this expectation of the return of Elijah should not be thought of as an example of a general principle of the possibility of reincarnation, but as the unique precursor of the Day of the Lord and the end of the present Age.

When one looks at the New Testament as a whole, it is inconceivable that Christians of that generation could have held reincarnation as a possible option. They were dominated by the belief that the world was coming to an end in the lifetime of the majority of them (see, for example, Mark 13:30; 1 Thess. 4:15; and 2 Peter 3: 3-10). There would simply not be enough time left to the world for there to be any more incarnations. The concept which inspires the New Testament writings is that of resurrection – Christ's as first-fruits, and our own in his train.

In subsequent Christian centuries, when the urgency of the expectation of the Coming of Jesus had somewhat abated, things were different. Christianity was making its way in the Mediterranean world of Greek and Hellenistic thought, and there were frequent attempts to assimilate the ideas of current philosophy within the Christian faith. The Fathers – especially of the third, fourth, and fifth centuries – can on occasions be seen to be toying with the idea of reincarnation. This must, however, not be over-estimated. As with the Old Testament references at which we glanced, so with many Patristic *dicta*; it is more often pre-existence than reincarnation which they discussed. Christian thinkers who write of the pre-existence of the soul do not necessarily teach that it pre-existed this incarnation by a previous earthly life. Pre-existence is usually thought of as being in a different *milieu* altogether. That is certainly true of the writer of the Wisdom of Solomon (8: 19-20) and of Origen[16] despite those who would claim him for the reincarnationist camp.

Eventually, speculations about reincarnation were banned from Christianity, and great 'No through road' notices erected. The methods by which this was secured, it needs to be admitted, were not always creditable. Those centuries included some particularly nasty examples of ecclesio-political skullduggery. The truths of doctrines were seldom left to shine by their own light. The ancients know quite as much as we do about how to pack Synods and make sure the voting went their own way. There is a lot of ancient Christian history of which the Church has little reason to be proud. But those who would have us believe that reincarnation was an accepted belief in the early Church and that it was eliminated by means of which the morality is highly dubious, are misreading the evidence. Speculations about reincarnation were attempts to make of Christianity what it did not profess to be, and they were entertained only by an unrepresentative minority of thinkers. They were unceremoniously thrown out, but they were never likely to have converted the Church as a whole. Those who today try to persuade Christians of the truth of reincarnation cannot credibly claim that they are restoring an ancient Christian doctrine to its true place. They are following in the wake of idiosyncratic thinkers who were never able to persuade the bulk of Christianity to their way of looking at things.

Today, we are in a more pluralistic environment, and speculation can be freer than has been possible for many centuries. There is, too, a new awareness of, and a new respect for, Eastern concepts which need to be examined on their merits. And, as we have seen, there is a deal of empirical evidence which, though not compelling in its implications, is at any rate compatible with a belief in reincarnation. In these circumstances, how are Christians to react?

The faith of the Church is expressed in the catholic creeds, which include an affirmation of belief in the Communion of Saints, the Resurrection of the Body, and the Life Everlasting. No doctrine of reincarnation can be acceptable that does not take full account of these beliefs. Any doctrine of the fate of the individual after death has to be a legitimate interpretation of, or a legitimate development from, them. In particular, it must be compatible with a belief in the Communion of Saints.

We who are Christians here are part of the same body –

incorporate – with all God's people; not only the world over, but throughout time. Oceans divide, the Eucharist unites; and that is as true of the wide blue Atlantic as it is of the narrow black waters of the Styx. 'Neither death nor life', said Paul (Romans 8:38-9), 'shall be able to separate us from the love of God, which is in Christ Jesus our Lord.' If we are incorporate with him before death, we are incorporate with him through death, and we remain incorporate with him after death. This is a status which death cannot destroy. In Christ we are united with all who are united with him – both sides of the grave.

That means we may communicate with them. Not that we must, nor that we shall, but that we may. Death is not an absolute bar to communication. It is possible to keep the channels open. Not always, not always consciously, not always verbally. But there *can* be communication. Sometimes it comes through intuition and a sense of presence. Sometimes it comes through subliminal activity. Sometimes it comes in automatic writing or trance speech. Sometimes it comes through so apparently ridiculous a means as poltergeist activity[17], as if the communicating entity is so frustrated at being unable to attract the attention of the surviving person that he has to use the silliest and most childish ways of drawing attention to himself and his need to be in touch. Sometimes it comes through a third person, a medium with a control. Sometimes it comes through auditory or visual hallucination. Sometimes it happens once and never again, sometimes it continues intermittently for decades, sometimes it happens (in automatic writing or through the practice of meditation) regularly at pre-set intervals. But it can happen. There is communication.

But we cannot demand it. It is obvious that not every departed person communicates and not every remaining partner receives communications. It does not seem to follow any particular rules or laws. It is not the cleverest, or the most prayerful, or the most spiritual, or even the most in need of reassurance, who receive communications. Some people receive messages without seeking for them, and others look in vain for years.

Not everyone is in communication. But we can all be in communion. Our links with the departed are in Christ, and in him there is certainty. 'Lo, I am with you always, even unto the end of the age' (Matthew 28:20). So the departed can help us and we can help them. The communion is a communion in prayer, in fellowship, and in Eucharist. The departed pray for us and we may pray for them.[18] We no more know how many of the departed are praying for us than we know how many of our Christian friends here on earth are doing the same. Nor do we know the power of their prayers for us, or the effect of our prayers on them. That is part of the mystery of prayer. All we *do* know is that prayer is a powerful instinct, given by God, and therefore not given by God to mock us. It must have a purpose, and it must have some effect. So we maintain our links with the unseen world by prayer and in the Eucharist. That is communion. Sometimes communication is added to communion. When it seems to be, we must first of all be cautious and critical, because in matters psychical it is so easy to be deceived. But if we are satisfied that this is indeed genuine communication, we should praise God for it, and use it to his glory. It is a marvellous and sacred thing.

Christians, therefore, hold on to the doctrine of the Communion of Saints as a communion which transcends death. They cannot accept any kind of reincarnationist doctrine which compromises that teaching.

Of course, doctrines develop. We do not today, for example, believe in the same kind of everlasting punishment as our forbears in the faith did, nor do we believe that we are condemned to it for the same reasons as they believed. But we have to be careful that any development of doctrine is along legitimate lines. Can there be any development of the doctrine of the Communion of Saints that leaves room for any form of reincarnationist teaching?

Any such doctrine will have to take account of the fact that we are all individuals and that individuals differ. It is no good suggesting that exactly the same thing happens to everybody. One of my difficulties in accepting Joe Keeton's accounts of hypnotic regression[19] is that he believes that everybody is reincarnated immediately upon death. That creates several difficulties. Not only does it put everyone into too tight a strait-jacket. It runs into trouble as soon as we consider the implications of a rising world population over the centuries. Either all souls are pre-existent and created at the same moment in time, or they may be created as required when bodies are ready for them. If the second is true, then there is no need to re-cycle souls; new ones can be created for new bodies, and after the death of the body they can be free to pursue whatever transmundane pilgrimage awaits them. If, on the other hand, there was an original creation of a finite number of souls, then only a certain number of these can be incarnate at any one time. As the world population grows, so the percentage of souls which are incarnate, rises with it. That knocks on the head any idea that reincarnation follows either immediately after the death of the body or at any invariable interval thereafter. Souls would have to queue up for bodies to inhabit. In the overcrowded world of the twentieth century, perhaps, that queue might be a short one, but in ancient times, when the world contained so much smaller a number of people, the wait must have taken centuries or even millenia.

We can avoid impasses like this if we realize that there may be different expectations for different individuals. Perhaps what the reincarnation debate is waiting for is that genius who will come to the problem and take a great quantum leap forward which will enable us to look at the debate from an entirely new standpoint, from which our difficulties and our mental blocks will look nothing like so intractable as they do at present. If, so, it is my hunch that that viewpoint will look even more novel to us than the viewpoint of Copernicus looked to his contemporaries. One thing that this new approach will free us from is the idea that a single set of options can apply to every distinct individual, or that there is any necessary pattern to be discerned in advance of a consideration of the character and spiritual pilgrimage of each separate person.

We have almost certainly been too timid by half in the kind of scenarios within which we have allowed ourselves to speculate. Why should the options be limited to the simple three of extinction for all, survival for all, and reincarnation for all? Why should each one of us have to conform to the same option? Is God not capable of tailoring our future to the needs of our present and the constraints that our past have put upon the personality which now describes us? Perhaps reincarnation is only necessary for some and not for all. Perhaps some of us – by the grace of God, certainly not through our deserving – find redemption through Christ and incorporation into his body and membership of the Communion of Saints in this world and can then (and therefore) progress after death through the lives of other worlds to come, whilst others of us do not meet Christ this time (or not in that conscious way which brings us into a saving relationship with him) and therefore do not become incorporate in him and don't become a part of the Communion of Saints and therefore by the grace and goodness and generosity of God have to be given a second chance, and can come back to this earth (perhaps time and time again) until that incorporation is granted to us and we can be redeemed through Christ from that terrible wheel of rebirth. I do not know. But that *might* be a form of the doctrine of reincarnation which could be consistent with a form of the doctrine of the Communion of Saints. It would be a universalist doctrine, in that it would require God to save every human soul in the end, and consign none to the damnation of the eternal loss of his presence in hell. But I am a universalist in any case, so that objection to the formulation would not worry me. Instead of hell, God might consign the impenitent or spiritually immature or those ignorant of him to another round of earthly life. It would be like returning to re-sit an examination in which we have not done well enough to proceed to another level of our education. Reincarnation must always be seen as a second best option; those who see it as desirable in itself have not begun to consider the length and breadth and depth and height of the love of God, and the things he has prepared for those who love him, which pass human understanding. Those who look forward to a further incarnation have – on this view – begun, by their very poverty of expectation, to deserve it.

Or here is another possibility. We know that our conscious mind is but the tip of the iceberg of the total human personality. Perhaps even what we think of as our total (conscious, preconscious, subconscious, and unconscious) human personality as known in any earthly incarnation is likewise only a fraction of our total self? If so, then perhaps different portions of our total self may come to earth in successive incarnations, bearing some kind of 'family resemblance' to each other, and perhaps having some degree of overlap with each other, so that there are moments or situations in which a human person on this earth, one segment of his Total Self, can realize his links with a previously-incarnated person who was a different segment of that same Total Self?[20] Dr Kenneth Ring surmises that the near-death experience, when it includes the meeting with a great Being of Light, may be an experience of becoming aware of that Self of which our incarnate personality is but a segment.[21] Perhaps different segments have to incarnate one by one until the whole has been exposed to the test of life on this earth, and can then move on as a totality to fresh pilgrimages in an extra-terrestrial environment. That is another reincarnationist speculation which might be formulated in such a way as not to deny the doctrines of the Communion of Saints and the Life of the World to come. It might, indeed, need to be united with some form of the preceding speculation before it was satisfactory as an option within Christian theology.

These are no more than speculations. They are intended to show that it is still admissable to allow our minds to entertain novel ideas, so long as they are tested against the touchstone of a Christian understanding. At this stage, when so many bewildering ideas are being floated, I would plead for that tolerance and openness of mind which is ready to look at any idea which is canvassed, and to try and see how it could be formulated in a way which maintains a Christian attitude to the world. The straightforward, monochrome, belief in reincarnation which is being pressed by the more unimaginative of its proponents seems to be to be an unattractive doctrine and one to which I find it difficult to warm. It is theologically suspect, empirically impossible to prove and philosophically difficult to justify. Theologically, much more can be made of a scheme which involves a series of lives in a series of future worlds than of one which requires us to come back here time and time again. I can see nothing appealing about a return to this earth, when there are so many transmundane explorations to look forward to. I have known Christ (fitfully, and often as through a glass, darkly) in this world and I long to be in a world where I can know him better. When this present pilgrimage is over, I want to come closer to seeing him face to face. Reincarnation would be a punishment, not a promise. Empirically, I can find non-reincarnationist explanations for all the reported cases 'suggestive of reincarnation'. Philosophically, I do not know what is meant by a 'soul' which can detach itself from one body and be inserted into another with no memories (or only a few and fitful memories) of its former life.

That is why reincarnation does not appeal to me. But I should like to think I am open enough to consider the possibility that there are forms of reincarnationist doctrine which might be consistent with Christian truth. At all events I would not like to deny a theological examination to such speculations as I have indulged in on these last few pages. There is need of a great deal more theological work in the whole area. If I had to end with a single sentence to sum up the position to date in this whole debate, I would take it from a Christian thinker of a generation ago who said 'Hold to Christ, and for the rest be totally uncommitted'.[22] I must hold to Christ, the incarnate Word of the Father, the Logos made flesh, God's ultimate Word which cannot be superseded. I am in business because Jesus is the Christ, and to him I will hold to my dying day, and I will do all in my power to bring others to hold to him. For the rest, I am still on pilgrimage. I do not hold myself to have apprehended all truth, but this one thing I do, I press toward the mark (Phil. 3: 12-14). Hold to Christ, and for the rest be totally uncommitted!

References

1. As reported in the Gallup Poll in the *Daily Telegraph* for 15 April 1979.

2. John Hick, *Death and Eternal Life* (Collins, 1976), esp. pp. 297-396.

3. Geddes MacGregor, *Reincarnation as a Christian Hope* (Macmillan Library of Philosophy and Religion, 1982).

4. Vol. 3, No. 4 (September 1979) and Vol. 4, No. 4 (December 1981). Published by the Churches' Fellowship for Psychical and Spiritual Studies, St Mary Abchurch, London EC4N 7BA.

5. Ian Stevenson, *Twenty Cases Suggestive of Reincarnation* (American Society for Psychical Research, 1966; second edition, revised and enlarged, University Press of Virginia 1974); *Cases of the Reincarnation Type* (University Press of Virginia; Vol. 1, *Ten Cases in India*, 1975, Vol. 2, *Ten Cases in Sri Lanka*, 1977, Vol. 3, *Twelve Cases in Lebanon and Turkey*, 1980).

6. Benjamin Walker, *Masks of the Soul* (Aquarian Press); David Christie-Murray, *Reincarnation – Ancient Beliefs and Modern Evidence* (David and Charles); Ian Wilson, *Mind out of time?* (Gollancz).

7. Arthur Guirdham, *The Cathars and Reincarnation*, and *We Are One Another* (1970 and 1974; paperback re-issue, Turnstone Press, 1982).

8. E.W. Ryall, *Second Time Round* (Neville Spearman, 1974).

9. Morey Bernstein, *The Search for Bridey Murphy* (Hutchinson, 1956).

10. Peter Moss and Joe Keeton, *Encounters with the Past* (Sidgwick and Jackson 1979). Similar material is presented by Glenn Williston and Judith Johnstone in *Soul Search: Spiritual Growth through a Knowledge of Past Lifetimes* (Turnstone, 1983).

11. B. Walker, *op. cit.* (n. 6 *supra*), p. 48.

12. See, for example, the review of Guirdham's *The Great Heresy* by A.J. Forey, Senior Lecturer in History at the University of Durham, in *The Christian Parapsychologist* Vol. 2, No. 2 (June 1978), pp. 52-4.

13. See especially Ian Wilson (*op. cit. supra*, n. 6), pp. 187-195.

14. *Op. cit. supra*, n. 6, *passim*.

15. Josephus, *Bell. Jud.* II, 8. 14.

16. See the careful analysis by Dr Gerald Bostock in *The Christian Parapsychologist* Vol. 4, No. 4 (December 1981), pp. 113-8, 'Origen and reincarnation'.

17. As it appeared to do in the case of Bishop Pike whose son committed suicide and allegedly communicated with him thereafter – see James A. Pike with Diane Kennedy, *The Other Side* (W.H. Allen, 1969). Doubt has been cast on the case by William Stringfellow and Anthony Towne in *The Death and Life of Bishop Pike* (NY, Doubleday, 1975) – see Leslie Price in *The Christian Parapsychologist* Vol. 1,

No. 9 (September 1977), pp. 148-9.

18. *Prayer and the Departed* – a report of the Archbishops' Commission on Christian Doctrine (SPCK, 1971).

19. Moss and Keeton, *op. cit.* n. 10 *supra.*

20. See Edwin Butler, 'Serial Consciousness' in *Light* Vol. 98, No. 1, (Spring 1978) pp. 17-24. The idea is akin to Hindu doctrines of successive incarnations of parts of the Atman. See David Christie-Murray 'The Evidence for Reincarnation' in *Psychical Studies* No. 32 (Summer 1983), p. 3.

21. Kenneth Ring, *Life at Death* (NY, Coward, McCann and Geoghegan, 1980), p. 240.

22. Who was this? My memory says it was Herbert Butterfield, but I have not been able to run this quotation to earth. Any help would be gladly received.

Part 6
Preaching

The essays and papers so far printed in this volume represent (so to speak) the tip of the iceberg of a considerable amount of study. If a Christian priest is to justify spending so much of his time on this subject, it is bound to reflect in his preaching. Not that I often find myself using parapsychology as grist to my sermonic mill. It is only one small part of total reality, and if I were to become one-track-minded about it in my proclamation of the Gospel, what a bore I should have become! But sometimes it surfaces, and I wish to end with a small selection of sermons where psychic studies have either provided the substance or the starting-point for a preachment.

The first is a sermon preached in Durham Cathedral on 14 February 1982, a few days before the hundredth anniversary of the formal constitution of the Society for Psychical Research. As with many of these sermons, it contains echoes from several of the pieces which have preceded it in this volume. I do not apologize for the repetition. It may show how the same material can be used in the two very different contexts of the pulpit and the lecture-hall.

The pulpit is not the only place for preaching. To preach is to proclaim the Gospel or good news of Christ, and this may be done in the market-place as well as in the holy place. Indeed, if it is to reach anyone other than the already-converted, it must begin in a very secular environment. My second sample, therefore, comes from a debate before the students of

Durham University at the Union Society on 30 April 1976. Alan Clarke was President that year – he is now ordained and the priest-in-charge of the church of St Herbert, Darlington. The debate that night was on the motion that 'This House believes that current fascination with the occult is a sign of spiritual ill-health'. It was proposed by the Worshipful the Reverend E. Garth Moore, who was President of the Churches' Fellowship for Psychical and Spiritual Studies and has for many years been Chancellor of the Diocese of Durham. The opposition was led by the late Maurice Barbanell, then editor of *Psychic News*. I seconded the motion with the speech printed below as 'Fascination with the occult'. Mr David Kennedy seconded the opposition. We won. Whether that reflected the excellence of our speeches, the force of our arguments, or the inherent religiosity of the Durham undergraduate, is not for us to say.

'Angels' was a sermon preached at two churches dedicated to St Michael and All Angels in the diocese and archdeaconry of Durham; at Lyons on Michaelmas day, 29 September 1982 and at Houghton-le-Spring on the following Sunday, 3 October. Sermons should not have footnotes revealing their sources, but the curious may wish to know that the long quotation in this one has been abbreviated from *Contemplations* by W.L. Wilmshurst, and is taken from the account of it in Raynor C. Johnson's *The Imprisoned Splendour* (Hodder and Stoughton, 1953), pp. 306-7.

The next two sermons were printed in *The Christian Parapsychologist*. 'The Mystery of Incarnation', preached at the Sunday morning eucharist on Christmas Eve 1978 at Durham Cathedral, appeared in volume 3, No. 9 (December 1980) pages 303-5, and 'Hell Harrowed', originally delivered in Trinity College Chapel, Cambridge on Sunday 22 April 1979, was printed in Vol. 4, No. 1 (March 1981), pp. 12-14. The conference to which it refers was the one at which I presented the paper on 'The Theological Approach to Survival', which appears in this book as Chapter 9.

The final offering was an All Souls' Day eucharistic sermon in Durham Cathedral on Sunday 2 November 1980, and was printed in *The Fellowship*, the Occasional Paper of the College of Preachers, No. 58 (June 1981), pp. 42-5.

15
A centenary sermon

A hundred years ago this week, a small group of friends – mainly philosophers and scientists from Cambridge – met formally to constitute a new Society, the Society for Psychical Research. Some of the things they wanted to investigate, such as thought-reading, divination, psychic sensitivity, and hauntings, had been known since the dawn of history. But they had come into prominence again during the previous thirty years. In 1848 the table-rappings in the household of Katie and Maggie Fox of Hydesville in up-state New York had been interpreted as communications from departed spirits, and a new religion called Spiritualism had got going – with the speed of a prairie fire. Within less than a generation, there were Spiritualists in all continents and at all levels of intellectual and social life.

But those friends who got together in February 1882 wanted to look at the world of the psychic in another way – not as a religion but as a subject for scientific enquiry. In the aftermath of Wallace and Darwin, relations between science and religion were at an all-time low, and this group of people hoped that here was a subject where they could discover the truth about man and the truth about human capabilities. Was it possible to read thoughts? Were there communications across the barrier of death? Was man immortal? They hoped to find answers to such perennial teasers through the

certainties of science instead of having to treat them as a matter of
religious belief. Their manifesto pledged that they would approach
the subject

> without prejudice or prepossession of any kind, and in the same spirit of
> exact and unimpassioned enquiry which has enabled Science to solve so
> many problems, once not less obscure nor less hotly debated.

It was a noble objective, faced with optimism and enthusiasm. I
wonder whether – if they could have seen a hundred years ahead –
those Victorian worthies would have been daunted? It proved to be
nothing like so easy and straightforward as they had expected. Psychical research turned out to be like some gigantic game of snakes
and ladders. Every time you made a small advance, there came a
great backwards slither which made the ultimate goal even more
difficult to reach. Every observation, every experiment, seemed to
have half-a-dozen equally likely interpretations; and the results of
one experimenter never seemed to be repeated by the next. Any
hopes that psychical research would be a kind of 'bridge' subject
between science and religion was dashed. A bridge is all very well,
but it's not much good if nobody will come near it, and it's not
much good if those who *do* come near it believe that it's a rickety
old structure that won't bear their weight. So the scientists looked
askance at it, and explained the results away – chance and
coincidence, they said; or bad experimental design; or downright
wicked fraud. And no matter how hard they tried, the psychical
researchers found that they just weren't allowed to win. Orthodox
science would have none of it.

And the religious establishment treated the subject pretty coolly,
too. Either it wasn't worth taking seriously, or it was tarred with a
very disreputable brush, and you were well advised to keep clear of
it. The whole enterprise was a seeking after evidence where faith
was a more appropriate stance, or the view was that Spiritualism
was a wicked and pernicious heresy, and psychical research was too
close to Spiritualism to be comfortable. You could almost smell the
sulphur.

This has always struck me as a pity. Just because a subject is
difficult, and because it is hard to get results, and because it is even
harder to be sure of the interpretation of your results, is no reason
for science to shy off it. Rather, it enhances its intellectual fascination and beckons to fresh efforts. And as for religion, why, surely
every Christian should welcome an exact enquiry, carried out

without prejudice or prepossession, whose purpose is to discover the truth about the mysterious capabilities of the human psyche? Who knows what might be revealed about God's creation, and man's place in it?

In any case, Christians dismiss the psychic aspect of life at their peril. It poses special pastoral and theological questions which have wide ramifications. For example, many of our bishops have their advisers to whom they refer people who come to them because they are troubled by poltergeist outbreaks, or troubled by their own psychic sensitivity. What counsel should they give? If there is such a thing as psychic sensitivity, is it essentially a gift from God like other gifts such as musical or artistic sensitivity? If so, can it be exercised (albeit with fear and trembling and in prayerful discretion) to God's glory? And should spiritual directors be aware of some of the human possibilities in this field, so that they may counsel wisely?

Of course it can be overdone. Of course it is possible to become a bore on the subject – or worse. Of course it is possible to become one-track-minded and see psychism as the centre and mainstay of one's religion. That is part of my quarrel with the Spiritualists. For the Spiritualist, a belief in communication with the spirits is almost the whole of his creed. The Christian can be much more relaxed about it all. The Christian believes that the dead survive (he believes a great deal more, but at least he believes that the dead survive); but a belief in communication is not part of the Christian creed, so it can be left to empirical observation, to scientific psychical research without prejudice or prepossession, whether they do or not.

Again, the Spiritualist seems to me to be more interested in survival than in God, and his religion is an essentially man-centred affair – *I* am central, and God is there, if he is there at all, to see that I am all right. The Christian is only interested in survival insofar as he is interested in God, and his own self-preservation plays a very small part in his religious understanding. The great reality is God, and our communion with him. We need to be put into our place and trust God to get on with his business in a way which will be to our eternal advantage.

So those who make the psychic the centre of their life are heading for spiritual trouble. But, conversely, those who are afraid of it, or antagonistic to it, or ignorant of it, are missing out on a facet of human existence, and are therefore taking a partial view of life. And no Christian should be satisfied with a partial view.

I believe that psychical research is a study which needs more Christian presence and more theological reflections. I began by speaking about the Society for Psychical Research. There is another body in this field, and that is the Churches' Fellowship for Psychical and Spiritual Studies. That is a body dedicated to the Christian understanding of the psychic, and it draws its membership from all the Christian churches. It is a difficult road to tread, between credulity and scepticism, between unhelpful rigidity in orthodoxy on the one hand and a lapse into heresy on the other, between encouraging wrong ideas if one is too 'soft' and dampening the smouldering wick of a person's uncertain faith if one is too 'hard'. But I believe it is a study – and a field – well worth the trouble of getting to know, so that the Christian Gospel can penetrate this mission field as it has penetrated so many others. So I would ask that you try to understand us, and that you protect us by your prayers. So may Jesus Christ be glorified in the search for truth, for he is alone the way and the truth and the life. To him be the glory for ever! Amen.

16
Fascination with the occult

Mr President:

According to the Canon Law of the Church of England, a Chancellor has an inhibiting effect upon an Archdeacon, because the Chancellor is a superior ordinary. About Chancellor Garth Moore, I am ready enough to acknowledge that he is superior. His title is the Worshipful whilst my own is merely the Venerable. One who deserves worship is clearly above one who only rates veneration. On the other hand, I do not think anybody would readily agree that he is ordinary. At all events, I am going to do my best tonight not to be inhibited by him. It is a pleasure to second a motion that he has proposed.

About Mr Barbanell I am not going to be at all inhibited. He is a distinguished editor with whose name I have long been familiar, although we had not met until this evening. Again, it is a pleasure to share a platform with him, even though we are on opposite sides of the Presidential throne. To tell you the truth, Mr President (and even an Archdeacon can do this from time to time) I would sooner be seeking common ground with him than arguing against him.

For a start, he and I both believe the occult exists. So many people think it is all a load of codswallop. *We* don't. We take it seriously. We both believe there are faculties about the human being that enable him to be in touch with an unseen world. We both believe that the veil between this world of our senses and the unseen world is a thin and shifting veil, and that from time to time it may blow aside so that we can catch a glimpse of what lies beyond. To put it crudely, Mr Barbanell would probably swallow a great deal more than I would, because I am of a less credulous disposition than he seems to be. I was trained in the physical sciences before I turned my collar round, and I'm more naturally inclined to be sceptical than to swallow all I am fed. But there is a lot we have in common.

But when we come to the motion that is before this House tonight, we part company. I am asking the house to agree with me that current fascination with the occult is a sign of spiritual ill-health.

First, though, let us get our terms right. Are we talking about the occult or are we only talking about the psychic?

A man is in touch with the psychic when he gets things that go bump in the night in his house, or when he sees things that aren't there. More often than not, these things happen because the person who experiences them is in touch with spirits rather than in touch with the spirits:

> Gin does more than ouija can
> To show an unseen world to man.

Or perhaps the house is over an underground stream and there are creaks and knocks and strange goings-on. Or perhaps somebody is playing tricks. But sometimes they are not, and there is a poltergeist in your house or you see a vision of a friend at the time of his death, even though he is miles away and you know nothing of what is happening to him.

That is just the psychic; it is not the occult. These sort of things happen, and you don't go after them — it's more like them going after you. Some of the saints were bothered with psychic disturbances as they deepened their ascetic and spiritual quest. But they regarded those sort of manifestations as a flaming nuisance because they got in the way of what they were really after. There was an engaging fellow in seventeenth-century Italy known as Joseph of Copertino, who went into a trance every time he tried to say his prayers, and would promptly be levitated. It was apparently an everyday occurence to have the holy friar flying above the altar instead of saying Mass in front of it. His brother monks forgave him this minor eccentricity and tried not to embarrass him by noticing him when he was doing it. The thing is, that psychic manifestations like that are – spiritually speaking – pretty low grade, and anybody who gets steamed-up about them is going to stick spiritually at a pretty low grade too.

Some people don't wait for the psychic to hit them. They go out for it. They may have discovered some sensitivity in themselves, and they develop it – generally for communication with the next world. Either trance mediums or planchette or automatic writing. You have got to watch that, too; when you go into trance, your conscious mind is inhibited (like an Archdeacon in front of a Chancellor) and all sorts of stuff that doesn't normally get through, gets through. Not all of it is from the world beyond. A lot of it may be just from our own subconscious murk. If it's sex there's not much harm in it; but, more often, what gets through is irrational violence. So planchette or the automatic writing spells out prophecies that one of the members of the circle is going to die very shortly, and the circle believe that it is true, and they believe it is a message from a departed spirit, and they believe that departed spirits know more about the future than we do: and the harm that such things can do and the disintegration of the personality that results can be very disturbing indeed. But when that happens, it is not the psychic. It isn't departed spirits. It is only the repressed violence of the subconscious dressing itself up and trying to scare the living daylights out of us. The trouble is, it often succeeds – sometimes more literally than we realize.

So I would say, don't play with planchette. Don't develop your mediumistic sensitivity. Don't go in for automatic writing; *unless* you have got an experienced spiritual guide who can stop it if you are going the way of self-delusion. And, even if you do get genuine messages from the departed, don't think you are going to get any more spiritual for being psychic. Psychic ability is an ability, which some people have and others don't, which some people develop and work at whilst others don't – like the ability to play the piano, or like the ability to paint. You develop your ability to become a good pianist, a good artist, a good psychic; but you don't *thereby* become any more spiritual. The two are not necessarily connected. Some mediums are highly spiritual; some have gone down the drain and left nothing but a nasty smell.

But all that is the psychic. What about the occult? The occult is the hidden, the secret, the mystic lore for the inner circle, the initiation into what makes the universe tick and why. The man who has been initiated into the arcane mysteries of the occult believes that he is at the source of power, that he can manipulate the levers that control the Universe, that he knows things about God or the gods which lesser mortals aren't in on. Sometimes he is a highly moral person and wants to use his occult power for good – like the druid or the white magician, the kind of person you used to find at Stonehenge on midsummer morning at sunrise before the Department of the Environment kept the crowds away. I have met them and talked to them. Most of them are simple, pre-scientific souls who believe in man's harmony with nature and think they can do a lot of good to a wicked world if they act in concert with the occult powers of good, which is done through magic spells and rituals. I have a sympathy with them, though as a scientist I don't follow their logic, and as a Christian I think I can show them a better way of being in line with the good in the Universe – a good which you can't manipulate, a good which is going to control you rather than letting you control him.

It's the other kind of occultist whom I would cross swords with. Not necessarily the black magicians. The black magician or the Satanist is often a mentally sick person. He hates the Church, he hates God, he hates Jesus, he hates the good, and he is cynical and perverted. Ultimately he is fighting a losing battle, but he knows what he is about: blasphemy is his stock-in-trade, and he knows that what the Christian calls 'spiritual health' is something to be spewed out and trampled on. He and I would only agree on one thing; and that is that we were both in dead earnest.

Where fascination with the occult is more dangerous than that is where it is less blatant. It is a dangerous sign of spiritual ill-health when a person has discovered the occult and got so hooked on it that he can't see his way out. He believes he is in touch with the hidden secrets of the Universe. He believes that he *knows*, and everybody else is outside the magic charmed ring. Now, whether he is right or not doesn't matter so much (I think he is wrong, but never mind that for the moment); what I am concerned with is his spiritual health. I fear it doesn't look too good to me. Whether he is concerned with astrological lore, or the mysteries of the Qabalah, or whether he is casting the Tarot cards or performing his occult rituals, he is attempting to control the forces of the Universe or to wrest from them their secrets, instead of seeking to *be* controlled by the God of the Universe. His soul, like that of Faust, is self-concerned; spiritually, he is in a position where growth is going wrong. It is all rather like an ingrowing toe-nail; the growth is all in the wrong direction. I would *not* describe as spiritually mature the man who was so concerned with the culture of his own soul, so concerned to probe into secrets which put him in a different class from his benighted fellow-men, so concerned to be one of the cognos-centi. That is not Christian spirituality. Christian spirituality is not soul-culture for soul-culture's own sake. It asks, instead, for hard work, intense discipline, powerful concentration; and it tells the man who sets out on the ascetic way that he must not introspect or be concerned with his own soul's well-being. The occultist seeks to save his soul through knowledge of secrets; the Christian knows that a man can only save his soul by being careless of it. The occultist knows mysteries which only the initiated can learn; the Christian mysteries are there for all the world to see. The veil before the holy of holies has been ripped open, and the tomb which leads to the world to come is empty and has the stone of concealment rolled away from the front of it.

A fascination with the occult is a sign of spiritual ill-health. It is a sign of a soul which is looking in the wrong direction. Those who follow the occult way will grow neither in wisdom nor in stature nor in favour with God or man. There is a different way and a better way. It can lead to mystic illumination, it can go through transcendental meditation, it can contemplate the profundities of the Godhead. It is a way of renunciation and of hard work, but it is a way of spiritual growth. Those who are fascinated by the occult will not find it.

17
Angels

There are only two subjects for medieval disputations that anybody nowadays seems to have heard about. One is 'Can an Archdeacon be saved?', and the other is 'How many angels can dance on the point of a pin?'. Since one subject is enough for a single sermon, and since everybody seems to think that Archdeacons can very well look after themselves, and since it's Michaelmastide, the feast of St Michael and all the angels, let's take the second of those questions.

How many angels can dance on the point of a pin? The question is not about the size of angels, or even about how tightly you can pack them in — as if they were students in a telephone box trying for an entry in the *Guinness Book of Records*. The thing is that the point of a pin is where the pin narrows down to nothing, so there isn't any room on it at all. Nothing can dance on the point of a pin, because there isn't any space there for *anything* to dance on.

Not even the tiniest angel?

Hold on a bit, though. The thing about angels is that they don't belong to this visible word, this universe of Archdeacons and pin-points. They don't actually take up any space at all. They exist in another world. So asking how many angels fit onto a pin-point is like asking how many nothings make up nothing — and the mathematicians tell us that any answer between nothing and infinity could be a correct one to *that* puzzler. We are asking how much space we need for the other world – the world of angels and of superhuman beings – to make its entrance into this world. And the answer is that the angels can slip in through the narrowest of cracks. 'Turn but a stone, and start a wing!' Any space, however small, any time, however momentary, is enough to find us materialistic creatures off our guard, and to show us something of the riches of God's unseen creation.

Let me read you part of what once happened to a worshipper in a little village church near the turn of this present century, whilst the *Te Deum* was being sung during morning prayer one Sunday:

My thought began to contrast the modest praises uttered in this humble place in the outward world, by its crippled organ, the puny voices of this juvenile choir and handful of villagers with the stupendous unimaginable paeans which must needs be heard above . . .

Whilst thus reflecting I caught sight, in the aisle at my side, of what resembled bluish smoke issuing from the chinks of the stone floor, as though from fire smouldering beneath. Looking more intently I saw it was not smoke, but something finer, more tenuous – a soft impalpable semi-luminous haze of violet colour, unlike any physical vapour . . . Upon the instant the luminous blue haze engulfing me and all around me became transformed into sudden glory, into light untellable . . . But the most wonderful thing was that these shafts and waves of light, that vast expanse of photosphere, and even the central globe itself, were crowded to solidarity with the forms of living creatures . . .

I saw moreover that these living beings were present in teeming myriads in the church I stood in . . . The heavenly hosts drifted through the human congregation as wind passes through a grove of trees; beings of radiant beauty and clothed in shimmering raiment.

As that vision faded, the worshipper found himself once more standing in the church, well and unmoved, and discovered that no-one else had been aware of what stupendous sights he had been seeing.

Only a few moments could have been occupied [he wrote] by an experience in the spirit, of which the incidents were so vivid and the details so numerous that my memory still fails to exhaust them. The singing of the 'Te Deum' had not concluded.

A host of angels needs no more than a point of a pin to dance on, and no more than a moment of our time in which to manifest itself.

For those to whom God grants a vision of the inner eye, space and time are unimportant. The angels do not inhabit our world, but the world of the seen and the world of the unseen can interpenetrate, and — sometimes, for some people — there is a moment when the breeze blows the veil to one side, and for a fleeting moment, the angels are seen by mortal men.

Something of that kind must have happened on the moonlit bank of a Bethlehem hillside to a group of shepherds watching their flocks by night; and, when it was over, they felt impelled to go to the village below to see if there really *was* a baby in a cowshed, or whether it had all been an illusion. Something of that kind must have happened to Peter and James and John on a mountain top where Jesus had been praying all night, and they saw — for a moment — the glory that was really his, and the splendour and the light was such that they could only hold their breath and their tongues, till Peter broke the spell by his pointless comment. Something of that kind must have happened to Paul, when he says that he was caught up into the third heaven and heard words beyond speech, which it is not lawful for a man to utter. Something of that kind must have happened to a man in Patmos, exiled because of his faith, whose visions have come down to us as the Book of the Revelation to John.

We don't see how the world of the angels and this world of ours can coexist, how they can be different worlds, inhabiting different spaces and different times, how an angel can dance on a pin-point and a revelation that lasts a lifetime can take but a single second. We try and make it more understandable by analogies or metaphors or parables; and different ages use different analogies to try to grasp what cannot be grasped.

So, in Biblical times, people imagined a kind of three-decker universe, with heaven above the bright blue sky and She'ol beneath the ground. That's a bit like the ideas of various 'planes of existence' like earth plane and astral plane that you come across in some more modern speculations. Other people, especially in this century of radio and television, try to think in terms of 'vibrations', so that this world and the world of the angels are characterized by different rates of vibration — they are like two different radio programmes on different wavelengths that don't interfere with each other because when you are tuned in to one, you cannot at the same time be tuned in to the other. Or, some people like to think of dimensions, so that the world of the angels is a multi-dimensional world interpenetrating ours, like a three-dimensional sphere can interpenetrate the flat, two-dimensional, world of a circle drawn on a piece of paper. All these are only analogies – ways of making the incomprehensible a bit more comprehensible to human minds. If they help you, use the analogies – but even as you use them, your mind will begin to boggle, because you will be trying to think of things which three-dimensional this-world human beings are not built to comprehend.

But don't ever say that angels cannot exist because there is no room for them on the point of a pin. The world God made is a great deal more marvellous than that bit of it we normally see. In the Creed we say that the Church believes in God the Father Almighty, maker of all that is – seen and unseen. The things that are seen, said St Paul, are temporal, but the things that are not seen are eternal.

At Michaelmastide, then, let us thank God that the world he has made is greater than our limited human imaginings can conceive. Some of that greatness should make us tremble and take care, because in the unseen world there is as much rebellion against God as there is in this visible world. There is Satan and there are the fallen angels of the devil, tempting, harming, ceaselessly working for our downfall. But set against them the myriads of creatures who are on God's side, who can speak to us of God, who can be his messengers and our protectors. Think of the guardian angels of children and of the young-at-heart and young-in-soul. Think of creatures who ceaselessly praise God in ways that make even the most splendid human worship seem very pallid and very amateur. Thank God that those who are for us are very many more than those who are against us, and join your own prayers – as the priest will join his in the Sanctus of this holy Eucharist – with angels and archangels and with all the host of heaven, singing Holy, Holy, Holy to the Lord – the Lord of the heavenly hosts, to whom be glory for ever. Amen.

18
The mystery of incarnation

Perhaps one of the most moving experiences in Durham Cathedral at Christmas time is the carol service for the mentally handicapped. They come with their parents, their nurses, their friends; some walk in, some are carried, and others arrive in wheelchairs. We hear the familiar lessons and we sing the familiar carols. Some of the congregation can join in; for some it just isn't possible. How much do they make of what's going on? I don't know. What I do know is that in the Cathedral that afternoon there is represented an immense amount of love — love given, love received: love offered without thought of reward, yet love creating its own reward. And if that isn't a powerful symbol of the message of Christmas, what is?

But that carol service for the mentally handicapped set me off thinking about Christmas in quite another way. It's that which I want to try and share with you this morning as we endeavour to let the mystery of the Incarnation soak into our hearts and minds.

Mental handicap happens because the brain is malfunctioning in some way, or because the internal electrical circuitry of the brain is incomplete. Something similar takes place if ever the brain is damaged through lack of oxygen — cardiac arrest, for example, for more than a few seconds; or in senile decay. The materialist will say that this is because thought and consciousness are simple functions of a certain level of brain organization, like doing sums is a function of a certain kind of electronic wiring in a computer. In the computer, if the wiring in the chip gets damaged, the sums don't get done; in the brain, if its circuits are mucked about with, the thinking and the self-awareness just doesn't happen.

That's one way of looking at it. It isn't *my* way of looking at it. The data allow us to believe – and I believe and I think most Christians believe – that the brain doesn't so much *create* consciousness as act as a kind of receiver or filter for it. There is something – let's call it the 'essential self' for lack of a better term, though many Christians would be traditional and call it the 'soul' – which uses the human brain in order to come to consciousness in this material world of ours. The brain is an incredibly delicate mechanism, and if it goes wrong, then the messages the essential self or the soul wishes to present to consciousness become distorted. Those mentally handicapped folk who were in the Cathedral last week were people whose brains can only allow the self to come through into thought and consciousness in fitful and distorted ways. If a person's brain is damaged his soul cannot express itself properly through his body. If a person goes senile, his self is not destroyed, it is isolated and cannot get through. There is medical evidence, for example, that some schizophrenics or sufferers from terminal meningitis become lucid and normal for a brief while before their death – as if the mind is becoming gradually disengaged from the malfunctioning body.

It's a bit like the distinction between a television transmitter and a television set. If you don't like the programme and you throw a hammer at the set, you don't stop the programme. That is still going on in the studio. All you have destroyed is the delicate mechanism whereby the programme can be perceived in your own home. The brain is not the self; it is the mechanism (like the television set) that the self uses to communicate.

Wait a minute, though. Are we sure that, even when it works normally, it is working perfectly? Might it be possible that *we* – compared with perfection – are ourselves the mentally handicapped? We have all experienced the frustration of knowing something and not being able to bring it to conscious recall, or of not being able to express what we feel and know. More than that, if our brains were perfect instruments, might we perhaps be aware of abilities, consciousness, powers, which at present transcend even our wildest dreams? Awarenesses such as are hinted at in that phrase of T.S. Eliot's about 'a tremour of bliss, a wink of heaven, a whisper', when the veil between the next world and this seems to be a very thin one, and it drifts aside for a tantalizing moment before things are ordinary again?

For most of us, these awarenesses are brief, infrequent, tantalizing. There *are* people about who have strange sensitivities which the rest of us can hardly guess at — people of intuition, of psychic awareness, people with healing powers — usually welling up intermittently and not entirely subject to their own human control. Perhaps they are indicators that it is possible — and will be possible, after this earthly life of ours is over — for the soul to work, not through a physical brain or a material body, but in another way altogether, in what the Christian calls 'the life of the world to come'. In that heavenly life, we may realize powers which this earthly body, this material brain, this imperfect instrument for allowing the essential self to express itself, this 'muddy vesture of decay', is too gross to allow. When we have exchanged this earthly body for a heavenly one, then the self may be capable of a consciousness and of powers such as eye hath not seen, nor ear heard, nor have entered into the mind of man to conceive. To quote C.S. Lewis, in that sermon of his which he published under the title of *The Weight of Glory*, 'when human souls have become as perfect in voluntary obedience as the inanimate creation is in its lifeless obedience, then they will put on its glory, or rather that greater glory of which Nature is only the first sketch'.

If it is possible that the human brain and human body is able to act as a receiver, a vehicle, for this kind of awareness, may it not be possible that a human frame could be the vehicle of an even greater glory? A glory that needed an all-but-incredible self-emptying to lodge within a human frame, a *kenosis* whereby eternity is contracted to a span, and of which we have to use such mind-bending paradoxes as

O wonder of wonders, for all to behold
The Ancient of Days is an hour or two old?

It is all-but-incredible, but it is the claim of Christian orthodoxy that God made the human frame *capax Dei* — fit for God himself to take lodgement in. The Word was made flesh and dwelt among us. 'Not', as the Athanasian 'Creed' has it, 'by conversion of the Godhead into flesh', but by using this inadequate human vehicle to realize and express, however imperfectly, the splendour and the glory that was communicating through it, and thus taking the Manhood into God.

Sometimes that splendour flashed through the material vehicle that it was using, and anyone who was percipient enough could see that divine things were afoot. That was what was happening in the healings, or the exorcisms. That was what was happening especially in the Transfiguration, or in the Resurrection, when the husk of the body was completely taken up into the unseen world which had controlled it. But most of the time, nobody could have realized it, unless he had been unusually in tune with what was going on. Most of the time, all that men saw was Jesus the prophet of Nazareth in Galilee; but some men, some times, could cry out, as Peter did, 'Thou art the Christ, the Son of the living God'.

Perhaps some of us will be able to say that, this Christmas. When some see a baby, and others listen to a myth, we may see God incarnate, the Word made flesh, a mystery and a miracle beyond our wildest imaginings, stretching the possibilities of humanity to their very limits. If that *is* what we see, then we may also have confidence in believing that by union with him (in the Holy Eucharist, for example) we too shall be made like unto him, for we shall see him as he is. To that consummation of bliss may the holy, incarnate, Son of God in his mercy bring us!

19
Hell harrowed

I was in London most of yesterday at a conference. I never discovered whether it was held on that day because it was the Saturday after Easter, but the subject of the conference was whether human beings survive death: so I suppose there's a kind of topicality in talking about that at Easter time. After all, Easter is about somebody who came back from the grave.

This conference was put on by a Survival Research Trust, and it included Christians, Spiritualists, and parapsychologists. We had the President of the College of Psychic Studies, a demonstration of platform clairvoyance, myself (I suppose) lending an air of Establishment respectability to the whole proceedings, and a panel of parapsychologists pulling the evidence to pieces and showing us that it wasn't all plain sailing.

And indeed there has been a lot of evidence recently.

1. There are stories of people whose hearts have stopped beating and who have been brought back to life on the operating theatre. Some of them have viewed their own bodies from a distance, inert on the table with the medics around it, and have floated away from it into other realms before being pulled back and regaining what we call 'consciousness'.

2. There are stories told by relatives, nurses, and doctors who have stood by the bedside of a dying patient and heard him meet up with his departed relatives and greet them with joy and surprise. Yes, there are still deathbeds today; they did not end when Victorian melodramatic romances went out of favour.

3. And then there are the mediums, who daily converse with those who though dead are still 'alive and well and living in the Great Beyond'.

Not that believers have it all their own way. The experience of seeing your own body from outside can be explained away as a compound of memory and imagination, eked out with a little hyperaesthesia and perhaps a bit of telepathy. What the dying see may be the kind of hallucination that you get when your brain cells are starved of oxygen; and as for mediums, the details they give us about the World of the Life to Come may be like Pooh-Bah said in the *Mikado*: 'corroborative detail added to lend artistic verisimilitude to an otherwise bald and unconvincing narrative'.

Of course, the arguments on either side are not as simple as that. What we have heard so far is just the first round – one fall each, and no submission yet. In the second round, the business gets a bit more sophisticated. That is why parapsychology is so intellectually fascinating to get mixed up in. But it all boils down to the fact that death is a very lively subject nowadays.

So the survival researchers organize a conference on it, and choose Easter as a topical time to hold it. And Christians have to say, 'What the hell do you think all this has got to do with Easter?' Yes, what the hell. I am not indulging in random profanity; I am choosing my words with some care.

Hell (as used in the Christian creeds) is the English word for what the Greeks called Hades and the Hebrews, She'ol. In so far as the men of the Old Testament were interested in what went on after death – and you have to confess that compared with the ancient Egyptians they were remarkably *un*-interested in it – but insofar as they *were* interested in life after death, the picture they drew of those who survived was not a very alluring one. It was a bit like the arrival platform at Liverpool Street station in an old-fashioned London pea-souper fog: a lot of coming, not very much going, everybody fed up, with a great deal of time on their hands and nothing to do with it; and the sun never coming out. Jehovah was not there, and since it was he who made life worth living, that says a lot for what sort of a place it was. No wonder Ecclesiastes the Preacher said that he would sooner be a living dog than a dead lion.

And it is Hell – She'ol – where the greater number of mediumistic communications seem to me to come from (those that are genuine, that is: some of them are). The descriptions many of them give of their goings-on strike me as coming from a realm where people are still caught on the treadmill of their earthly desires, still trying to be satisfied with the trite and colourless pastimes which are the best they can imagine, still encapsulated in such appalling poverty of spirit. If this is all there is to everlasting life, then I would soon get bored to death with it.

So survival is not necessarily good news. It could be very bad news indeed. It could mean that you had discovered what a crashing great bore you were, and that you couldn't even get out of range of yourself by dying. My God – is there any escape from survival? Or are we condemned to an everlasting life sentence of immortality?

Part of the Christian message of Easter (because I am not going to try to get the *whole* of the theology of Easter into one sermon) is that – to use the classical phrase – Jesus has harrowed hell. Easter is about Jesus going down to She'ol and transforming it. It is about God performing an act of resurrection. And it is resurrection alone which rescues us from the futility of survival. The ancient Hebrews – you remember my saying it – believed that She'ol was where Jehovah wasn't. The Christian claim is that in Jesus, God has penetrated right down to hell, and that from now on, even the dead have the hope of resurrection.

In theological terms, survival is part of the doctrine of creation. If men survive death in the way in which the parapsychologists study the survival of death, they do so because they are human beings and this is the way human beings are made. But resurrection (theologically speaking) is part of the doctrine of redemption. By resurrection, God redeems a person from his former manner of life and transforms him in so radical a way that you have to use a new word to describe it: no longer just 'life' (what T.S. Eliot called 'living and partly living') but 'eternal life' – life of a new dimension, a new quality. *That* is the result of resurrection. Not floating ethereally around the séance-room giving a bit of comfort to Cousin Edna, or talking about an astral summerland of higher vibrations; but enjoying the kind of life that tingles with the vitality of God the life-giver.

You didn't ask to be born. You can survive death without doing anything about it. But you cannot be resurrected without your consent, because resurrection involves the redeeming work of God on the expectant and individual soul. You cannot be resurrected until you have seen the futility of the old life and until you have desired — more than you have ever desired anything else — the new life which only God can give. Self-knowledge, repentance, faith — and *then* God can perform resurrection! Some people are resurrected in *this* life; some of us know eternal life now. Others may have to wait until the next life before they can see clearly enough to choose God and hand their old self over to him for transformation. But all of us — so I believe — are destined to be resurrected, when God has had his will with us and we have accepted his gift.

What evidence have I got for this? Not the kind of evidence that would count for much with the Survival Research Trust. But there *is* some evidence, even about resurrection. I don't just mean Jesus of Nazareth, although — who knows? — there may even be a bit of scorched linen somewhere tucked away in an Italian cathedral which got left behind when the resurrection happened. No. The evidence for resurrection *ought* to be seen in Church on a Sunday, when Christians gather together.

Si monumentum requiris, circumspice. If you want evidence for resurrected Christians, for those who have had the touch of God upon them and who are living in the power of the risen Jesus, you ought to be able to look around and find it — here. That is why Easter is as much a challenge as a comfort to Christians. Do you know Jesus well enough to walk the risen life with him? Can you be recognized as a person whose quality of life is different? Has Jesus harrowed your hell?

The message of Easter is that you can be resurrected before you die, and, if so, then death holds no terrors for you. The para-psychologists may look for the evidence of life after death, but it takes a Christian to provide evidence for life before death.

20
All souls

The trees are turning; the leaves are falling. November is in the air and winter cannot be far away. The very season of the year reminds us of our own mortality. Like the leaves on the trees, we too shall wither and decay. But is that all? Is there a spring to follow our winter, or are we all of us so much compost?

There has been a lot of scientific research of late into deathbeds and what is known as the 'near-death experience'. It seems that a number of people at the moment of death (or just before it) behave as though they are being welcomed at the threshold of a new existence by departed friends or by spiritual beings. Their faces light up and they tell us they are being met by friends whom they recognize. And it seems – from sophisticated statistical analysis of many such cases – that this kind of experience can be sharply differentiated from diseased hallucination or from wish-fulfilment fed by religious or cultural pre-expectations.

It seems, too, that patients who have suffered cardiac arrest and been resuscitated may come back from the experience with travellers' tales about having experienced the separation of mind from body, about having known a review of their past life, and about the expansion of the self into surroundings of inexpressible light and beauty and peace. The research is very new, and there is a great deal of sifting of data and arguing of conclusions to be done:

but the preliminary suggestions are that death is not necessarily the end. It looks as if scientific research is telling us that the human self may survive the dissolution of the physical body.

Christians will not be surprised. They may be gratified that they are getting some kind of independent corroboration of something they had long believed in on other grounds. But they will not be surprised. Nor will they over-estimate the significance of all this research. What it is like at the moment of death is only the beginning of it. Survival of death is only, as it were, the way in. What is it we survive *to*?

On such a subject we cannot speak dogmatically. We can only speak of our own convictions, yet humbly and hesitantly. *My* conviction is that however traumatic the experience of death may be, and however much of a culture shock we may be in for when we exchange this present body of flesh and blood for whatever takes its place in the next world, that won't immediately change the kind of persons we are. What *will* happen, I believe, is that we shall be able to see what kind of persons we have made ourselves into. I don't know you, but I do know myself well enough to be sure that in my case it will not be a pretty sight. None of us is a completely integrated personality. Each of us is a mass of inconsistencies. Some of our desires are desires towards love and God and altruism. Many of them are – inconsistently – desires towards anger, or lust, or self-aggrandisement. But all of them are *us*. That mixed-up bundle is what we have become. These disparate desires do not live well with each other, and when they all well up in an unrepressed way, and the lid is off, we are not in for a quiet time. So none of us can contemplate life after death without great misgivings.

But I do not believe that in the next world we are going to be left to rot in self-encapsulated isolation. We shall get help. Some of that will (I believe) be from our human friends – those who have died before us, and those who remain on earth and say their prayers. Some will (I believe) come from non-human beings – the angelic creation, our guardian angels. Most of it will (and this I most strongly believe) come from God himself, who will be closer to us than we can ever conceive on this earth, and who will be able to work with us more directly than is ever possible here and now. He will guide us through the desert of what we have made of ourselves, to the paradise-garden where we can become a coherent bundle of unified desires, and where we can enter into that rest of the spirit that comes from knowing that we are where we were *meant* to be. 'Thou hast made us unto thyself', said St Augustine, 'and our hearts are restless until they find their rest in thee.'

How and when that will happen, and how long it will take, I cannot say. 'When?' and 'How long?' are questions that smack of clocks and calendars, and in the next world I do not suppose time will be the same as it is for us here. But what we *can* say is that our departed friends and loved ones — those whom we especially wish to remember before God on All Souls' Day, the second of November — need this purification if they are to find their rest in God. And so shall we. So *do* we.

Because this is so, we remember them. We remember them in love, and we believe that love is stronger than death. More importantly, we remember them in God, and we *know* that God is stronger than death. We know this, because God was in Christ, reconciling the world to himself, and Christ could not be held by death.

So we know that the power of God over the fate of those who have departed this life is greater than any other power. It is greater than any human power, so no soul can ultimately resist the love of God. It is greater than any subhuman or superhuman power, so no devil or demon can claim any soul as his own.

And because the love of God is stronger than death, and because we love them still, though they have passed through death, we love them within the Communion of Saints, and we commend them to God's purifying love. We pray that his will may be done in them, as it needs to be done in us, both now and hereafter.

Periodicals

Many of the contributions to this volume have appeared in print elsewhere before, and the introductions to each section give the exact whereabouts. The list below details all the publications concerned.

Bres (six issues *per annum*). Published by European Universities Press, Amsterdam. In Dutch. Subscriptions to Zuidegroep Abonnementen Service, Postbus 245-2501 CE, Den Haag, Netherlands.

Catholic Digest (monthly). Published by the College of St Thomas, 2115 Summit Avenue, St Paul, Minnesota 55105, USA. Subscriptions to Catholic Digest, St Paul's Square, PO Box 1812, Des Moines, Iowa 50336, USA.

The Christian Parapsychologist (quarterly). Published by the Churches' Fellowship for Psychical and Spiritual Studies, St Mary Abchurch, Abchurch Lane, London EC4N 7BA.

Contact (occasionally). Sponsored by the Clinical Theology Association, the Institute of Religion and Medicine, the Association for Pastoral Care and Counselling, the Westminster Pastoral Foundation, and the Irish Pastoral Association. Subscriptions to A.O.B. Dick, 59 South St, St Andrews, Fife.

Epworth Review (three times *per annum*). Available only on subscription from the Methodist Publishing House, Wellington Road, Wimbledon, London SW19 8EU.

The Expository Times (monthly). Published by T. and T. Clark Ltd., 36 George St, Edinburgh EH2 2LQ.

The Fellowship (occasional). For private circulation only, to members of the College of Preachers Fellowship. Enquiries to the College of Preachers, The Guild Church of St Margaret Pattens, Eastcheap, London EC3M 1HS.

The Journal of Religion and Psychical Research (formerly the *Journal* of the Academy of Religion and Psychical Research) (quarterly). Published by ARPR, PO Box 614, Bloomfield, Connecticut 06002, USA. ARPR is an academic affiliate of Spiritual Frontiers Fellowship (see below).

Journal of the Society for Psychical Research (three times *per annum*). Published by SPR, 1 Adam and Eve Mews, London W8 6UG.

Light (quarterly). Published by the College of Psychic Studies, Ltd., 16 Queensberry Place, London SW7 2EB.

The Modern Churchman (quarterly). Published by the Modern Churchmen's Union, Hon. Sec. the Revd F.E. Compton, The School House, Leysters, Leominster, Herefordshire, HR6 0HS.

One World (monthly). Published by the Communications Department of the World Council of Churches, 150 route de Ferney, PO Box 66, 1211 Geneva 20, Switzerland.

Parapsychology Review (six times *per annum*). Published by the Parapsychology Foundation, Inc., 228 East 71st Street, New York, NY 10021, USA.

Psychical Studies (occasional). Published by the Unitarian Society for Psychical Studies, 20 Wetherill Road, London N10 2LT.

Psychic News (weekly). 23 Great Queen Street, London WC2B 5BB.

Spiritual Frontiers (quarterly). Published by Spiritual Frontiers Fellowship, Inc., 10819 Winner Road, Independence, Missouri 64052, USA.

Theta (quarterly). Published by the Psychical Research Foundation, Inc., 214 Pittsboro Street, Chapel Hill, North Carolina 27514, USA.

The Times (daily except Sunday), PO Box 7, 200 Gray's Inn Road, London WC1X 8EZ.

Transpersonal Books, 46 Evelyn Gardens, London SW7 3BH.

Index

1. Subjects

Academy of Religion and Psychical Research, 13, 218
Adam, 165
altered state of consciousness, 34, 69, 74
angels, 99, 131, 202ff., 215
apparition, 43, 98, 114, 162
Archbishops' Commission on Christian Doctrine, 10, 45
ars moriendi, 93f., 107
automatic writing, 44, 114, 184, 199

body, 91, 122, 126ff., 133, 134f., 141
boggle threshold, 62
brain hemispheres, 79
Bridey Murphy, 167, 171, 177, 189 n.9

Churches' Fellowship for Psychical and Spiritual Studies, 13, 24, 27, 33, 53, 112, 149, 150, 196, 217
College of Psychic Studies, 112, 133, 143, 210, 218
Committee for the Scientific Investigation of Claims of the Paranormal, 62
communication, 116, 134, 184, 195

Communion of Saints, 13, 126, 183ff.
conversion, 118
Copernicus, 56, 186
creation, 117, 146
cryptomnesia, 167, 172

dabbling, 9, 48
death, 85ff., 118, 134
deathbed visions, 97ff., 104, 114, 142, 211, 215
déjà vu, 176, 177
deliverance, ministry of, 12, 144
dervish, 70, 74
devil, 45, 75, 105, (*see also* Satan)
dimensions, 116, 125, 204
direct voice, 72
discarnate existence, 138
disclosure, 42, 48, 158, 163
divination, 30

England, Church of, 12
ethical committees, 15
'Eve', 172f.
evidence, 34, 114f.
exorcism, 12, 46, 144, 209

faith, 30, 34, 52ff., 115, 164
flashback, 100f.
flesh, 127
Fortean Times, 55, 65

fraud, 57

genius children, 176, 177
Gospels, 152

Hades, 75, 211 (*see also* Sheol)
hallucinations, 99, 184
healing, 30, 209
heaven, 124, 145, 146
hell, 146, 210ff.
hemispheres of brain, 79, 179
hereafter, 125
historical evidence, 152ff.
hyperaesthesia, 58, 167

images, 136
immortality, 93, 118, 212
incarnation, 206
Inner Space Interpreters' Service, 33
International Association for Near-Death Studies, 96, 108 n.2
interpretation of data, 57, 121

Jekyll and Hyde, 172
Jesus, visions of, 99, 101
judgement, 106, 129, 141, 146

kahin, 70, 74

Lambeth conference, 9, 27, 113

lysergic acid diethylamide, 106

magic, 200
Mary, Virgin, visions of, 99
mediumship, 7, 30, 44, 46, 67ff., 114, 123, 184, 211
metaphor, 124
miracles, 31, 161
Modern Churchman's Union, 37, 218

near-death experience, 100ff., 214
next world, 122ff., 126
numinous, 41, 48, 80, 88

occult, 48, 197ff.
oracles, 30
ouija, 44, 198 (see also planchette)
out-of-body experience, 74, 100f., 102, 103, 114, 210, 214

paradise, 123
Piltdown Man, 57, 78
planchette, 43, 44, 199
planes of existence, 123, 204
Plato, 89, 91
poltergeist, 43, 46, 143, 184, 195, 198
possession, 69ff., 167
prayer, 30, 184
pre-existence of soul, 181
Presbyterians, 10, 15
promotor fidei, 31
prophets, 70f., 73f., 81
Ptolemy, 55
purgatory, 141, 146
purity, 145

redemption, 117
reincarnation, 34, 99, 116, 131, 149, 167ff.
regression, hypnotic, 167, 168, 171ff., 178f.
religion, 29
repeatability, 27, 58
requiem, 144
resurrection, 30, 75, 76, 80, 93, 116, 118, 128, 135, 146, 149, 151ff., 182, 209, 212
resurrection appearances, theories, 159ff.
resurrection narratives, 153ff.
rites of passage, 89
'Rosemary', 170

salvation, 117
Satan, 23, 27, 68, 76, 118f., 200

Scotland, Church of, 10, 12, 27
second order desires, 144
secondary personality, 172f., 179
seer, 73, 81
sensitivity, psychic, 14, 27, 81, 195, 199, 208
shaman, 67, 70, 74
Sheol, 75, 76, 92, 123, 146, 204, 211
Society for Psychical Research, 8, 20, 22, 26, 32, 38, 53, 97, 125, 136, 149, 191, 193, 218
Socrates, 89, 91f.
soul, 91, 181, 188, 207
Spiritual Frontiers Fellowship, 13, 24, 33, 37, 111, 218, 219
Spiritualism, 8, 10, 12, 28, 32, 34, 45, 53, 105, 111, 119, 146, 193ff.
stigmata, 31, 173
suicide, 102
super-ESP, 61, 114
survival, 14, 27, 33, 111ff., 151, 195, 212
Survival Joint Research Committee Trust, 111, 210

theory, 60
Tibetan Book of the Dead, 116, 129, 139f., 147 nn 7, 8, 9.
trance, 69, 184
tradition, 180
transcendent, 41
transfiguration, 79f., 209
tunnel experience, 100f., 104

Underhill Report, 10, 27, 45, 119, 120 n. 6
unidentified flying objects, 34, 55
Unitarianism, 38, 52
Unitarian Society for Psychical Studies 53, 218
Urim, 66, 74

vibrations, 124, 204, 212
visions, 30, 99, 101

wavelength, 124
witchcraft, 7, 23, 32
Witch of En-dor, 66ff.
World Council of Churches, 19, 24, 25, 218

yamdoot, 99

2. Names
Augustine, St, 141, 215

Badham, P., 82 n. 11, 135, 136, 147 n. 2, 148 n. 18
Barbanell, M., 111, 192, 197
Barrett, W.F., 97, 108 n. 4
Beard, P., 111, 112, 126
Belloc, H., 56, 65 n. 5
Bennett, B.M., 35 n. 1, 79, 82 n. 13, 83 n. 15
Benson, Mrs E.W., 9, 33
Bernstein, M., 169, 189 n. 9
Blacker, C., 35 n. 2
Blackmore, R.D., 174
Blackmore, S.J., 103, 108 n. 14, 114, 120 n. 3
Bloxham, A., 167 n. 1
Bluck, J., 19
Bostock, W.G., 189 n. 16
Brown, J., 26, 32
Brown, W., 45
Burge, Bishop, 17 n. 3
Burrows, Fr., 43
Burt, C., 58, 103, 108 n. 15
Butler, E., 190 n. 20
Butterfield, H., 190 n. 22

Carlyle, 94
Carpenter, W.B., 27, 33
Cassirer, M., 68
Cayce, E., 167, 168
Chari, C.T.K., 120
Christie – Murray, D., 150, 168, 176, 189 n.6, 190 n.20
Clarke, A., 192
Cleckley, H.M., 173
Cobbe, F.P., 97
Coggan, F.D., 12
Coly, L., 35 n.1, 83 n. 13
Copertino, Joseph of, 198
Crehan, J., 43
Creery, A.M., 9
Crookall, R., 102, 108 n. 12
Cuddon, E., 169
Cupitt, D., 158, 159 ff.
Currie, I., 114, 117, 120 n.2

Dean, E.D., 83 n. 14
de Morgan, A., 65 n. 3
Dickens, C., 65 n. 8
Donne, J., 94
Downing, B., 34
Dryden, D., 97

Edwards, O., 85
Eisenbud, J., 35 n. 5
Eliot, T.S., 41, 50 n. 1, 207, 212
Elliott, G.M., 35 n. 3

Evans, C.F., 92, 95 n. 1, 153, 157, 164, 165 n. 1
Evans-Wentz, W.Y., 147 n. 7

Farmer, W.R., 155, 165 n. 5
Fletcher, J., 173, 176, 178
Fletcher, R., 134
Forey, A.J., 189 n. 12
Fox sisters, 193
Fremantle, F., 147 n. 7
Fryer C.E.J., 83 n. 17
Fuller, M., 95 n. 3
Fuller, R.H., 153, 154, 165 n. 6

Goedicke, H., 82 n. 6
Goldney, K.M., 50 n. 4
Goodacre, D.L., 85
Grattan-Guinness, I., 20
Gregory, A., 57, 65 n. 7
Grensted, L.W., 45
Grof, S., 107
Grosso, M., 35 n. 5, 105, 109 n. 19
Guirdham, A., 167, 168, 170, 176, 178, 189 nn 7, 12

Haddow, A.M., 17 n. 3, 33
Halifax, J., 107
Hampe, J.C., 100, 104, 108 n. 8, 108 n. 16, 131
Haraldsson, E., 98, 99, 142, 147 n. 11
Haskins, M.L., 95 n. 2
Haynes, R., 31, 61, 65 n. 12, 149
Heisenberg, W., 54, 64 n. 1
Herman, N., 50 n. 3
Heron, L.T., 34, 35 n. 7
Hertzberg, H.W., 67, 82 n. 2
Heywood, R., 51 n. 11
Hick, J., 24, 135, 136, 147 nn 2, 3, 170, 175, 189 n. 2
Howell-Everson, D., 148 n. 15
Hyslop, J., 97

Johnson, R.C., 192
Johnson, S., 85
Johnstone, J., 189 n. 10
Josephus, F., 181, 189 n. 15

Kampmann, R., 172
Keats, J., 50 n. 2
Keeton, J., 171, 177, 185, 189 n. 10, 190 n. 19
Kelsey, M.T., 9, 17 n. 2
Kelly, E.F., 35 n. 6
Kennedy, David, 192
Kennedy, Diane, 147 n. 13, 189 n 17
Kerr, J.S., 51 n. 14

Kohl, M., 108 n. 8
Kübler-Ross, E., 107, 109 n. 21

Lambert, G.W., 51 n. 12
Lambertini, P., 31
Lang, C.G., 10, 45
Lees, R., 32
Lester, R., 53
Levitt, Z., 105, 109 n. 18
Lewis, C.S., 43, 137, 208
Lewis H.D., 135
Lindblom, J., 70, 72, 74, 82 nn 6-9
Locke, R.G., 35 n. 6
Loewe, L., 35 n. 2
Longford, E., 32

McCormick, D., 60, 65 n. 9
MacGregor, G., 175, 189 n. 3
McHarg, J.F., 103, 114, 120 n. 4
MacKenzie, A., 50 nn 4, 5
McLenon, J., 65 n. 10
Markwick, B., 57, 65 n. 6
Martin, H., 50 n. 3
Marxsen, W., 156ff., 166 n. 7
Matthews, W.R., 27, 33, 45
Mendel, 57
Mihalasky, J., 83 n. 14
Moody, R., 100, 105, 108 nn 8, 9, 131
Moore, E.G., 192, 197
Morison, F., 152
Moss, P., 189 n. 10, 190 n. 19
Moule, C.F.D., 159 ff.
Murphy, G., 132
Murray, M., 61

Neale, J.M., 147 n. 10
Neff, R., 35, 35 n. 9
Nineham, D.E., 51 n. 11

Origen, 183, 189 n. 16
Osis, K., 59, 61, 65 n. 9, 98, 99, 104, 114, 142, 147 n. 11
Otto, R., 88

Pahnke, W., 106, 109 n. 20
Parker, S.B., 69 ff., 82 n. 5
Penelhum, T., 134, 135
Perrin, N., 153
Perry, M.C., 35 n. 4, 50 n. 4, 50 n. 9, 51 n. 13, 82 n. 12, 83 n. 16, 147 n. 12, 166 n. 12
Petitpierre, R., 51 n. 11, 147 n. 14

Phillips, J.B., 43, 50 n. 4, 137, 147 n. 5
Pike, J., 143, 147 n. 13, 189 n. 17
Pope, A., 56, 65 n. 4
Price, H.H., 125, 128, 136 f., 144, 147 n. 4
Price, L., 17 n. 11, 112, 189 n. 17
Prince, M., 172
Pritchard, J.B., 82 n. 6

Rajneesh, 52
Ramsey, I.T., 38, 42, 46, 50 n. 10, 113, 158, 163
Rawlings, M., 104 f., 108 n. 17
Ring, K., 102, 104, 108 n. 2, 108 n. 11, 131, 187, 190 n. 21
Ritchie, G., 101, 108 n. 10
Robinson, J.A.T., 127, 155, 165 n. 4
Rogo, D.S., 35 n. 5, 97, 108 n. 3, 147 n. 14
Roll, W.G., 65 n. 11
Ryall, E.W., 173, 176, 178, 189 n. 8

Sabom, M., 108 n. 11
Sai Baba, 31
Saunders, C., 107
Shackleton, B., 57
Shanti Devi, 167, 178
Shapin, B., 35 n. 1, 83 n. 13
Sherrill, E., 108 n. 10
Shorten, B., 163
Simpson, M., 96, 108 n. 1
Sizemore, C., 173
Smith, G.R., 145, 148 n. 17
Smythies, J.R., 147 n. 4
Soal, S.G., 57
Stevenson, I., 167, 168, 171, 176, 178, 189 n. 5
Stoddard, S., 107
Stringfellow, W., 189 n. 17
Suso, 107
Swann, I., 79

Tanous, A., 59
Thigpen, C.H., 172
Thomas, K., 7, 17 n. 1, 32, 68, 82 n. 3
Thouless, R.H., 116, 120
Thurston, H., 35 n. 5
Tighe, Mrs, 169, 177
Towne, A., 189 n. 17
Toynbee, A., 147 nn 4,6
Tribbe, F., 112
Trungpa, C., 147 n. 7
Tuckett, C.M., 165 n. 5
Tugwell, S., 50 n. 6

Twigg, E., 143
Tyrrell, G.N.M., 21, 26, 121

Underhill, E., 45
Underhill, F., 45

Victoria, Queen, 26, 32

Walker, B., 150, 167, 176, 178, 189 nn 6, 11
Walters, J., 150
Waterhouse, J., 174
Weatherhead, L.D., 83 n. 16
Weldon, J., 105, 109 n. 18
Whitby, G.S., 37, 38, 53
White, R.A., 35 n. 5
Williams, C., 125
Williams, H.A., 165, 166 n. 18
Williston, G., 189 n. 10
Wilmshurst W.L., 192
Wilson, I., 150, 170ff., 176, 178, 189 nn 6,13, 14

Zorab, G., 83 n. 16

3. Biblical references

Gen. 44.5,15,	74
Lev. 19.31,	73
Lev. 20.6,	73
Lev. 20.17,	73
Num. 20-24,	74
Deut. 6.16,	118
Deut. 18.9ff.,	73
Josh, 13.22,	74
1 Sam. 9,	70
1 Sam. 9.9,	73
1 Sam. 10.5-7,	70
1 Sam. 10.10,	74
1 Sam. 19.20ff.,	70
1 Sam. 28,	66ff., 146
2 Kings 5.26,	74
2 Kings 6.7,	80
2 Kings 6.11f.,	79
2 Kings 23.24,	73
1 Chron. 10.13	73
Job 1.21,	91
Job 14.7-12,	75
Job 14.14,	181
Ps. 88.5,	75, 92, 146
Ps. 90.3,	181
Ps. 139.8,	92
Prov. 8. 22-31,	181
Eccles. 1.9-11,	181
Eccles. 3.19f.,	75
Eccles. 9.5f.,	75, 146
Eccles. 11.3,	118
Isa. 8.19,	50 n. 7, 71, 73, 76
Isa. 14.10,	75
Isa. 29.4,	72
Isa. 40.6,	75
Jer. 1.4-5,	181
Dan. 10.7,	80
Mal. 4.4f.,	181
Wisd. 8. 19-20,	181, 183
Bel & Dragon,	77
2 Macc. 7.11,	127
2 Macc. 14.46,	127
Matt. 4.7,	118
Matt. 9.4,	79
Matt. 11.14,	182
Matt. 16.13f.,	182
Matt. 24,	79
Matt. 28.20,	184
Mark 9.5,	51 n. 15
Mark 9.9f.,	157
Mark 13.30,	182
Mark 15.34,	92
Luke 16.26,	126
Luke 21,	79
Luke 22.44,	92
Luke 24. 19-21,	164
Luke 24.39,	155
John 1.21,	182
John 2.24,	79
John 9.2,	182
John 11.24,	154
John 12.28,	80
John 14.2,	126
John 21,	156
John 21.28,	90
Acts 10.10ff.,	80
Acts 16. 16-19,	81
Acts 22.17,	80
Rom. 6.4,	89
Rom. 7.18f.,	144
Rom. 7.25,	144
Rom. 8.38f.,	184
1 Cor. 3.16,	141
1 Cor. 15,	153
1 Cor. 15.14,	151
1 Cor. 15.26,	91
1 Cor. 15.50,	127
2 Cor. 11.14,	50 n. 8
Phil. 1.23,	90
Phil. 3.10f.,	93, 146
Phil. 3.12ff.,	65, 188
1 Thess. 4.15,	182
Heb. 2.14,	91
2 Pet. 1.5,	53
2 Pet. 3. 3-10,	182
1 John 4.1,	76
Rev. 6.9,	116